Start & Run Your Own Profitable Service Business

IRVING BURSTINER

PRENTICE HALL
Englewood Cliffs, New Jersey 07632

Library of Congress Cataloging-in-Publication Data

Burstiner, Irving
Start & run your own profitable service business / by Irving Burstiner.
p. cm.
Includes index.
ISBN 0-13-842733-X
1. New business enterprises—United States—Handbooks, manuals, etc. 2. Service industries—United States—Handbooks, manuals, etc. I. Title. II. Title: Start and run your own profitable service business.
HD62.5.B85 1992 92-31197
658′.041—dc20 CIP

Printed in the United States of America

10 9 8 7 6 5 4 3

ISBN 0-13-842733-X(PBK)

PRENTICE HALL
Career & Personal Development
Englewood Cliffs, NJ 07632
A Simon & Schuster Company

On the World Wide Web at http://www.phdirect.com

Prentice-Hall International (UK) Limited, *London*
Prentice-Hall of Australia Pty. Limited, *Sydney*
Prentice-Hall Canada Inc., *Toronto*
Prentice-Hall Hispanoamericana, S.A., *Mexico*
Prentice-Hall of India Private Limited, *New Delhi*
Prentice-Hall of Japan, Inc., *Tokyo*
Simon & Schuster Asia Pte. Ltd., *Singapore*
Editora Prentice-Hall do Brasil, Ltda., *Rio de Janeiro*

To Razel, with love

Preface

If you are thinking about, or have ever thought about starting a business of your own, you owe it to yourself to find out more about the opportunities that abound in today's service industries.

Astonishing and unparalleled growth has propelled the service sector to where it is now: (1) generates a greater share of our Gross National Product, (2) employs more people (28 million), and (3) creates more new jobs each year than both the retail and wholesale trades combined.

The service sector is a most attractive arena for the aspiring entrepreneur. Many service enterprises can be launched with far less money than the amount of capital typically needed to open a manufacturing, wholesale, or retail business. Many new service operators are able to begin at home, thus avoiding the expense of renting, buying, or constructing business premises. Moreover, end-of-year earnings in the service sector compare favorably with the profit margins enjoyed by most other types of enterprise.

About This Book

This book is directed at two important groups: (1) the 500,000 to 600,000 enterprising souls who, each year, dare to launch businesses of their own, and (2) the 6 to 8 million others who think, and dream, about pursuing the great American dream.

I believe the book fills a void. Books on entrepreneurship are, of course, readily available. Some are quite specific; they address the challenges associated with starting and managing a restaurant, retail store, mail-order business, travel agency, or consulting service. A few deal exclusively with the marketing of services. To my knowledge, however, this is the first book that demonstrates how to plan, organize, launch, and manage a successful service business.

It is a how-to book with a straightforward approach. It is an easy-to-read operations manual designed to guide the reader through all of the steps needed to succeed.

Among the book's unique features are:

- End-of-chapter bibliographies for further reference

- Tables, charts, and other figures that accent important concepts and add to reader interest
- Illustrations of the legal forms used to set up a sole proprietorship, partnership, or corporation
- An outline designed to help the reader prepare a comprehensive plan for the new business
- Four chapters devoted to the intricacies of service marketing
- Three chapters on the financial aspects of managing a company
- Three chapters about the promotion mix
- An appendix containing examples of filled-out income tax returns for the different legal forms of business

Part One lays the foundation for reader understanding of the opportunities and challenges associated with entrepreneurship. After providing specifics about various types of manufacturing, wholesale, and retail enterprises, it explores the burgeoning service sector of the economy in some detail. It then offers a procedure designed to help the reader select the type of service operation to open.

Part Two presents useful approaches for targeting consumer and organizational markets and describes how marketing research can be used to aid management decision making. It reviews the pros and cons of three routes to entrepreneurship, discusses the legal forms of operation, and comments on the ethics and social responsibilities of business owners. It clarifies the terms on balance sheets and operating statements, shows how to determine the amount of capital needed to launch the business, and demonstrates how to calculate the firm's breakeven point. Insights into the planning process and a useful outline for creating a business plan complete this section of the book.

Part Three offers counseling on choosing a location; reviews the business structure of a typical city; outlines the benefits and drawbacks of renting, buying or building business premises; and covers the topics of layout and decor. It then provides a thorough grounding on management functions as well as information about locating, hiring, paying, training, and motivating employees.

Part Four centers on the firm's marketing mix. It presents a comprehensive overview of the pricing area, including price-setting approaches, promotional pricing methods, and discounts. It then delves into the promotion mix, covering such topics as advertising budgets, the mass media, effective advertising and sales promotion techniques, and publicity. A separate chapter on personal selling analyzes the selling process, provides specifics on polishing the selling skills of salespeople, and advocates greater use of the telephone to boost sales and profits.

Part Five is devoted to the financial aspects of business management. Among other topics, it covers recordkeeping, cash flow, budgeting, and credit management. It shows how ratio analysis can be used to keep tabs on the progress of the business. It suggests measures for protecting company assets and holding down theft. After presenting a brief overview of business law, it offers a detailed treatment of the tax responsibilities faced by the business owner.

Part Six focuses on the future of the new business. It describes the business life cycle, suggests directions for company growth, and cautions that both the firm's finances and its organizational needs should be reviewed before embarking on a growth plan. Suggestions on management succession and how to keep the family business running conclude the book.

–Irving Burstiner

Table of Contents

Part One

EXPLORING OPPORTUNITIES IN THE SERVICE SECTOR

CHAPTER 1

SHOULD YOU GO INTO BUSINESS?

Every year, regardless of the state of the economy, as many as half a million venturesome souls launch businesses of their own. Every year, millions more dream about stepping away from their jobs and moving into entrepreneurship. And, at some point in their lives, most people who have not by then dared to pursue this exciting path will surely give the idea serious consideration.

This introductory chapter aims at helping you to decide whether or not *you* should go into business. It begins with a review of the benefits people seek from entrepreneurship as well as the disadvantages that it offers. You will discover that many new enterprises do not survive their first few years of operation. You will gain insights into the causes of business failure and learn what kinds of personal characteristics, background, and experience are of value in helping the entrepreneur succeed. Finally, you will be advised to surround yourself with several specialists to whom you may need to turn to ensure the success of your new business.

STARTING YOUR OWN BUSINESS: THE PROS AND CONS

Have you ever wondered why many people do go into business for themselves? Have you ever asked yourself what could have motivated them to take this action?

The Pros

Listed below are four of the more commonly heard statements made by budding entrepreneurs when asked why they wanted to go into business. Note that all four responses were expressed in terms of personal wants. Look them over; match them against your own thoughts and feelings. Perhaps one or more of them may touch a responsive chord.

1. "I want to be independent." A craving for independence can indeed be a significant motivator. You may dislike, or even resent, having to take orders from others or being told what you should or should not do, being pushed to work harder, or listening to complaints about your performance. You may have already reached the point where you daydream occasionally of the freedom associated with business ownership.

2. "I want to run my own show." You would like an opportunity to put your own knowledge, skills, and talents to work for you, instead of other people. You are positive that you would enjoy making all decisions and building a successful enterprise through your own efforts.

3. "I want an opportunity to strike it rich." As a jobholder, you may have realized by now that it is almost impossible for you to save more than a miniscule portion of each year's earnings. Even without suffering the effects of inflation, whether creeping or galloping, your savings will be limited by the taxes you must pay. Think about it. Yes, you will accumulate some funds as you go along. But, like so many other people, you cannot visualize winding up five years down the pike with much more than a few thousand dollars in your savings account.

4. "I want to feel secure." With a business of your own, you are sure that you can shed the common concerns of many employees: getting fired, losing out on a promotion, being furloughed for weeks (or months) when company revenues or incoming orders slow down, and the like.

The Cons

What holds many people back from deciding to launch ventures of their own? Perhaps it is because they feel that the disadvantages of running a business outweigh the potential benefits.

You can look forward to long hours and lots of hard work. Unlike working at a job, you will find yourself spending many evenings and weekends wrestling with business affairs. You will carry a heavy burden of responsibilities and be compelled to make many decisions on your own.

Chances are excellent, too, that you will not be able to draw a salary during your first few months of operation. A year or more may pass by before you reach the level of earnings you enjoyed on your last job. There is also the dire possibility that you will not succeed in getting your business off the ground. If this happens and you are forced to close down, you will most likely lose a sizable chunk, if not all, of your investment.

No, Not Every New Venture Succeeds!

Starting a business of any type is like gambling. The outcome is never certain; you may win or you may lose. The American economy itself is one vast, bustling arena—a battleground replete with continuous motion, challenges, successes, defeats, and ongoing change. This dynamism that characterizes our entire business community is underscored by the following quotation:

> Every year thousands of firms are started, many either fail or discontinue, and others transfer ownership or control. Each business day, over 35,000 changes are made to the Dun & Bradstreet database of over 9 million businesses at our National Business Information Center. New businesses are added and closed businesses are deleted, name styles altered, and financial information revised. This is all evidence of the dynamic change and turnover constantly taking place in the business population.*

Unfortunately, many new businesses are unable to survive for more than a few years. Note the information, in Figure 1–1, about 60,432 businesses that

FIGURE 1–1
Ages of 60,432 businesses that failed in 1990*

Age of Business	Services	Manufacturing	Wholesale Trade	Retail Trade	All Types Combined**
1 year or less	8.6%	8.5%	7.3%	9.6%	8.0%
2 years	10.3	11.3	10.0	13.0	10.3
3 years	10.3	10.5	10.0	12.2	10.3
4 years	9.3	9.0	10.5	10.1	9.5
5 years	8.5	7.8	9.3	8.2	8.4
Total 5 years or less	47.0%	47.1%	47.1%	53.1%	46.5%
6 to 10 years	26.3	25.1	25.5	23.1	25.4
Over 10 years	26.7	27.8	27.4	23.8	28.1
Total	100.0%	100.0%	100.0%	100.0%	100.0%

*These are preliminary statistics for 1990.

**Other categories included in total, although not shown, are: agriculture, forestry, and fishing; mining; construction; transportation and public utilities; and finance, insurance, and real estate.

Source: Economic Analysis Department, The Dun & Bradstreet Corporation, *Business Failure Record: 1989 Final/1990 Preliminary* (New York: The Dun & Bradstreet Corporation, 1991), 17. Used with permission.

*Economic Analysis Department, The Dun & Bradstreet Corporation, *Business Failure Record: 1989 Final/1990 Preliminary.* (New York: The Dun & Bradstreet Corporation, 1991), inside front cover. Used with permission.

failed in 1990. The data, tabulated by industry and age of the business, reviewed nine sectors of the economy: (1) agriculture, forestry, and fishing; (2) mining; (3) construction; (4) manufacturing; (5) transportation and public utilities; (6) wholesale trade; (7) retail trade; (8) finance, insurance, and real estate; and (9) services.

Across all industry, 46.5 percent of all these failures occurred during the first five years of operation. Retail trade bore the dubious distinction of having the highest mortality rate (53.1 percent) during the five-year period. Failures in the service sector were on a par with both the manufacturing and wholesaling trades.

It is important to point out at this juncture that the number of enterprises that close down their operations but are not designated "failures" is far greater than the actual number of companies that fail. Note how Dun & Bradstreet differentiates between business failures and business discontinuances in their *Business Failure Record:*

> Business failures do not represent total business closings, which consist of both business failures and business discontinuances. As defined in Dun & Bradstreet's statistics, business failures consist of businesses involved in court

FIGURE 1–2
More significant causes of business failures, 1990.*

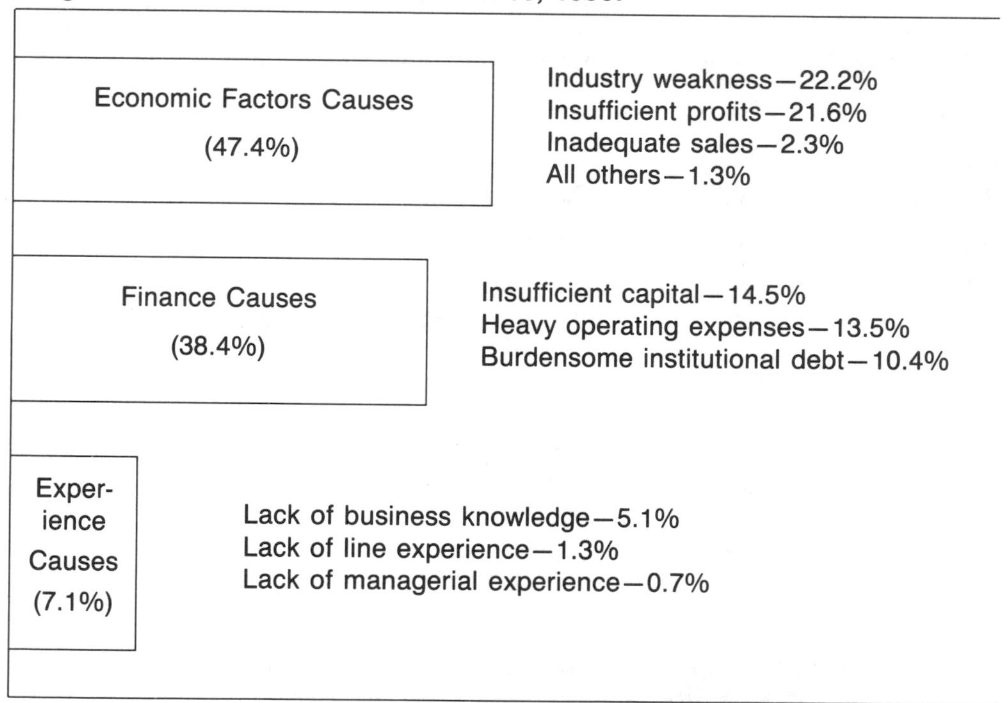

*These are preliminary statistics for 1990. Less often cited causes of business failures included neglect causes (3.4%), disaster (1.5%), strategy causes (1.1%), and fraud (1.0%).

Source: Adapted from: Economic Analysis Department, The Dun & Bradstreet Corporation, *Business Failure Record: 1989 Final/1990 Preliminary* (New York: The Dun & Bradstreet Corporation, 1991), 19. Used wtih permission.

proceedings or voluntary actions involving losses to creditors. In contrast, businesses that discontinue operations for reasons such as loss of capital, inadequate profits, ill health, retirement, etc., are not recorded as failures by Dun & Bradstreet if creditors are paid in full. Although they represent only a percentage of total closings, failures have the most severe impact upon the economy.*

Why do some businesses fail? The chart in Figure 1–2 discloses the more significant causes of business failures that occurred during 1990. Topping the list were the "economic factors," reported as the primary cause of failure by nearly five out of every ten failed companies. The major economic problems that these organizations faced were: (1) industry weakness and (2) insufficient profits.

Some 38.4 percent of the firms attributed their failures to "finance causes." Insufficient capital, heavy operating expenses, and burdensome institutional debt were the three big problem areas in this category. A fraction over 7 percent of the organizations labeled "experience causes" as the major culprit. Even fewer companies pointed to such other categories as "neglect causes" (3.4 percent), "disaster" (1.5 percent), "strategy causes" (1.1 percent), and "fraud" (1.0 percent).

REQUIREMENTS FOR SUCCESS IN BUSINESS

Rushing into business, no matter how attractive an opportunity beckons you, is never a wise move. You can double your chances of succeeding simply by deferring the decision to proceed until you have weighed all aspects judiciously and prepared a sensible and comprehensive plan for your new venture. (See the section on "How to Write Your Business Plan" in Chapter 7.)

What else will you need to ensure success? First and foremost, of course, you must have some capital to invest. How much will you need? The amount will depend on:

- the kind of business you intend to launch
- whether you plan to start a brand-new business, buy someone else's established operation, or contract for a franchise unit
- how much you will need to live on while you are getting your business off the ground

You must have: (1) initial capital to get you started, (2) working capital to pay your operating expenses—and to support yourself—until your new enterprise starts generating enough profit to keep you going, and (3) reserve funds to be held in abeyance for contingencies.

But money alone is not enough. You need to prepare yourself personally to do an outstanding job in business. Three essential personal qualifications for would-be entrepreneurs are a good education, the right kind of business experience, and excellent health.

Education—A quality education can serve as one of your strongest assets. A working knowledge of psychology and skill at communicating your ideas will

*Ibid.

enable you to deal competently with customers, employees, suppliers, media people, and others. Some exposure to business fundamentals is also desirable. Try to take at least one introductory-level college course in finance, management, and marketing.

After you have completed your formal education, be sure to keep up with what goes on in the world by reading widely: newspapers, magazines (general, news, business, and trade publications), and books. Joining a trade association will also help to keep you abreast of timely information.

Get Appropriate Experience—Try to obtain hands-on experience in the same type of business as the one you plan to start. While there, strive to move up the ladder into the middle management ranks—or even higher. A promotion or two will help you to see things from a different, and higher, perspective. Try to gain exposure to all phases of the business: buying, selling, financial management, inventory control, and so on.

Work at Maintaining Good Health—Operating a business can be extremely taxing. You will need abundant energy to keep up the pace of running your organization. Count on having to take work home with you most evenings and weekends, and on occasionally having to deliberate about business affairs into the wee hours of the morning.

Work Toward Self-Improvement—You should also begin to work toward strengthening: (1) certain helpful personality traits, for example: empathy, resourcefulness, self-confidence, and sensitivity to others; (2) useful capabilities such as your ability to analyze situations, communication and listening skills, the ability to motivate others, and skill at prioritizing; and (3) behaviors that are both ethically and morally correct and demonstrate your understanding of what good interpersonal relations should be.

Contact the U.S. Small Business Administration

Defer all planning for a business of your own until after you have visited a field office of the U.S. Small Business Administration (see Figure 1–3). The SBA is an excellent source of information. While there, arrange for an appointment with a member of SCORE (the Service Corps of Retired Executives) or ACE (the Active Corps of Executives). When you meet with the counselor, you can expect to get answers to many of the questions you have as well as advice about the benefits and drawbacks of going into business.

CHOOSE CAPABLE PROFESSIONALS TO ADVISE YOU

Not too long after you have managed to secure a foothold in the business community, you are likely to discover that daily chores are beginning to consume a disproportionate share of your time and energies. You may feel overtaxed, busier than you have ever been before—running the operation, promoting your service(s), and generally trying to keep tabs on the continuous ebb and flow of

FIGURE 1–3
Offices of the U.S. Small Business Administration*

Agana, Guam
Albany, N.Y.
Albuquerque, N. Mex.
Anchorage, Alaska
Atlanta, Ga.
Augusta, Maine
Baltimore, Md.
Birmingham, Ala.
Boise, Idaho
Boston, Mass.
Buffalo, N.Y.
Casper, Wyo.
Charleston, W. Va.
Charlotte, N.C.
Chicago, Ill.
Cincinnati, Ohio
Clarksburg, W. Va.
Cleveland, Ohio
Columbia, S.C.
Columbus, Ohio
Concord, N.H.
Corpus Christi, Tex.
Dallas, Tex.
Denver, Colo.
Des Moines, Iowa
Detroit, Mich.
Eau Claire, Wis.
Elmira, N.Y.
El Paso, Tex.
Fairbanks, Alaska
Fargo, N. Dak.
Fresno, Calif.
Gulfport, Miss.
Harlingen, Tex.
Harrisburg, Pa.
Hartford, Conn.
Hato Rey, P.R.
Knoxville, Tenn.
Las Cruces, N. Mex.
Las Vegas, Nev.
Little Rock, Ark.
Los Angeles, Calif.
Louisville, Ky.
Lubbock, Tex.
Madison, Wis.
Marquette, Mich.
Marshall, Tex.
Memphis, Tenn.
Miami, Fla.
Milwaukee, Wis.
Minneapolis, Minn.
Montpelier, Vt.
Nashville, Tenn.
Newark, N.J.
New Orleans, La.
New York, N.Y.
Oklahoma, City, Okla.
Omaha, Nebr.
Philadelphia, Pa.
Phoenix, Ariz.
Pittsburgh, Pa.
Portland, Oreg.
Providence, R.I.
Rapid City, S. Dak.
Richmond, Va.
Rochester, N.Y.
St. Louis, Mo.
Salt Lake City, Utah
San Antonio, Tex.
San Diego, Calif.
San Francisco, Calif.
Seattle, Wash.
Sioux Falls, S. Dak.
Spokane, Wash.
Helena, Mont.
Holyoke, Mass.
Honolulu, Hawaii
Houston, Tex.
Indianapolis, Ind.
Jackson, Miss.
Jacksonville, Fla.
Kansas City, Mo.
Springfield, Ill.
Syracuse, N.Y.
Tampa, Fla.
Washington, D.C.
Wichita, Kans.
Wilkes-Barre, Pa.
Wilmington, Del.

*Note: For addresses and telephone numbers, look under "United States Government" in the appropriate telephone directories.

Source: C.R. Stigelman, "Franchise Index/Profile: A Franchise Evaluation Process," *Small Business Management Series No. 35* (Washington, D.C.: U.S. Small Business Administration, 1986), 55.

your finances. Eventually, you will come to realize that if you continue spreading yourself so thin, one or more aspects of your operation may start to suffer. Furthermore, situations occasionally arise that call for expertise in areas about which you know little or nothing. You may find that you must seek the help of specialists.

For their own protection and to ensure the safety of their organizations, all entrepreneurs should choose and enlist the services of several professionals prior to starting out in business. Every business needs:

- An accountant
- An attorney
- An insurance agent/rep
- A banker

Your Accountant

Most new business owners are quick to realize that they need help in filling out their income tax returns. So, once each year, many turn to a tax preparation service (H&R Block, for example). Some prefer to ask "knowledgeable" relatives or friends to assist them. Unfortunately, though, many are convinced that they cannot afford to pay an accountant to handle their returns. How mistaken they are! Tax return preparation should not be the sole motive for enlisting the services of an accountant.

Do you need an accountant to handle your books? No, not at all. It is easy enough to hire a bookkeeper on a part-time basis, preferably one who is knowledgeable about your type of business and who you believe will be attentive to your needs and eager to "grow" along with your growing business. Or, you can do your own bookkeeping.

Still, hiring an accountant at the outset to set up your books would be a wise move. If your books are set up properly, you will be able to keep close tabs on what is happening in your operation. Most likely, you will also become aware of developing problem situations before they grow too serious to handle.

The U.S. Small Business Administration offers this information about the value of accounting services:

> Most businesses fail not for lack of good ideas or goodwill, but rather for lack of financial expertise and planning . . . Your accountant will help set up your books, draw up and analyze profit and loss statements, advise on financial decisions (e.g., buying a computer), and give advice on cash requirements for your start-up phase. He or she can make budget forecasts, help prepare financial information for a loan application, and handle tax matters.
>
> * * * * *
>
> Your accountant is your key financial advisor. He or she should alert you to potential danger areas and advise you on how to handle growth spurts, how to best plan for slow business times, and how to financially nurture and protect your business future.*

Your Attorney

Another professional to add to your advisory staff (preferably, on a monthly retainer basis) is a capable attorney. This person can help you from the very start: in setting up your legal form of business, negotiating the lease on your premises, securing the necessary licenses and permits, preparing a partnership agreement or filing for a corporate charter, and so on. Your attorney can also inform you about local ordinances and government legislation that can affect your operation. These run the gamut from minimum wage, equal pay, and civil

---

*Lynne Waymon, *Starting and Managing a Business from Your Home* (Washington, D.C.: U.S. Small Business Administration, 1986), 31–2.

rights laws through health and safety regulations to various tax responsibilities. As time goes on, you will most certainly need to seek legal advice to help get you through different kinds of situations.

Your Insurance Agent

Naturally, you will also want to protect your business and its assets from fire and other perils. (See the section on "How to Safeguard Your Firm's Assets" in Chapter 15.) Find an insurance agent or representative experienced in handling service companies like yours. Have this person prepare and present to you an insurance program to meet your particular needs.

Your Banker

Visit a commercial bank in the neighborhood of your new service business. Introduce yourself to the branch manager and ask to open a business checking account. Tell the manager about your plans and find out how to go about securing a loan, should you need one, at some future date. Call upon the manager in the future for advice on neighborhood trends and general economic trends.

FOR FURTHER INFORMATION

Books

Burstiner, Irving, *The Small Business Handbook,* rev. ed. New York: Prentice Hall Press, 1989.

Cunningham, William H., Ramon J. Aldag, and Christopher M. Swift, *Introduction to Business,* 2d ed. Cincinnati: South-Western, 1989.

Eyler, David R., *Starting and Operating Your Home-Based Business.* New York: Wiley, 1989.

Hodgetts, Richard N., *Effective Small Business Management,* 3rd ed. San Diego, Calif.: Harcourt Brace Jovanovich, 1989.

Lowry, James R., Bernard W. Weinrich, and Richard D. Steade, *Business in Today's World.* Cincinnati: South-Western, 1990.

Mauser, Ferdinand F. and David J. Schwartz, *American Business: An Introduction,* 6th ed. San Diego, Calif.: Harcourt Brace Jovanovich, 1986.

Ryan, J. D. and Lee A. Eckert, *Small Business: An Entrepreneur's Plan,* 2d ed. San Diego, Calif.: Harcourt Brace Jovanovich, 1990.

Walthall, Wylie A. and Michael J. Wirth, *Getting into Business: An Introduction to Business,* 5th ed. New York: Harper & Row, 1988.

Business Development Publications Available from the U.S. Small Business Administration*

MANAGEMENT AND PLANNING

MP 11–"Business Plan for Small Service Firms" ($.50)
MP 12–"Checklist for Going into Business" ($1.00)
MP 15–"The Business Plan for Home-based Business" ($1.00)

*Contact the nearest SBA field office to secure a copy of Form 115A (for ordering publications and videotapes on starting and managing a small business). For additional information on SBA business development programs and services, call the SBA Answer Desk in Washington, D.C. at: 1-800-368-5855. (In the District of Columbia, call 653-7561.) Send your orders to: SBA Publications, P.O. Box 30, Denver, CO 80201-0030. Make checks payable to: U.S. Small Business Administration. When ordering two or more items at one time, include $1.00 for domestic shipping and handling.

CHAPTER 2

IS THE SERVICE SECTOR FOR YOU?

This chapter begins by accompanying you on a rapid tour through three of the four business arenas that are the most attractive to new entrepreneurs. You will be introduced to the manufacturing, wholesale, and retail sectors and be made aware of the financial operating results reported by many types of firms in these areas. We then present an overview of the service sector, emphasizing its astonishing rate of growth over the past two decades. Finally, we examine several characteristics of service offerings that tend to make the marketing of services considerably more difficult than the marketing of goods.

THE MAJOR BUSINESS ARENAS: AN OVERVIEW

The federal government identifies, classifies, and tracks business activity through its Standard Industrial Classification (SIC) system. Each type of business is assigned its own set of code numbers. The first two numerals in the set identify the particular industrial category. Classifications and subclassifications within each category are represented by the third and fourth numerals.

The principal categories in the SIC system are:

- Agriculture, forestry, and fishing
- Mining
- Construction

- Manufacturing
- Transportation, communications, and electric and gas utilities
- Wholesale trade
- Retail trade
- Finance, insurance, and real estate
- Services
- Public administration

Here are some examples of SIC numbers assigned to different manufacturing, wholesaling, retailing, and service enterprises:

Sic Number	Type of Business
#2335	Manufacturers—women's dresses
#2369	Manufacturers—children's clothing
#3089	Manufacturers—miscellaneous plastic products
#3911	Manufacturers—jewelry and precious metals
#5023	Wholesalers—floor coverings
#5146	Wholesalers—fish and seafood
#5148	Wholesalers—fresh fruits and vegetables
#5169	Wholesalers—chemicals and allied products
#5411	Convenience food stores
#5661	Shoe stores
#5812	Restaurants
#5942	Bookstores
#4724	Travel agencies
#6411	Insurance agents/brokers
#7841	Videotape rental services
#8111	Legal services

Over the past several decades, the majority of new ventures have appeared in four sectors of the economy: manufacturing, wholesaling, retailing, and services. The first three of these business arenas are briefly discussed over the next several pages. Because of the exceptional growth we have witnessed in the service sector in recent years, we have deferred our treatment of the fourth arena to the next section of this chapter.

Manufacturing

Most manufacturing firms convert raw materials and/or components into finished products for consumer and/or organizational markets. They may produce these goods by hand or by machine. Some manufacturers are assemblers who make useful products by combining various components. To function, most types of manufacturing companies require machines, a plant to house the machinery, the continuous purchase and inflow of raw or semifinished materials to be used in the production process, and a constant stream of supplies.

Approximately 380,000 manufacturing establishments are currently operating in the United States. The more common types are displayed in Figure 2–1.

FIGURE 2–1
Manufacturing: Popular types and number of establishments*

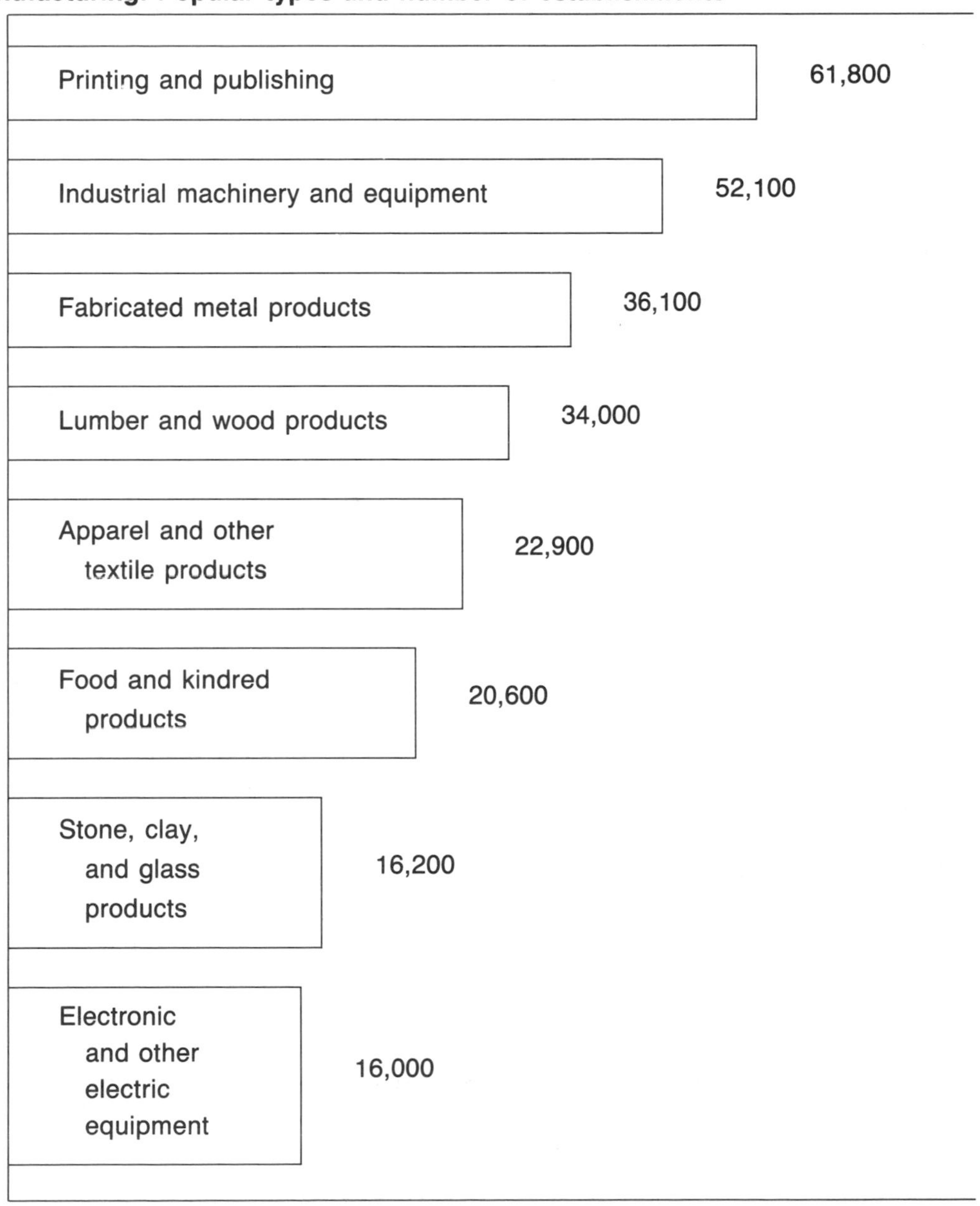

*Establishments with payroll.

Source: U.S. Department of Commerce, Bureau of the Census, *Statistical Abstract of the United States, 1990,* 110th ed. (Washington, D.C.: U.S. Government Printing Office, 1990), 735–39.

Heading the list are printing and publishing manufacturers, with 61,800 establishments. The 52,100 producers of industrial machinery and equipment constitute the second most popular type of manufacturing business; third place is occupied by the 36,100 plants that turn out fabricated metal products.

Figure 2–2 offers some interesting operating results for 1990–1991 for selected manufacturing types. Expressed in terms of *percentages of net sales,* the data reveal the cost of sales, gross profit, operating expenses, and operating profit for type. (*Note:* The term *gross profit* is applied to that amount left over after subtracting the cost of sales from the net sales figure.)

The gross profit percentages that appear in Figure 2–2 range from a low of 36.3 percent (jewelry and precious metals–SIC #3911) to a high of 50.9 percent (signs and advertising specialties–SIC #3993). The range of operating profit extends from 2.7 percent (electrical lighting fixtures–SIC #3645, 46) and wood household furniture, except upholstered–SIC #2511) to 10.6 percent (industrial chemicals–SIC #2861, 65, 69).

Wholesaling

Wholesalers purchase goods and/or services from manufacturers and other producers and resell them to organizations and/or to consumers. The 1987 Census of Business tabulated approximately 467,000 wholesale establishments in operation.* Four out of every five of these were "merchant wholesalers"–firms that buy goods in large quantities, store them in warehouses, and then "break bulk" by preparing smaller quantities to fill customer orders. These include general merchandise, single-line, and specialty wholesalers. Some of these distributors are known as "limited-service wholesalers" because they fail to provide all the services that resellers (retailers) and organizational buyers have come to expect from a wholesale operation. Mail order distributors, cash-and-carry wholesalers, and drop-shippers are in this category.

A sizable majority of the nation's wholesalers deal in durables, goods that deliver long-lasting satisfaction to those who purchase them: motor vehicles, furniture, machinery, electrical goods, apparel, and so on.

Among the requirements for most types of wholesaling are a heavy investment in inventory for resale, an efficient inventory control system, a warehouse for temporary storage of the goods, equipment for moving the merchandise about, and a sales contingent to sell the goods.

The more popular kinds of wholesale operations are listed in Figure 2–3. Topping the list in 1987 were the 114,100 establishments engaged in the whole-

*U.S. Department of Commerce, Bureau of the Census, *Statistical Abstract of the United States, 1991,* 111th ed. (Washington, D.C.: U.S. Government Printing Office, 1991), 779.

FIGURE 2–2
Financial data for selected manufacturing businesses*

SIC Number	Type of Business	Cost of Sales	Gross Profit	Operating Expenses	Operating Profit
2051	Bread and other bakery products, except cookies and crackers	49.9%	50.1%	42.1%	8.0%
2064	Candy and other confectionery products	53.0	47.0	42.2	4.8
2759	Commercial printing, letterpress and screen	49.2	50.8	46.0	4.9
3645, 46	Electric lighting fixtures	63.5	36.5	33.9	2.7
2861, 65, 69	Industrial chemicals	57.0	43.0	32.3	10.6
3911	Jewelry and precious metals	63.7	36.3	27.3	8.9
3089	Miscellaneous plastic products	59.2	40.8	31.5	9.3
3993	Signs and advertising specialties	49.1	50.9	45.4	5.4
3949	Sporting and athletic goods	57.5	42.5	37.2	5.3
2511	Wood household furniture, except upholstered	61.8	38.2	35.6	2.7

*Based on statement studies of firms with fiscal year-ends April 1, 1990 through March 31, 1991. All statistics are expressed in terms of percentages of annual sales volume. (*Note:* Only data for firms with from $0 to $1 million in sales have been shown since this would be characteristic of the beginning business.)

Source: Robert Morris Associates, *Annual Statement Studies, 1991.* (Philadelphia: Robert Morris Associates, 1991). Copyright 1991 by Robert Morris Associates. Used with permission. (*Note:* See the following "Interpretation of Statement Studies Figures.")

Note Regarding Interpretation of Statement Studies Figure

RMA cautions that the Studies be regarded only as a general guideline and not as an absolute industry norm. This is due to limited samples within categories, the categorization of companies by their primary Standard Industrial Classification (SIC) number only, and different methods of operations by companies within the same industry. For these reasons, RMA recommends that the figures be used only as general guidelines in addition to other methods of financial analysis.

FIGURE 2–3
Wholesaling: Popular types and number of establishments*

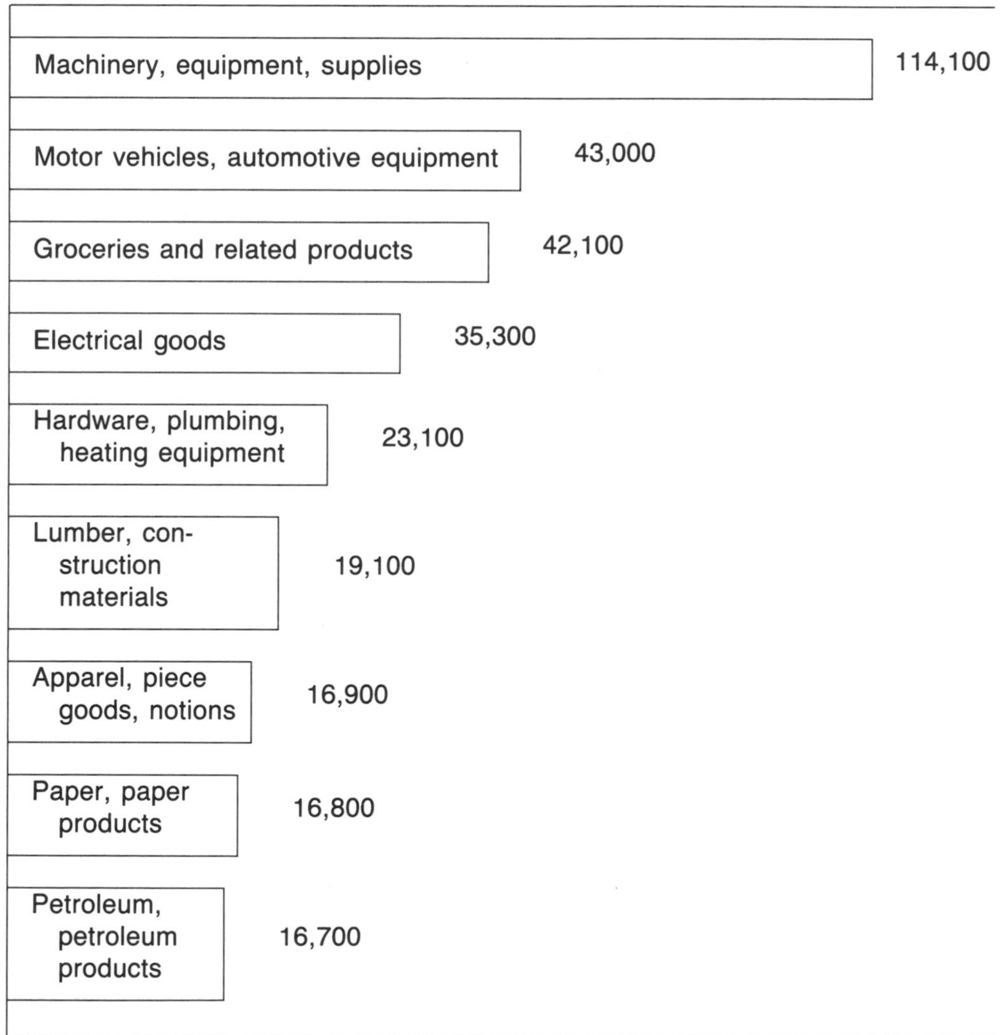

*Number of establishments in business at any time during the year 1987.

Source: U.S. Department of Commerce, Bureau of the Census, *Statistical Abstract of the United States, 1991,* 111th ed. (Washington, D.C.: U.S. Government Printing Office, 1991), 779.

sale distribution of machinery, equipment, and supplies. Distributors of motor vehicles and automotive equipment placed a poor second (43,000 establishments). Close behind this group were 42,100 wholesalers of groceries and related products.

Operating information for selected types of wholesale distributors is provided in Figure 2–4. The gross profit percentages reported by these wholesalers ranged from 30.7 percent (general groceries–SIC #5141) to 42.1 percent (general merchandise–SIC #5199).

The lowest operating profit came to a lackluster 0.7 percent (building materials–SIC #5032); the highest amounted to 5.9 percent of sales (fresh fruits and vegetables–SIC #5148).

FIGURE 2–4
Financial data for selected wholesaling businesses*

SIC Number	Type of Business	Cost of Sales	Gross Profit	Operating Expenses	Operating Profit
5032	Building materials	62.5%	37.5%	36.8%	0.7%
5169	Chemicals and allied products	60.3	39.7	35.5	4.2
5063	Electrical supplies and apparatus	60.0	40.0	35.8	4.2
5023	Floor coverings	60.7	39.3	38.4	0.9
5148	Fresh fruits and vegetables	59.0	41.0	35.1	5.9
5021	Furniture	61.8	38.2	35.2	3.0
5141	General groceries	69.3	30.7	28.6	2.1
5199	General merchandise	57.9	42.1	36.7	5.4
5072, 5198	Hardware and paints	64.2	35.8	34.3	1.4
5112	Stationery supplies	64.3	35.7	33.4	2.4

*Based on statement studies of firms with fiscal year-ends April 1, 1990 through March 31, 1991. All statistics are expressed in terms of percentages of annual sales volume. (*Note:* Only data for firms with from $0 to $1 million in sales have been shown since this would be characteristic of the beginning business.)

Source: Robert Morris Associates, *Annual Statement Studies, 1991*. (Philadelphia: Robert Morris Associates, 1991). Copyright 1991 by Robert Morris Associates. Used with permission. (*Note:* See the following "Interpretation of Statement Studies Figures" at end of Figure 2–2 on page 18.)

FIGURE 2–5
Retailing: Popular types and number of establishments*

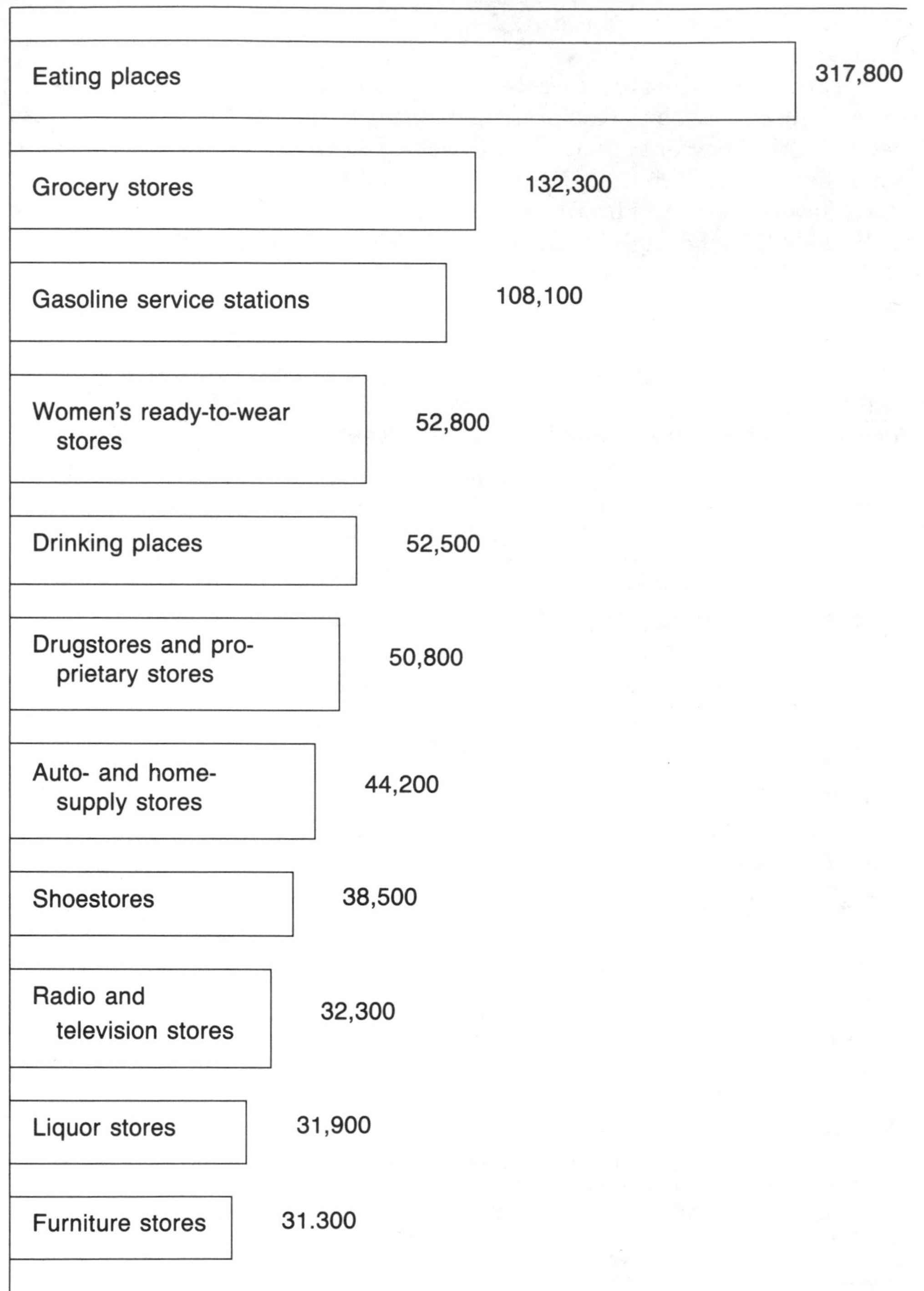

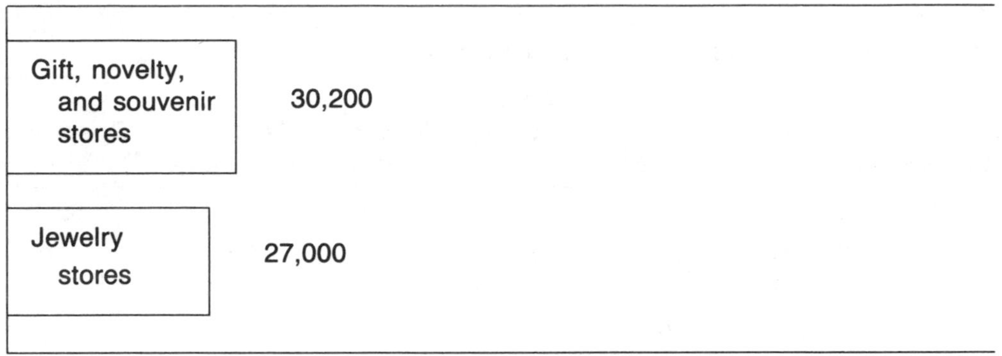

*Number of establishments in business at any time during 1988.

Source: U.S. Department of Commerce, Bureau of the Census, *Statistical Abstract of the United States, 1991,* 111th ed. (Washington, D.C.: U.S. Government Printing Office, 1991), 769.

Retailing

Retail sales in 1988 were in excess of $1.6 trillion.* Retailers buy goods and services from producers, wholesalers, and service providers and then resell them to satisfy consumer needs. About 1.5 million retail establishments serve the American consumer population. Although most retailers operate from store premises, many do not. The three most popular "nonstore" retailing types are direct selling companies (house-to-house canvassers, party-plan operators, and so on), mail order houses, and vending machine operators. Peddlers and flea marketers are two other nonstore types that come readily to mind.

Generally, store retailers require a good location, suitable space, fixtures, an initial stock of merchandise, and attractive displays.

The more popular types of retailing are indicated in Figure 2–5. Eating places (317,800), grocery stores (132,300), and gasoline service stations (108,100) are the three most commonly found.

Figure 2–6 offers financial operating data for some types of retailing. The highest gross profit percentage earned in this group was 57.3 percent (restaurants–SIC #5812); the lowest, 25.7 percent (convenience food stores–SIC #5411). Operating profit percentages reported for these retailers ranged from 2.3 percent (shoestores–SIC #5661) to 6.5 percent (bookstores–SIC #5942).

*Ibid., 772.

FIGURE 2–6
Financial data for selected retailing businesses*

SIC Number	Type of Business	Cost of Sales	Gross Profit	Operating Expenses	Operating Profit
5942	Bookstores	59.6%	40.4%	33.9%	6.5%
5734	Computers and software	55.0	45.0	39.0	6.0
5411	Convenience food stores	74.3	25.7	22.6	3.0
5651	Family clothing	59.1	40.9	36.2	4.6
5251	Hardware	63.2	36.8	32.6	4.1
5722	Household appliances	64.4	35.6	31.3	4.3
5944	Jewelry stores	52.3	47.7	42.5	5.2
5812	Restaurants	42.7	57.3	53.2	4.1
5661	Shoestores	59.2	40.8	38.6	2.3
5621	Women's ready-to-wear	59.6	40.4	37.1	3.3

*Based on statement studies of firms with fiscal year-ends April 1, 1990 through March 31, 1991. All statistics are expressed in terms of percentages of annual sales volume. (*Note:* Only data for firms with from $0 to $1 million in sales have been shown since this would be characteristic of the beginning business.)

Source: Robert Morris Associates, *Annual Statement Studies, 1991.* (Philadelphia: Robert Morris Associates, 1991). Copyright 1991 by Robert Morris Associates. Used with permission. (*Note:* See "Interpretation of Statement Studies Figures" at end of Figure 2–2 on page 18.)

CHARTING THE AMAZING GROWTH OF THE SERVICE SECTOR

In recent years, the astounding rate of expansion in the service sector has far outpaced growth in all other arenas of American private enterprise.

What are services, anyway? According to the American Marketing Association, services are "activities, benefits, or satisfactions which are offered for sale or are provided in connection with the sale of goods."*

Figure 2–7 presents the most popular types of service businesses. In 1988, the leading three categories—and the number of establishments in each—were health services (417,200); business services (250,500), and personal services (177,300).

*Committee on Definitions, *Marketing Definitions: A Glossary of Marketing Terms* (Chicago: American Marketing Association, 1960), 21.

FIGURE 2–7
Number of establishments in service industries (1988)*

Industry	Number of Establishments** (000)	Representative Businesses
Health services	417.2	Offices and clinics of doctors of medicine, dentists, chiropractors, and other health practitioners; nursing and personal care facilities; medical and dental laboratories; hospitals
Business services	250.5	Advertising agencies, mailing services, services to buildings, employment agencies, computer and data processing services, detective services
Personal services	177.3	Laundry, dry cleaning, beauty shops, funeral parlors
Automotive repair, services, and parking	145.5	Car rental agencies, automotive repair shops
Legal services	135.7	(Not broken down)
Social services	104.8	Individual and family services, child day care services, residential care
Amusement and recreation services	70.5	Recreation clubs, membership clubs
Accounting, auditing, and bookkeeping services	66.2	(Not broken down)
Miscellaneous repair services	61.8	Electrical repair shops
Hotels and other lodging places	49.0	(Not broken down)
Educational services	33.2	Elementary and secondary schools, colleges and universities

*Firms subject to Federal income tax.
**Represents the number of establishments in business at any time during 1988.

Source: U.S. Department of Commerce, Bureau of the Census, *Statistical Abstract of the United States, 1991,* 111th ed. (Washington, D.C.: U.S. Government Printing Office, 1991), 784.

In 1988, the nation's service industries contributed more than $872 billion to our Gross National Product. In 1970, they produced no more than $120 billion. Over the 18-year period, then, the service sector's contribution expanded more than sevenfold.* Services now account for nearly 18 percent of our total GNP—a greater proportion than that contributed by both the wholesale and retail trades combined.

Figure 2–8 summarizes the contributions to the GNP by selected service industries. Note the exceptionally large increases in both business and legal services between 1970 and 1988.

FIGURE 2–8
Gross national product: selected service industries, 1970–1988*

Industry	1970 (in billions of dollars)	1988 (in billions of dollars)	Growth Percentage (1970–1988)
Business services	18.0	200.3	+1,012.8%
Legal services	7.3	67.4	+823.3
Miscellaneous professional services	10.3	89.4	+768.0
Health services	31.4	248.5	+691.4
Auto repair, services, and garages	6.3	41.6	+560.3
Hotels and other lodging places	6.3	40.9	+549.2
Miscellaneous repair services	2.7	15.9	+488.9
Amusement and recreation services	4.8	26.5	+452.1
Motion pictures	2.3	12.2	+430.4
Social services, membership organizations	10.0	50.1	+401.0
Educational services	7.1	33.1	+366.2

*In *current* dollars.

Source: U.S. Department of Commerce, Bureau of the Census, *Statistical Abstract of the United States, 1991,* 111th ed. (Washington, D.C.: U.S. Government Printing Office, 1991), 766; *Statistical Abstract, 1990,* 110th ed., 766.

*U.S. Department of Commerce, Bureau of the Census, *Statistical Abstract of the United States, 1991,* 111th ed. Washington, D.C.: U.S. Government Printing Office, 1991), 766.

The Service Sector Is Where the Jobs Are

During the 1980s, eight or more out of every ten new jobs that were created were in the service sector. Back in 1970, the country's service operations employed a total of 11.4 million people. By 1988, this number had more than doubled—to 25 million. No slackening of this growth pattern has since been witnessed nor is it expected. By the end of this century, the service sector may be staffed by 33.7 million (see Figure 2–9). In stark contrast to this projected expansion, note that

FIGURE 2–9
Employment in manufacturing, domestic trade, and services: 1970, 1988, and projected to the year 2,000 (in millions)*

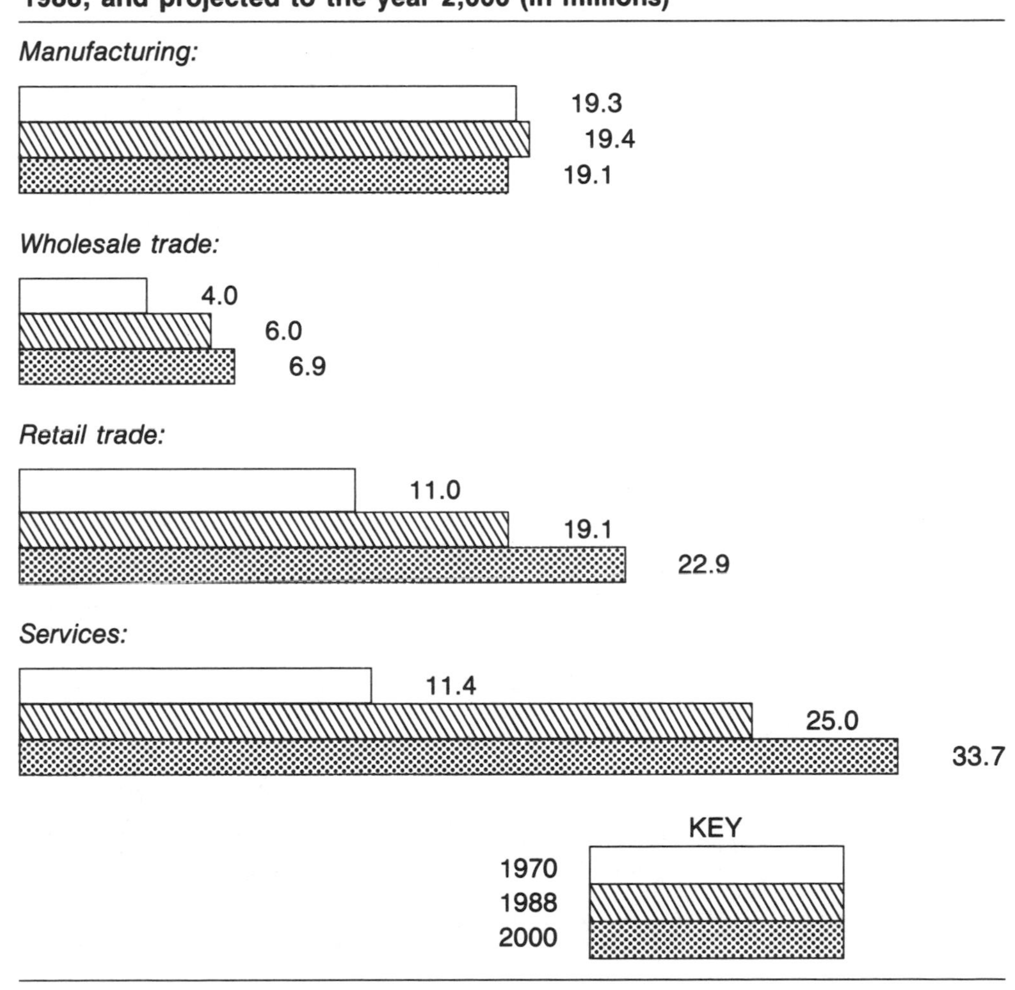

*Based on assumptions of moderate growth.

Source: U.S. Department of Commerce, Bureau of the Census, *Statistical Abstract of the United States, 1991,* 111th ed. (Washington, D.C.: U.S. Government Printing Office, 1991), 401.

an insignificant increase in employment in the manufacturing sector occurred between 1970 and 1988—and that a small decrease is actually projected by the year 2,000.

The three service industries that added the most employees between 1970 and 1988 were: (1) legal services—up 261 percent (616,000 additional employees); (2) business services—up 232 percent (nearly 3.9 million more people); and (3) health services—up 134 percent (over 4 million more workers). (See Figure 2–10.)

The financial requirements for starting a new service business can vary drastically from one type of operation to another. Obviously, launching a car rental agency, motel, laundry, medical laboratory, or nursing care facility calls for an exceptionally heavy investment. On the other hand, the initial funding for many service operations can be rather minimal—especially when compared to the amount of capital required to go into the majority of manufacturing, wholesaling, or retailing enterprises.

Many new service businesses are launched with modest investments by persons who offer a special skill, talent, or information base. They may need to purchase no more than one or two relatively inexpensive pieces of equipment, have some business cards printed up, install a business telephone, and place some advertising. Often, their own home or apartment serves as their place of business until their operation outgrows its surroundings.

By way of illustration, here are just a few of the kinds of service businesses that have been launched in just that manner:

bookkeeping service
child care
cleaning service
correspondence course(s)
handbag repairs
house painting
lawn care
maid service
newsletter publishing
resume preparation
translation bureau
tutoring

FIGURE 2–10
Fastest-growing service industries in numbers of employees, 1970–1988

Industry	Numbers of Employees 1970 (000)	1988 (000)	Percentage of Gain, 1970–1988
Legal services	236	852	+261.0%
Business services	1,676	5,570	+232.3
Health services	3,053	7,144	+134.0
Auto repair, services, garages	391	837	+114.1
Amusement and recreation services	468	918	+96.2

Source: U.S. Department of Commerce, Bureau of the Census, *Statistical Abstract of the United States, 1991,* 111th ed. (Washington, D.C.: U.S. Government Printing Office, 1991), 401.

Figure 2–11 summarizes operating results for various types of service businesses. Note that the cost of sales and gross margin columns do not appear in this figure, as they did in connection with the financial data on manufacturing, wholesaling, and retailing businesses. The reason is that no inventories were involved.

FIGURE 2–11
Financial data for selected service businesses*

SIC Number	Type of Business	Operating Expenses	Operating Profit	All Other Expenses	Pre-tax Profit
8721	Accounting, auditing, and bookkeeping	83.8%	16.2%	3.1%	13.2%
4119	Ambulance, limousine, and other local transportation services	89.3	10.7	1.9	8.8
7538	Auto repair—general	93.2	6.8	1.9	4.9
7933	Bowling center	91.7	8.3	5.5	2.8
7349	Building cleaning and maintenance	90.7	9.3	2.7	6.6
7542	Car wash	91.6	8.4	13.0	−4.6
7371	Computer programming	93.4	6.6	2.2	4.4
8351	Day care—child	86.8	13.2	6.1	7.2
7331	Direct mail advertising	95.0	5.0	1.4	3.6
7361	Employment agency	92.1	7.9	1.1	6.8
7359	Equipment rental and leasing	82.1	17.9	7.9	9.9
7231, 41	Hair stylist	92.8	7.2	1.5	5.7
6411	Insurance agent/broker	93.1	6.9	1.9	5.0
7211, 16	Laundry/dry cleaner's	89.3	10.7	3.6	7.1

FIGURE 2–11
Continued

SIC Number	Type of Business	Operating Expenses	Operating Profit	All Other Expenses	Pre-tax Profit
7515	Leasing—passenger cars	84.5	15.5	9.2	6.3
8111	Legal services	84.3	15.7	0.6	15.1
4214	Local trucking and storage	94.9	5.1	2.0	3.1
8742	Management consulting	87.8	12.2	6.9	5.3
8071	Medical laboratory	90.4	9.6	3.6	6.0
7011	Motels, hotels, and tourist courts	81.1	18.9	15.6	3.2
7991	Physical fitness facility	93.3	6.7	5.6	1.1
6531	Real estate agent/broker	76.8	23.2	15.0	8.2
7999	Skating rink—ice or roller	91.7	8.3	5.1	3.1
4724	Travel agency	94.9	5.1	0.6	4.5
7841	Video tape rental	91.7	8.3	1.9	6.4

*Based on statement studies of firms with fiscal year-ends April 1, 1990 through March 31, 1991. All statistics are expressed in terms of percentages of annual sales volume. (*Note:* Only data for firms with from $0 to $1 million in sales have been shown since this would be characteristic of the beginning business.)

Source: Robert Morris Associates, *Annual Statement Studies, 1991.* (Philadelphia: Robert Morris Associates, 1991). Copyright 1991 by Robert Morris Associates. Used with permission. (See "Interpretation of Statement Studies Figures" at end of Figure 2–2 on page 18.)

The highest percentage for operating expenses reported within this group was 95.0 percent (Direct mail advertising—SIC #7331). Lowest percentage for the group was 76.8 percent (Real estate agent/broker—SIC #6531).

Reported pre-tax profit by one type hit a high of 15.1 percent (Legal services—SIC #8111). Another type actually reported a negative figure—a loss that amounted to −4.6 percent of sales. (Car wash—SIC #7542)!

HOW SERVICES DIFFER FROM PRODUCT OFFERINGS

Service marketing can be far more challenging than the marketing of products because of these three distinctive characteristics of service offerings:

- Services are intangible.
- Services are perishable.
- Services cannot be separated from the service providers.

Services Are Intangible

Products are concrete objects. They are tangible–things that can be seen, touched, and examined. Some goods, like articles of clothing, can be tried on to determine whether or not they fit us well or if they improve our appearance. We are able to taste, smell, or listen to some products before we decide to purchase (or not purchase) them. If we are so motivated, we can shop around and compare competitive merchandise on price, quality, materials, style, and/or other criteria.

Services, on the other hand, are not tangible objects. They are abstract concepts. Consequently, our five senses are of little value in evaluating a service before we decide to buy it.

What a difficult task it would be to try to compare and evaluate the services offered by each of two pediatricians, career counselors, commercial photographers, public relations agencies, or campgrounds for recreational vehicles!

Services Are Perishable

Unlike products, services cannot be fabricated in advance and then warehoused while awaiting future orders. No inventory buildup is possible. The production, delivery, and consumption of a service all occur simultaneously.

Services that, for whatever reason, are not consumed at the time of production represent lost income to the service provider. Available rental cars that do not move off the lot, empty seats on an airliner or at a concert, vacant alleys at a bowling center, and idle machines at a slenderizing salon are all familiar illustrations of situations where potential revenues fail to materialize.

Services Cannot Be Separated from the Service Providers

It is almost impossible to disassociate a service from the people responsible for its production and delivery. Consider, for example, the broad category of instructional services: in arts, crafts, dance, golf, music, tennis, and other areas. Note that both instructor and instruction are intricately intertwined. This element of inseparability pervades the service sector. We perceive it readily in accounting, banking, and other financial services; engineering and legal services; health care; lodging and food services; plumbing and electrical repairs; pet care; and most other service industries.

The inseparability factor is the root cause of variability in service quality, something we see only occasionally in product manufacturing. Finished articles coming off the same production line are typically clones, duplicates of each other. They are produced according to established standards and subjected to quality control techniques. Because they are designed for mass marketing, they have been "standardized" in the manufacturing process.

Quality control methods, though, are difficult to apply to services. Services resist attempts at standardization. Variations in service quality are often noted when the same service is delivered by different providers. Quality will also vary in situations where the same producer provides the same service to different clients—or when a service is delivered several times to the same customer.

Some Directions for Services Marketing

What, then, can be done to reduce the effects of these singular characteristics of services? Some useful suggestions follow:

Intangibility—Introduce into the picture one or more tangible elements—things that both prospective buyers and your present clientele will come to associate with your service(s). Among the many articles that service firms have found of value for this purpose are banners, booklets, buttons, certificates, copies of the company's code of ethics, guarantees, membership cards, mottos, special awards, symbols, and warranties. Items of apparel (blouses, caps, shirts, jackets, and so on) are also possibilities.

Another worthwhile approach is to capitalize on the potential of your business premises. You can imbue your service(s) with more "physicality" by presenting a sensible layout, tasteful decor, well-chosen furnishings and fixtures, state-of-the-art equipment, and good lighting. Proper attention to atmospherics may well result in your clients "seeing" and "experiencing" the service(s) you offer.

Perishability—To ameliorate the problems associated with this characteristic, increase your production capabilities. Expand your present premises. If you cannot, open a branch (or two) elsewhere. Another possibility is to bring a mobile unit into play, if this is feasible in your type of business.

If machinery or equipment is used to deliver your service(s), replace antiquated models with newer ones and/or install additional units.

Add personnel as needed during busy periods (of the day, week, or month). Build up demand during slow periods by offering discounts and/or by using other methods of sales promotion.

Inseparability—Take advantage of the relationship that exists in people's minds between any service and the service provider(s). Review your selection procedures. Look to hire applicants who can communicate well, are courteous and dependable, and have good interpersonal skills. Train them well and set high performance standards for them.

Also, think about moving toward the standardization of some operations—and away from total dependency on your employees. Increase your personnel's efficiency by mechanizing operations wherever you can (as banks have done with automatic teller machines). Consider, too, systems packaging (like the tour packages offered by travel agencies and the group health plans offered by insurance companies).

FOR FURTHER INFORMATION

Books

Albrecht, Karl and Ron Zemke, *Service America! Doing Business in the New Economy.* Homewood, Ill.: Business One Irwin, 1985.

Burstiner, Irving, *Basic Retailing,* 2d ed. Homewood, Ill.: Irwin, 1991.

_______, *Run Your Own Store,* 2d ed. New York: Prentice Hall Press, 1989.

_______, *The Small Business Handbook,* rev. ed. New York: Prentice Hall Press, 1989.

_______, *Mail Order Selling,* 2d ed. New York: Prentice Hall Press, 1989.

Connor, Richard A., Jr. and Jeffrey P. Davidson, *Marketing Your Consulting and Professional Services.* New York: Wiley, 1985.

Cunningham, William H., Ramon J. Aldag, and Christopher M. Swift, *Introduction to Business,* 2d ed. Cincinnati: South-Western, 1989.

Eyler, David R., *Starting and Operating Your Home-Based Business.* New York: Wiley, 1989.

Kotler, Philip and Paul N. Bloom, *Marketing Professional Services.* Englewood Cliffs, N.J.: Prentice-Hall, 1984.

Lovelock, Christopher H., *Services Marketing,* 2d ed. Englewood Cliffs, N.J.: Prentice-Hall, 1990.

Mauser, Ferdinand F. and David J. Schwartz, *American Business: An Introduction,* 6th ed. San Diego, Calif.: Harcourt Brace Jovanovich, 1986.

Wheatley, Edward W., *Marketing Professional Services.* Englewood Cliffs, N.J.: Prentice-Hall, 1983.

CHAPTER 3

CATEGORIES OF SERVICE INDUSTRIES

Over the previous two chapters, you became acquainted with the opportunities and the challenges associated with entrepreneurship, scanned three major arenas of economic activity (manufacturing, wholesale, and retail), and explored the rapidly growing service sector. More information about this sector is presented in this final chapter of Part I. It offers an approach that can help you determine the one type of service operation to go into that would best suit your needs and personal situation. A listing of more than 200 types, arranged by categories, is then provided for your studied consideration in arriving at a decision.

Opportunities abound in the service sector. Many service companies market directly to consumers. Many others cater only to organizations. Some straddle the fence, offering their services to both. (Note: Consumer and organizational markets are treated in more detail in Chapter 4.)

Many types of service businesses can be launched for less than $1,000. Others may require 10, 20, or 50 times that figure, or even more. Many new operations are started at home, in spare time, by people who are still working at their jobs.

CHOOSING THE RIGHT SERVICE BUSINESS: A SUGGESTED PROCEDURE

To help you decide on the best service business for you to go into, follow this simple procedure: (1) study the five factors listed below that are bound to influence your decision and (2) begin evaluating, one by one, the many kinds of service operations in light of those factors:

- *How much you are willing to invest*–For safety's sake, at least 50 percent of the capital needed to launch the business should be your own funds. If you do not have enough money, consider: (1) taking on one or more partners, (2) borrowing an additional sum, or (3) forming a corporation and selling some of its stock. (Note: See the section on sources of capital in Chapter 6.)
- *The level of preparation you can bring to the business*–Carefully review your educational background, work experience, specialized knowledge, and any skills you have. In short, try to answer this question, "How well qualified am I to succeed in this type of business?"
- *Your personality*–Do a self-analysis. List your major strengths and weaknesses. Examine your likes, preferences, and dislikes. Ask yourself, "Am I the right kind of person for this type of business?"
- *The business itself*–Think about the kind of environment you will need to work in if you choose to go into this type of business. Determine how you feel about the nature of the work that will be involved and about the people with whom you will have to deal.
- *The likely payoff*–Try to assess the nature of the opportunity that you believe exists in service enterprises of this type. How soon do you think the business may prove profitable? How high a salary will you be able to draw?

Over the next several pages are listed, for your consideration, more than 200 different kinds of service businesses. Each was assigned to one of three groups, according to the amount of capital likely to be needed for start-up purposes, as indicated below:

Initial Investment Required	Defined as:
Low	Under $5,000
Moderate	$5,000 to $25,000
High	Over $25,000

Each type was then evaluated in light of the level of knowledge, skills, training, and expertise called for by that business, as follows:

Category	Level Required
A	Minimum
B	Moderate
C	High

At this point, you can begin checking through the following list of service operations. As you consider each one, be sure to keep the five factors firmly in mind.

CONSUMER SERVICES

Low Initial Investment–Category A

apartment/house cleaning service
apartment/house painting
babysitting service
bicycle repair
date reminder service
exterminating
gardening
housesitting
lawn care
maid service
mail forwarding service
party planning
personal shopping service
personalizing products
pet boarding
resume preparation
secretarial services
sewing
shoe bronzing
typing service
wedding planning
window washing

Low Initial Investment–Category B

appliance repair
badge-making service
bridal consultant
ceramics instruction
craft instruction
flower arranging
frame-making
hair styling
home care
imprinting
lamp repair
manicurist
monogramming
pet grooming
sharpening service (knives, scissors)
small appliance repair
tailoring
tax form preparation
toy repair
vinyl repair
wallpapering

Low Initial Investment–Category C

air conditioning service
art instruction
career counseling
clock/watch repair
drama coaching
dressmaking
engraving
interior decorating
locksmith
music instruction
musical instrument repair
tool repair
tutoring
typewriter repair
VCR repair
videotaping

Moderate Initial Investment–Category A

bicycle rental
carpet cleaning service
dating service
delivery service
packing/mailing service
self-storage warehouse
telephone answering service
videotape rental service

Moderate Initial Investment–Category B

catering service
child-care center
day camp
instructional seminars
pool-cleaning service
travel agency

Moderate Initial Investment–Category C

car repairs
car tune-up service
facsimile machine repair
furniture refinishing
home security services
jewelry repair
motorcycle repairs
reupholstering
self-defense training
TV repair

High Initial Investment–Category A

bar
billiard parlor
bread-and-breakfast inn
boat rental
bowling alley
campgrounds
car rental/leasing
car wash
check cashing
consignment store
dancehall
employment agency
laundromat
limousine service
lunchwagon service
miniature golf course
moving van service
parking lot
racquetball court
self-storage warehouse
taxi service
tour bus
tourist court

High Initial Investment–Category B

art gallery
barber shop
beauty salon
drycleaning service
golf course
movie theater
nail salon
night club
restaurant
private school
trailer park

High Initial Investment–Category C

automobile painting
car transmission services
correspondence school
dance studio
fitness center
home security system installation
hotel/motel
laundry
oil change/lube shop
photography shop
photoprocessing laboratory
printing services
roofing services
shoe repair shop
ski lodge
slenderizing salon
trade school
weight-control center

BUSINESS SERVICES

Note that a company that intends to market services to organizations, rather than to consumers, typically requires more capital to get the new business off to a good start. Consequently, you will find that the majority of service operations listed in this section fall into the moderate or high initial investment category.

Low Initial Investment–Category A

carpet cleaning
gardening
janitorial services
messenger service
mailing service
painting
typing services
window washing

Low Initial Investment–Category B

bookkeeping
property management services
secretarial services
sign painting
translation bureau
window dressing

Low Initial Investment–Category C

business seminars
fax machine repair
management consultant
marketing consultant
sales training programs

Moderate Initial Investment–Category A

clipping bureau
commercial art supply
copying services
delivery service
guard services
plant rental service
speakers' bureau
telephone answering service

Moderate Initial Investment–Category B

maintenance services
newsletter publishing

Moderate Initial Investment–Category C

accounting services
auditing
business machine repair
commercial photography
computer programming
data processing
desktop publishing
public relations agency
printing services
research bureau

High Initial Investment–Category A

bus service
car rental and leasing
collection agency
equipment rental and leasing
mailing list broker
mailing list company
mailing services
property management
security services
temporary personnel agency
transportation service
truck rental/leasing

High Initial Investment–Category B

hotel
motel
sign shop

High Initial Investment–Category C

advertising agency
air conditioning/refrigeration services
photoprocessing laboratory
printing services

LEGAL, MEDICAL, AND OTHER PROFESSIONAL SERVICES

For rather obvious reasons, we made no attempt to categorize legal, medical, and other professional services as we did with consumer and business services. College-level courses, advanced degrees, and/or a much higher level of sophistication are frequently required for the delivery of such services.

Of course, you may be able to go into a business of this nature without having the necessary training and/or expertise. For example, you might be able to start your own pharmacy, so long as you place a pharmacist on your payroll (or take one in as a partner). Some other possibilities you may consider are forming a law, engineering, or financial planning firm, starting a dental or medical laboratory, opening a nursing care facility, or launching a vision center. Of course, you may need special licenses and/or permits in addition to the professionals you hire.

FOR FURTHER INFORMATION

Books

Albrecht, Karl and Ron Zemke, *Service America! Doing Business in the New Economy.* Homewood, Ill.: Business One Irwin, 1985.

Burstiner, Irving, *Mail Order Selling,* 2d ed. New York: Prentice Hall Press, 1989.

Connor, Richard A., Jr. and Jeffrey P. Davidson, *Marketing Your Consulting and Professional Services.* New York: Wiley, 1985.

Cunningham, William H., Ramon J. Aldag, and Christopher M. Swift, *Introduction to Business,* 2d ed. Cincinnatti: South-Western, 1989.

Eyler, David R., *Starting and Operating Your Home-Based Business.* New York: Wiley, 1989.

Gray, Douglas A., *Start and Run a Profitable Consulting Business,* 2d ed. Bellingham, Wash.: Self-Counsel Press, 1986.

Haynes, William G., *Start and Run a Profitable Craft Business,* 3rd ed. Bellingham, Wash.: Self-Counsel Press, 1990.

Johnson, Eugene M., Eberhard E. Scheuing, and Kathleen A. Gaida, *Profitable Service Marketing.* Homewood, Ill.: Business One Irwin, 1986.

Kahn, Sharon and The Philip Lief Group, *101 Best Businesses to Start.* New York: Doubleday, 1988.

Kotler, Philip and Paul N. Bloom, *Marketing Professional Services.* Englewood Cliffs, N.J.: Prentice-Hall, 1984.

Lovelock, Christopher H., *Services Marketing,* 2d ed. Englewood Cliffs, N.J.: Prentice-Hall, 1990.

Lowry, James R., Bernard W. Weinrich, and Richard D. Steade, *Business in Today's World.* Cincinatti: South-Western, 1990.

Mauser, Ferdinand F. and David J. Schwartz, *American Business: An Introduction,* 6th ed. San Diego, Calif.: Harcourt Brace Jovanovich, 1986.

McHatton, Robert J., *Total Telemarketing.* New York: Wiley, 1988.

Putman, Anthony O., *Marketing Your Services: A Step-by-Step Guide for Small Businesses and Professionals.* New York: Wiley, 1989.

Sheedy, Edna, *Start and Run a Profitable Home-Based Business.* Bellingham, Wash.: Self-Counsel Press, 1990.

Walthall, Wylie A. and Michael J. Wirth, *Getting into Business: An Introduction to Business,* 5th ed. New York: Harper & Row, 1988.

Wheatley, Edward W., *Marketing Professional Services.* Englewood Cliffs, N.J.: Prentice-Hall, 1983.

Withers, Jean and Carol Vipperman, *Marketing Your Service: A Planning Guide for Small Business.* Bellingham, Wash.: Self-Counsel Press, 1987.

Business Development Publications Available from the U.S. Small Business Administration

Management and Planning

MP 11–"Business Plan for Small Service Firms" ($.50)
MP 12–"Checklist for Going into Business ($1.00)
MP 15–"The Business Plan for Home-based Business" ($1.00)

Booklets Available from the Superintendent of Documents

S/N 003-009-00596-5–Franchise Opportunities Handbook, 1991–$16.00
S/N 045-000-00232-4–Starting and Managing a Business from Your Home–$1.75.

Part Two

PLANNING YOUR SERVICE OPERATION

CHAPTER 4

SELECTING YOUR TARGET MARKET(S)

Part One of this book focused on (1) helping you decide whether or not you should go into business for yourself, (2) exploring the manufacturing, wholesale, retail, and service sectors, and (3) reviewing the various categories of service industries.

All four chapters in Part Two offer guidance in planning your service enterprise. This first chapter begins by introducing two massive marketplaces in which a firm can operate: the consumer and organizational populations. You will be encouraged to choose the kinds of prospects to whom you intend to offer your service(s), for finding, satisfying, and keeping customers are the principal keys to success in any business. You will learn about the strategies that companies adopt to market their goods and/or services—and how to discover, target, and reach potentially profitable submarkets. Finally, a discussion of marketing research and its usefulness to company management conclude the chapter.

DECIDING WHO YOUR CUSTOMERS WILL BE

Perhaps the most important step you can take at this early planning stage is to select your target customers. Will they be consumers or organizations? Both populations are huge—in size and in sales potential. Both purchase goods and services to satisfy their needs and wants. Of course, their needs and wants differ.

Consumers buy because they seek to satisfy their needs or desires for affection, comfort, convenience, entertainment, good health, happiness, pleasure, recognition, relaxation, self-improvement, and many other things. Organizations buy to keep their operations running in good order and to earn profits.

At this point, further useful insights may be gleaned by comparing the more outstanding characteristics of both populations:

The Consumer Marketplace

1. It embraces a tremendous number of buyers. Of course, not all of our 265 million consumers buy. Infants, for example, cannot buy for themselves.
2. Because they are so dispersed, consumers cannot be reached easily through promotional effort.
3. Consumers buy in much smaller quantities than organizations do.
4. They also buy more often than do organizations.
5. Consumers are not trained buyers.
6. Frequently, emotions play a role in consumer buying.

The Organizational Marketplace

1. Organizations number far fewer than consumers; there are, at most, some 17 million organizations.
2. Because they are more geographically concentrated than consumers, organizational markets can be more easily reached through promotion.
3. Organizations buy in greater quantities than consumers do.
4. Organizational purchasing agents do not buy as often as consumers do.
5. Usually, these purchasing agents are specialists who buy logically and avoid allowing their emotions to affect their buying.

After you have chosen the arena in which you will operate, begin acquiring a clear understanding of your intended targets. You will need answers to such questions as:

Who are your customers?

What are they like?

Where can they be found?

Why do they buy?

When do they buy?

How do they buy?

SEGMENTING THE GIGANTIC CONSUMER MARKETPLACE

After you have decided to sell to consumers or to organizations (or, possibly, to both!), you should then select your strategic marketing approach. Three choices are available: (1) undifferentiated, (2) differentiated, and (3) concentrated marketing.

Few companies implement the first strategy. Those that follow an *undifferentiated,* or *mass marketing,* approach believe that the vast majority of consumers or organizations are potential users/buyers of their products and/or services. Thus, they devise a single "marketing mix" for attracting and selling all customers. (Note: The term "marketing mix" refers to the decisions made by a firm in all four areas of marketing activity: goods and services, pricing, promotion, and distribution.)

Often cited as examples of organizations engaged in undifferentiated marketing are sugar and salt manufacturers, makers of antifreeze for car engines, and newspaper publishers.

Differentiated marketing is far more popular. Where this strategy has been adopted, company management searches for large, promising submarkets within the total population. It looks for groups that are:

- fairly homogeneous as to their needs or wants,
- sufficiently large to warrant going after,
- accessible to company promotional effort, and
- financially able to pay for their purchases.

Once these groups have been pinpointed, they are then researched in depth and a different marketing mix is prepared for each one. The procedure is known as "market segmentation."

The third strategy, *concentrated marketing,* is in reality a variation of market segmentation. A company that adopts this strategy locates and then concentrates on a single segment, ignoring the rest of the population.

For most new service operations, strategies #2 or #3 are recommended.

Bases for Segmenting the Consumer Marketplace

The more popular approaches for carving out consumer subgroups are: geographic, demographic, psychographic, benefit, and usage-rate segmentation.

Geographic Segmentation—By far the oldest method of segmenting consumer subgroups, this technique categorizes consumers by where they reside. States, regions, and climates are the more commonly-used bases for categorization.

Demographic Segmentation—This is the most popular of all segmentation approaches. Sex, age, family size, yearly income, occupation, and level of education are among the more useful population variables used in identifying consumer submarkets. Once the characteristics, needs, and wants of these subgroups have been studied, appropriate marketing mixes are developed to reach and sell them.

Consider, for example, how some service companies can benefit from segmentation involving no more than a single demographic variable:

1. segmenting consumers according to *family size* can be of value to laundromats, babysitting services, music schools, amusement parks, shoe-bronzing companies, physicians, and dentists.
2. segmenting consumers by *income level* can be profitable for hotels, travel agencies, bowling alleys, stock brokerages, golf courses, income tax form preparers, and pool construction companies.

In recent years, geodemography has emerged as a new segmentation tool. This technique groups consumers by their zip-code numbers, on the assumption that people residing in the same area have many characteristics in common and enjoy rather similar lifestyles.

Psychographic Segmentation–This method attempts to classify consumers on the bases of their interests, their opinions, and the activities they engage in. It is, however, a difficult technique to apply because of the extensive investigation of consumer behavior that must precede any attempt at classification. One rather interesting psychographic approach is lifestyle segmentation. It seeks to identify submarkets on the basis of the lifestyles displayed by their members.

Benefit Segmentation–Marketers may also uncover potentially profitable segments by assigning consumers to categories based on the kinds of benefits they look for in a particular product or service.

Usage-rate Segmentation–This is an unusual, though quite useful, technique that identifies and differentiates the "users" of a product or service from the nonusers in the population. Users are then divided into three groups: "heavy," "moderate," and "light" users. Profiles of typical members of the three user groups are developed and these submarkets are targeted with appropriate marketing mixes. The heavy user group often accounts for a substantial proportion (20 to 35 or more percent) of all purchases in many product and service categories.

HOW TO TARGET ORGANIZATIONAL MARKETS

The organizational marketplace in the United States is comprised of three huge and distinct markets:

- Manufacturers and other producers
- Resellers (wholesalers and retailers)
- Governments (all levels)

Manufacturers and Other Producers

The nation's manufacturers continually buy large quantities of the raw materials, semi-processed goods, and/or components they need to produce finished products. They also purchase facilities, installations, equipment, supplies, and other types of goods and services essential to the various manufacturing processes.

In addition to product manufacturers, the producer market spans a wide range of industries, institutions, and service providers. Here are just a few examples:

- Mining companies, construction firms, cattle ranches, farmers, bottling plants
- Utilities (electric, gas, water), telephone companies, railroads, subways, bus lines, truck transport, airlines
- Banks, savings-and-loan institutions, brokerage houses
- Religious institutions
- Schools, colleges, and universities
- Hospitals, physicians, optometrists, and other health-care providers
- Racetracks, football stadiums, theaters, theme parks
- Hotels, motels, inns, RV parks
- Employment agencies, lawyers, accountants

Resellers

More than 400,000 wholesalers and 1.9 million retailers make up the reseller market. These organizations buy all kinds of products for resale to consumers and/or organizations at a profit. They also purchase many additional goods and services needed for running their operations: tools and equipment; stationery and supplies; cars and trucks; business insurance; cleaning and maintenance services; accounting, legal, and transportation services; and so on.

Government

The federal government employs more people than any other employer in the nation. Each year, it also spends more on goods and services than all our state and local governments combined. Government agencies, departments, and bureaus at all levels purchase an unbelievable variety of products and services to meet organizational needs. They buy real estate, office furniture, and furnishings; typewriters, telephones, computers, copiers, and facsimile machines; stationery and office supplies; janitorial, window-cleaning, and plant maintenance services; motor vehicles, gas, oil, and automotive repair services; food and transportation services; and a myriad of other goods and services. The military branches, of course, also buy uniforms, trucks, ships, aircraft, weapons, and countless tons of other essential equipment as well as foodstuffs and medical supplies.

Post exchanges, navy stores, and commissaries are among the relatively few government operations that also purchase goods for purposes of resale.

Segmenting Organizational Markets

Although opportunities for selling goods and services abound in all three organizational markets, many companies decide to carve their niches in no more than one area. Again, as in the consumer marketplace, each firm chooses to follow an undifferentiated, differentiated, or concentrated marketing strategy. Market segmentation techniques can prove as valuable in selling goods and services to manufacturer/producer, reseller, and government sectors as they are in dealing with the consumer marketplace.

With the aid of the federal government's Standard Industrial Classification (SIC) system, business organizations can readily be grouped by industry and by the type of economic activity in which they are engaged. Another popular segmentation method classifies organizations by their size (by sales volume, share of market, number of employees, and so on). Other viable approaches include geographic and usage-rate segmentation, both of which have already been discussed in connection with selling to consumers.

USING MARKETING RESEARCH TO HELP YOU MAKE DECISIONS

Marketing research is a powerful management tool for collecting information relative to marketing issues that can help to facilitate better decision making. As indicated in Figure 4–1, it can be used to investigate any aspect of a company's marketing mix.

FIGURE 4–1
Scope of marketing research

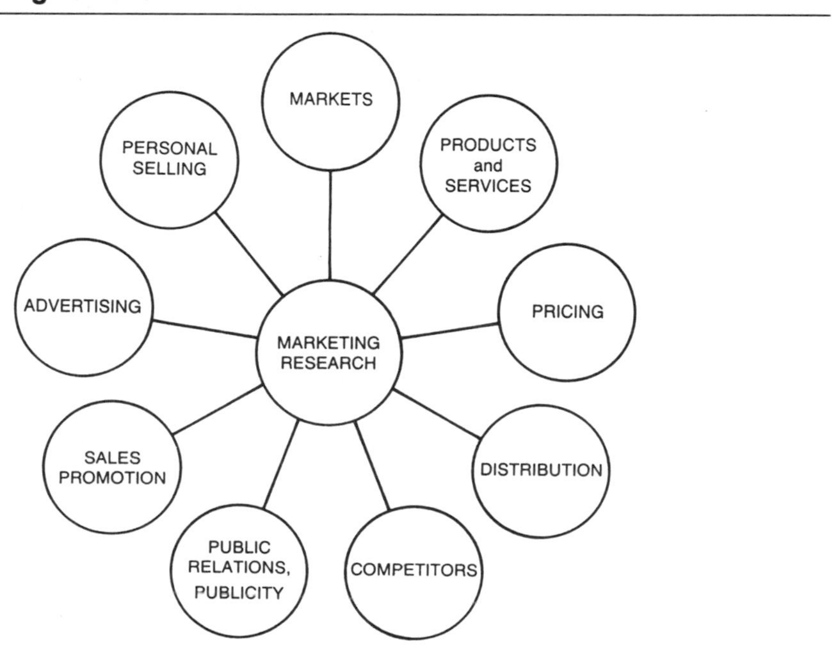

Most problem situations that organizations face are common or repetitive annoyances that are quickly resolved without the need for formal research study. Occasionally, though, management may find itself unable to solve an important and unusually difficult problem with only the information it has at hand. When this happens, a marketing research project may be indicated.

Here are the steps to follow when conducting a formal research study:

1. Specify the problem you want to solve.
2. Decide on the kind of information you need to solve the problem.
3. Choose an appropriate method for getting the information.
4. Collect the information.
5. Analyze the information.
6. Draw conclusions based on your analysis.
7. Act on your conclusions.

As a reminder, a chart of the process is offered in Figure 4–2.

Getting the Information

You may be able to locate additional, helpful facts that have already been compiled and published by government agencies; business and trade organizations; business, news, and consumer publications; and other agencies. Researchers label facts that are already available as *secondary data.* Facts that no one has collected as yet and that you will need to gather through your own efforts and at your own expense are called *primary data.*

Secondary Data

The most prolific source of secondary data in the United States is, of course, the federal government. Worthwhile information can be found in many of its publications, for example: the *Census of Population* (and census tracts), the *Census of Business,* the *Survey of Current Business,* and the *Statistical Abstract of the United States.* Local and state departments and agencies are also excellent sources of secondary data.

Among other useful information sources are the Wall Street Journal Index, New York Times Index, Business Publications Index, a number of Dun & Bradstreet publications, and various directories that are available in public, university, and business libraries. Secondary information may also be found in trade association reports, business periodicals, consumer publications, and a company's own, internal records.

Primary Data

If primary information is deemed essential to the resolution of a problem situation, an appropriate technique for collecting the required data must be selected.

FIGURE 4–2
Formal research procedure

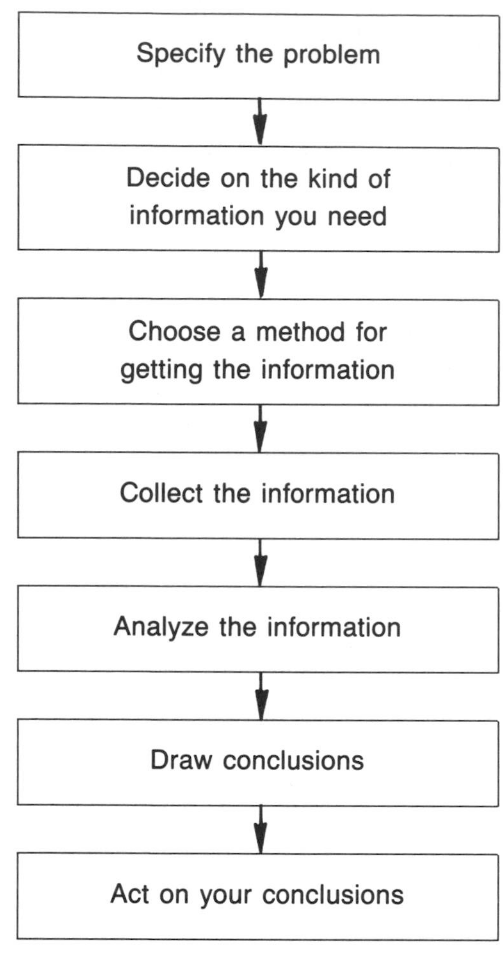

Three different methods are available for this purpose: surveys, observation, and experimentation.

Surveys—Surveys are by far the most popular fact-gathering approach used by business organizations. They can be applied to many types of problem situations. They may be conducted in person, by mail, or over the telephone. Personal interviews are usually best for collecting the maximum amount of information from an interviewee. They can, however, be costly and time-consuming, for interviewers should be well-trained before they are sent into the field. Because of these and other drawbacks, mail and telephone surveys are often preferable to in-person surveys.

Survey questionnaires must be worded carefully and the questions offered in sensible sequence.

Observation—Occasionally, a market researcher will employ trained observers or special equipment, such as camcorders, movie cameras, or tachistoscopes, to record people's behavior. A serious disadvantage of observational techniques is that they only record human behavior and reveal little or nothing about people's needs, preferences, opinions, attitudes—or whatever else goes on in their minds.

Experimentation—Another, more exacting method for gathering primary data is experimentation. It is not used all that often. It involves setting up a situation in which one aspect is subjected to some sort of test while all other factors that could conceivably affect the outcome of the experiment are carefully controlled. A major drawback to the technique is that it is much more difficult to set up a valid experiment in a real environment than to set one up in a laboratory.

The Semantic Differential

An often useful substitute for the survey questionnaire is the semantic differential instrument. Easy to prepare, it can be applied to many kinds of business problems.

The typical semantic differential instrument is a single printed sheet of paper that displays from 8 to 15 "scales." Each scale consists of two phrases (or adjectives) that are diametrically opposed to each other and are separated by a series of dashes. If, for example, you want to determine how your customers regard your company and the service(s) you offer, you might use such scales as the following to collect information:

A reliable company	— — — — — — —	An unreliable company
Prices are low	— — — — — — —	Prices are high
Top-quality service	— — — — — — —	Poor-quality service
Liberal credit policies	— — — — — — —	Strict credit policies

Usually, an odd number of spaces separate the two "polar" phrases to leave room (the middle space) for the respondent who cannot arrive at a decision. Instructions for completing the instrument are given at the top of the sheet. Numbered headings and short adjectives identify each column for respondents. People who regard your firm as reliable are to place checks in Columns 1 ("extremely" reliable), 2 ("very" reliable), and 3 ("somewhat" reliable), according to the opinions they hold. Those who feel differently may check off Columns 5, 6, or 7. (See Figure 4–3 for an example of a completed semantic differential instrument.)

Here are some additional scales you may find useful for your service business:

A progressive company	—	—	—	—	—	—	—	A backward company
Salespeople are warm and friendly	—	—	—	—	—	—	—	Salespeople are cold and businesslike
Company is sensitive to customer needs	—	—	—	—	—	—	—	Company is insensitive to customer needs
Quick service	—	—	—	—	—	—	—	Slow service
Advertisements are appealing	—	—	—	—	—	—	—	Advertisements lack appeal
Fine customer relations	—	—	—	—	—	—	—	Poor customer relations
Attractive displays	—	—	—	—	—	—	—	Unattractive displays
Adjustments made readily	—	—	—	—	—	—	—	Adjustments handled poorly
Superior guarantees	—	—	—	—	—	—	—	Inferior guarantees

FIGURE 4–3
An interviewee's completed semantic differential instrument*

	Extremely	Very	Somewhat	Don't Know	Somewhat	Very	Extremely	
A reliable company	___	___	✓	___	___	___	___	An unreliable company
Slow service	___	___	___	___	✓	___	___	Fast service
Sensitive to customer needs	___	___	✓	___	___	___	___	Insensitive to customer needs
Salespeople are cold and businesslike	___	___	___	___	___	✓	___	Salespeople are warm and friendly
Prices are low	___	___	___	___	✓	___	___	Prices are high
Advertisements lack appeal	___	___	___	___	✓	___	___	Advertisements are appealing
Inferior guarantees	___	___	___	✓	___	___	___	Superior guarantees
Top-quality service	___	___	✓	___	___	___	___	Pooro-quality service
Unattractive displays	___	___	___	___	___	___	✓	Attractive displays
Liberal credit policies	___	___	✓	___	___	___	___	Strict credit policies
Poor customer relations	___	___	___	___	✓	___	___	Fine customer relations
Adjustments readily made	___	___	✓	___	___	___	___	Poor adjustment policy

*Note how this instrument intermingles positive and negative polar phrases instead of showing all of one type on the same side. This forces interviewees to exercise more care when checking off the scales.

FIGURE 4–4
Service company profile based on opinions of 85 respondents

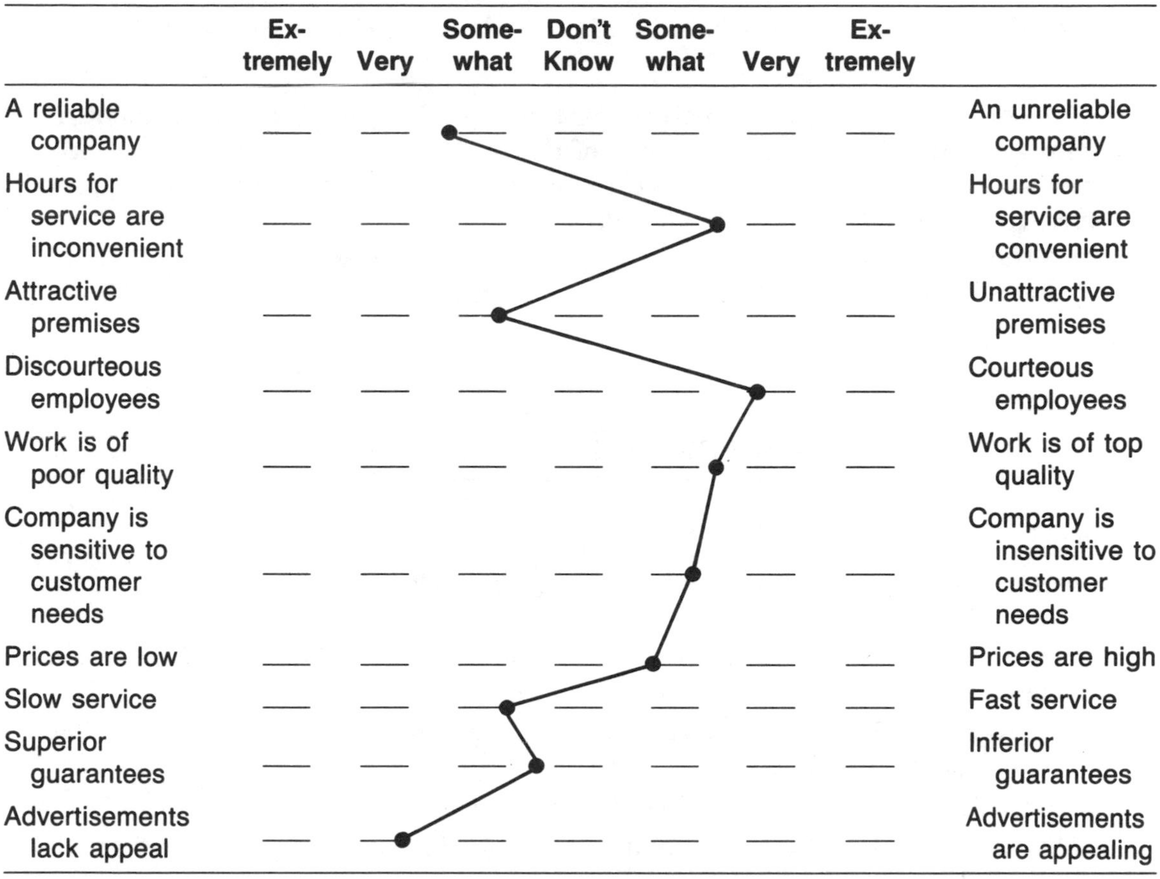

	Extremely	Very	Somewhat	Don't Know	Somewhat	Very	Extremely	
A reliable company	___	___	___	___	___	___	___	An unreliable company
Hours for service are inconvenient	___	___	___	___	___	___	___	Hours for service are convenient
Attractive premises	___	___	___	___	___	___	___	Unattractive premises
Discourteous employees	___	___	___	___	___	___	___	Courteous employees
Work is of poor quality	___	___	___	___	___	___	___	Work is of top quality
Company is sensitive to customer needs	___	___	___	___	___	___	___	Company is insensitive to customer needs
Prices are low	___	___	___	___	___	___	___	Prices are high
Slow service	___	___	___	___	___	___	___	Fast service
Superior guarantees	___	___	___	___	___	___	___	Inferior guarantees
Advertisements lack appeal	___	___	___	___	___	___	___	Advertisements are appealing

To determine the collective opinions of a group of respondents, regardless of its size, follow this procedure for scoring a set of semantic differential instruments:

1. Score each scale on the instrument separately from the others.
2. Count the total number of papers that have checkmarks in the first column of the scale. Record this number.
3. Total all checks that appear in the second column of the papers. Multiply this figure by 2 (for column #2). Record the result.
4. Add all third-column checks, then multiply the number by 3. Record this new figure.
5. Continue in the same manner across the scale—all the way through to the seventh column. (By this time, of course, you will need to multiply the number of checks by 7!)
6. Total the figures you have recorded for all seven columns in the scale.

7. Divide the total in #6 above by the number of people who completed the instrument. The result will be an "average" or "mean" score for the scale.
8. Continue to score the balance of the scales on the instrument in the same fashion.

To produce a composite "picture," or profile of the group's opinions about the company, you will need another copy of the instrument–one that has not been filled out at all. Mark each scale with a heavy dot in the space that most closely approximates the "mean" that you have determined for that scale. Then, draw lines from one dot to the next all the way down the page.

For an illustration of such a profile, see Figure 4–4.

FOR FURTHER INFORMATION

Books

Andreasen, Alan R., *Cheap But Good Marketing Research.* Homewood, Ill.: Business One Irwin, 1988.

Bonoma, Thomas V. and Benson P. Shapiro, *Segmenting the Industrial Market.* Lexington, Mass.: D. C. Heath, 1983.

Gorton, Keith and Isobel Doole, *Low-Cost Marketing Research: A Guide for Small Businesses,* 2d ed. New York: Wiley, 1989.

Kress, G., *Marketing Research,* 3rd ed. Englewood Cliffs, N.J.: Prentice-Hall, 1988.

Loudon, David L. and Albert J. Della Bitta, *Consumer Behavior: Concepts and Applications,* 2d ed. New York: McGraw-Hill, 1984.

Luck, David J. and Ronald S. Rubin, *Marketing Research,* 7th ed. Englewood Cliffs, N.J.: Prentice-Hall, 1987.

Peter, J. Paul and Jerry C. Olson, *Consumer Behavior: Marketing Strategy Perspectives.* Homewood, Ill.: Irwin, 1985.

Pratt, Shannon P., *Valuing a Business.* Homewood, Ill.: Business One Irwin, 1989.

———, *Valuing Small Business and Professional Practices.* Homewood, Ill.: Business One Irwin, 1986.

Schiffman, Leon G. and Leslie Lazar Kanuk, *Consumer Behavior,* 4th ed. Englewood Cliffs, N.J.: Prentice-Hall, 1991.

Settle, Robert B. and Pamela L. Abreck, *Niche Marketing: How to Pinpoint Target Markets.* New York: Wiley, 1989.

Tull, Donald S. and Del I. Hawkins, *Marketing Research: Measurement and Method,* 4th ed. New York: Macmillan, 1987.

Walters, C. Glenn and Blaise J. Bergiel, *Consumer Behavior: A Decision-Making Approach.* Cincinnati: South-Western, 1989.

Weiers, Ronald M., *Marketing Research,* 2d ed. Englewood Cliffs, N.J.: Prentice-Hall, 1988.

Wilkie, William L., *Consumer Behavior,* 2d ed. New York: Wiley, 1990.

Business Development Publications Available from the U.S. Small Business Administration

Marketing

MT 2–"Marketing for Small Business: An Overview" ($1.00)
MT 8–"Researching Your Market" ($1.00)

CHAPTER 5

HOW TO JOIN THE SERVICE SECTOR

We begin this chapter with a presentation of the advantages and disadvantages offered by each of the three paths that can lead you to a service business of your own. You may decide to buy an established firm, take on a franchise, or launch a brand new enterprise. The choice, of course, is yours to make.

You are then introduced to, one by one, the three common legal forms of business: the sole proprietorship, the partnership, and the corporation. Each form's benefits and drawbacks are reviewed in some detail to help you decide which is best suited to your needs.

Finally, a discussion of the social responsibilities and ethical behavior of the business owner completes the chapter.

BUYING AN ESTABLISHED SERVICE BUSINESS

The most direct path to entrepreneurship is to purchase someone else's successful operation. If you choose to follow this route, you will avoid many of the problems associated with starting a new business.*

---

*For useful reading on this subject, see: Verne A. Bunn, *Buying and Selling a Small Business.* (Washington, D.C.: Superintendent of Documents, 1969).

The Pros

The business that you buy offers you a ready location; premises that have already been designed and decorated; and equipment, fixtures, merchandise, and supplies on hand for immediate use. You can also expect to inherit a basic clientele. Because of the goodwill built up over time by the firm's previous owner(s), you will not have to struggle through a protracted period before ringing up sales. Indeed, you will most likely do business on the very day you open. Moreover, you will be able to count on experienced employees to help guide you through the first few weeks.

There may also be financial benefits. Depending on how strongly motivated the seller is, you may be fortunate enough to be able to buy the business at a favorable price. You may also succeed in working out favorable payment terms for yourself.

After you have bought the firm, you may find that the experience of the former owner(s) is of great help to you. Moreover, access to internal records should yield worthwhile information about the firm's past performance, assist you in understanding its present situation, and furnish insights into its future potential. You will also benefit by having ready sources of supply at your fingertips.

The Cons

Notwithstanding the foregoing section on the advantages of buying an established business, this avenue does present several drawbacks. First and foremost, problems may exist at the location you chose despite the fact that the firm had apparently enjoyed some degree of success in those premises. The site may not be the best one for your purposes. Perhaps the area has been deteriorating, or local traffic has been thinning out, or some of the neighboring businesses are not of the right kind to complement your operation.

Then, too, the premises themselves may no longer be suited to your needs. Too much, or too little space may be available. Some remodeling may be required. You may have to repair the heating or cooling systems, the plumbing, or electrical wiring. The firm's machinery and/or equipment may be outmoded or in need of repair. The inventory may be outmoded, out of balance, or otherwise unsalable.

The exercise of poor customer relations by the firm's employees and the former owner(s) may have curtailed goodwill toward the firm. Perhaps satisfactory adjustments were not readily made. You may also find out that those experienced employees you acquired do not demonstrate the amount of drive and the selling skills to be able to live up to your expectations. If your subsequent attempts to motivate and train them prove unsuccessful, you may have to replace one or several of them.

As for the financial aspects, you may discover that you paid more for the business than you should have paid. Perhaps your appraisal of the operation's real worth was inaccurate. Or, you were too quick to absorb most of the seller's claims and paid too little attention to existing records. Or, the records were incomplete. Perhaps the business was overloaded with debt; this would make it difficult for you to turn the company around.

What Information Should You Have Before You Buy?

Before you enter into negotiations to buy a going business, you will need to ferret out a great deal of important information. Those facts you must consider will fall into two categories: (1) internal (within the company) and (2) external.

Internal Information—Prepare to dig deeply into all major segments of the operation: the financial side, the clientele, past and present sales, the personnel, legal aspects, and the business premises.

Financial Information—To prepare yourself for the "buy/do not buy" decision, ask for balance sheets and operating statements covering the last five years. If at all possible, try to go back even further—perhaps to as many as 10 years. Request copies of past tax returns as well. Reserve the right to have your accountant audit the seller's records.

Customers—You will need to find out who the firm's customers are, what they are like and what their needs may be, where they are, when they buy, and how they buy. If the firm sells primarily to organizations, try to gather additional information such as the major types of organizations that are being serviced, organization size in terms of sales volume, and who does the buying. If the clientele consists of consumers, check into the demographics: sex, age, size of family, type of residence, income bracket, educational level, and so on.

Sales History—Check into all available sales data. Analyze the information by service(s) and/or products, by customers, and by salespeople. Check through the invoice file to determine the amount of goods, if any, purchased for resale. If company policy included the granting of credit to customers, a review of the accounts receivable records should prove of value. Unfortunately, though, few small businesses maintain adequate sales records. Checking through the records of sales tax payments made to the state may, however, be useful in this connection.

Personnel—Examine payroll records and employee files to become familiar with salary levels, commission structure (if any), worker benefits, and the like. Observe employees in action and talk with them to determine each one's capabilities and efficiency and to ascertain the morale level of the entire group.

Legal Aspects—You will need to look into many legal details. Among other aspects, review zoning ordinances, licenses, permits, building codes, leases, liens and mortgages, and any contracts that are still in effect. Check the documentation for patents, trademarks, and trade-name registration.

The Premises—Walk around the neighborhood to get a good sense of its good and bad points. Go over the business premises with consummate care. Observe the appearance and layout of the place. Have experts check the plumbing, heating, and lighting.

External Information—A wealth of important information lies outside the firm. A sensible first move would be to conduct a thorough analysis of the market—its size, purchasing power, and other demographics, along with likely future patterns. Delve into the firm's position within the market, what competing businesses there are, and what the competition is like. For help, tap your trade association, local banks, the chamber of commerce, and your suppliers.

How to Establish the Price You Should Pay

Typically, both parties to any buy-sell situation seek to get the better of the deal. Sellers ask for as much as they believe they can get, and often more—and buyers are reluctant to pay one cent more than what they think they should pay.

How do you decide how much to offer for the business you are interested in buying?

People who purchase established companies generally rely on one of two approaches in deciding how much to pay: (1) the net-worth method or (2) the return-through-profits technique. The first approach focuses on the appraised value of the firm's assets, less its liabilities, at the time of negotiation. The second technique revolves around the buyer's expectations of future profits and return on investment.

Which procedure should you follow? Although it is the weaker of the two, the net-worth method is by far the more popular approach only because it is easier to work with. For best results, though, we suggest you follow the return-through-profits technique even though you may find it somewhat difficult to make projections of both future profits and return on investment.

The Net-worth Method—A company's net worth can readily be determined by subtracting the dollar value of its liabilities from the total value of its assets. Net worth, liabilities, and assets are all terms you will shortly meet in Chapter 6. At this point, though, it would be useful to identify them, however briefly. A company's *assets* include the financial resources and all other property it uses in its operation. Cash, machinery, equipment, and inventories are some examples. *Liabilities* are debts that the company must repay. Included in this category are short- and long-term loans, unpaid taxes, mortgages, accounts payable (monies owed to suppliers), and other business obligations. To arrive at a company's *net worth,* subtract the total amount of its liabilities from the total value of its assets.

If you choose to follow this method, be sure to secure the seller's permission for an audit. You will need to send in your accountant to appraise the value of all property owned by the firm and to check into all its liabilities as well. Special attention should be paid to the condition of all assets.

The Return-through-profits Technique—To use this method, you will first need to work up forecasts of company sales and profits for the next five years. Based on these figures, estimate how many years it will take for you to break even on your investment (the price you should offer to pay for the business). If you can recoup that amount in four years, then you will have earned an annualized 25 percent return on your investment. Getting your money back in five years would be equivalent to a 20 percent return each year; a six-year recovery period would work out to about 16.3 percent annually. If it would take you any longer than six years to recover your investment, you would probably be better off not bidding for the business.

The Buy/Sell Contract—Even though the owner(s) and you may have agreed on the price for the business, other details need to be worked out. A formal contract should be drawn up and approved by both sides. Among other aspects, the contract should cover the sale, purchase price, method of payment, obligations of both parties, and the seller's agreement not to enter into competition with you.

A government booklet points out the following:

> To protect the interests of both parties, the contract must cover possible problems that are often far from the minds of the buyer and the seller at the time.
>
> What if the buyer defaults on his installment payment of the purchase price? What if the seller's financial statements, which the buyer relied on, turn out to be inaccurate or false? What if the seller turns out to have liabilities that have not been taken into account in the price? What if some of the assets purchased turn out not to be owned by the seller or are subject to undisclosed liens? What if material changes in the business occur before the buy-sell transaction is closed? What if the seller opens a competing business of the same type in the immediate vicinity?*

Refer to Figure 5–1 for the list of the topics covered in the typical buy-sell agreement.

TAKING ON A SERVICE FRANCHISE

Opening a unit of a well-known and well-established franchising organization is usually the safest pathway to starting your own business. At least eight out of every ten franchise units now operating in the United States are believed to be profitable.

What *is* franchising? By way of explanation, here are two quotations from the *Franchise Opportunities Handbook,* a publication of the U.S. Department of Commerce:

> Franchising is both an old and new concept. The term from the French originally meant to be free from servitude. Its meaning in the context of present-day

*Bunn, "Buying and Selling a Small Business," 51.

FIGURE 5–1
Major parts of a typical buy-sell contract

1. Date of the agreement
2. The names of the parties to the agreement
3. The purpose of the agreement
4. The name and location of the business
5. The purchase price of the business
6. The method of payment by the buyer
7. Adjustments to the purchase price to be made at the time of closing
8. The buyer's assumption of business liabilities and contracts
9. The seller's warranties (designed to protect the buyer in the event of undisclosed debts, title defects, fraudulent information, and other unknowns)
10. The seller's obligations up to the date of closing
11. The seller's assumption of risk of loss up to the date of closing
12. The seller's covenant not to compete with the buyer
13. Conditions precedent to closing
14. When and where the closing is to take place
15. Indemnification by the seller (for liabilities not assumed by the buyer, damage, misrepresentation, and the like)
16. Security deposit to be held in escrow
17. Details relating to the arbitration of any disputes that may arise

Source: Adapted from Verne A. Bunn, *Buying and Selling A Small Business,* (Washington, D.C.: U.S. Small Business Administration, 1969), 51–7.

promotions is the opportunity for an individual to own his or her own business, even if they are inexperienced and lacking adequate capital.*

. . . .

Franchising is a form of licensing by which the owner (the franchisor) of a product, service or method obtains distribution through affiliated dealers (the franchisees). The holder of the right is often given exclusive access to a defined geographical area.

The product, method or service being marketed is identified by a brand name, and the franchisor maintains control over the marketing methods employed.**

Basically, two types of franchising are found in our economy: (1) product and trade name franchising, and (2) business format franchising.

---

*U.S. Department of Commerce, *Franchise Opportunities Handbook* (Washington, D.C.: U.S. Department of Commerce, January 1988), xxix.

**Ibid.

Here is how the Department of Commerce differentiates the two types:

> Product and trade name franchising began in the United States as an independent sales relationship between supplier and dealer in which the dealer acquired some of the identity of the supplier. Franchised dealers concentrate on one company's product line and to some extent identify their business with that company. Typical of this segment are automobile and truck dealers, gasoline service stations, and soft drink bottlers.*
>
> Business format franchising is characterized by an ongoing business relationship between franchisor and franchisee that includes not only the product, service, and trademark, but the entire business concept itself—a marketing strategy and plan, operating manuals and standards, quality control, and a continuing process of assistance and guidance. Restaurants, nonfood retailing, personal and business services, rental services, real estate services, and a long list of other service businesses fall into the category of business format franchising. Business format franchising has been responsible for much of the growth of franchising in the United States since 1950 and will continue to offer opportunities for those individuals seeking their own businesses.**

By 1988, sales for the nation's business format franchisors were expected to hit $190 billion, up from $28.7 billion in 1972. Over the same 16-year period, nearly 179,000 new establishments were added in this category. This amounted to an increase of 94.3 percent.† Among the many causes of this rapid expansion were: rising personal income, high levels of consumer optimism, increased competition among companies for market share, changing patterns in household formation, more working women, and new technology.‡

The chart in Figure 5–2 points up the explosive growth in some areas of service franchising.

Among today's better-known franchising organizations in the service sector are Budget Rent A Car, Century 21 Real Estate, Diet Center, H&R Block, Holiday Inns, Kampgrounds of America (KOA), Jiffy Lube, Nutri/System, and Sir Speedy.

For your information, Figure 5–3 (page 66) offers a listing of selected franchisors—along with their home cities, number of franchisees, and brief descriptions of the businesses they are in.

If you contact any franchising organization for further information, expect to receive a rather impressive sales pitch. Be careful. Avoid jumping into any kind of arrangement without serious investigation. You owe it to yourself to research the whole situation thoroughly before signing anything.

Begin by checking all information contained in the prospectus, or "disclosure statement," issued by the franchisor. Also, be sure to review the helpful

---

*U.S. Department of Commerce, *Franchising in the Economy: 1986–1988* (Washington, D.C.: U.S. Department of Commerce, February 1988), 1.

**Ibid., 3–4.

†Ibid., 4.

‡Ibid., 5.

FIGURE 5–2
Selected franchise types: Numbers of establishments, 1970–1988*

Franchise type	1970	1988	Change
Printing and copying services:	329	6,361	+ 1,833.4%
All business aids and services:	10,487	62,977	+ 500.5%
Recreation, entertainment, and travel services:	2,667	8,926	+ 234.7%
Hotels, motels, and campgrounds:	4,000**	10,358	+ 159.0%
Employment services:	2,927	6,881	+ 135.1%
Tax preparation services:	4,708	8,640	+ 83.5%
Rental services (auto/truck, equipment):	10,742	13,886	+ 29.3%
Gasoline service stations:	222,000	112,000	− 49.5%
Laundry and drycleaning services:	4,113	2,570	− 60.0%

*Based on actual figures for 1970 and estimated figures for 1988.
**Estimated.

KEY
1970 (open bar)
1988 (hatched bar)

Source: Andrew Kostecka, *Franchising in the Economy: 1986–1988* (Washington, D.C.: U.S. Department of Commerce, February 1988), 28, 35.

"Checklist for Evaluating a Franchise" contained in Figure 5–4 (page 68). Visit several franchise units to query their owners about their level of satisfaction (or disenchantment) with both their businesses and the franchisor. Discuss the advisability of opening your own unit with your local banker and Chamber of Commerce. Finally, consult an attorney before thinking of signing up.

The Advantages

Even if you, as a would-be franchisee, know little about business in general and next to nothing about the particular type of business you want to get into, the parent organization will most likely teach you just about everything you will need to know. Usually, too, you can count on their help in finding a location, laying out and decorating your premises, furnishing the necessary equipment and machinery, setting up your books, and perhaps installing an inventory control system. They will provide management training, promotional help, and follow-up supervision.

From the very beginning, you will enjoy the customer goodwill that stems from a successful business history and a clear, positive company image. Your franchise will also profit from the enhanced purchasing power of a large chain operation. The premises you occupy will be near-duplicates of the original successful units or, possibly, will reflect a more recent and improved prototype.

You may discover, too, that the parent company maintains throughout the year extensive, professionally-developed promotional programs—in advertising, sales promotion, publicity, and public relations.

The Disadvantages

The most significant drawback to opening a franchised unit is, of course, the requirement that you share all profits with the franchisor. For the life of your contract, you will have to pay the parent company a specified percentage of your net sales. Note that the percentage you pay is based on net sales, not on the profit your unit earns. Depending on the franchisor you sign up with, this percentage can run from 3 or 4 percent to 7 or 8 percent and possibly higher.

There is also the initial franchise fee requested by most successful franchising organizations. This is a single, up-front payment of anywhere from several thousands of dollars to as much as $50,000 and more.

In many cases, you will not be able to interest a company in granting you a franchise unless you can back up your initial investment with a substantial amount of reserve capital. You may, of course, locate a few service franchisors who are willing to talk to investors who command no more than $5,000 or $10,000 in assets. Other companies will only consider applicants whose total assets reach a minimum of a quarter of a million dollars. Some of the better-known fast-food restaurant franchises fall into this category.

Another significant drawback is the insistence on the part of many franchisors that each unit also contribute some percentage of its sales to a promotion

FIGURE 5–3
Selected Franchisors in the Service Sector

Franchisor	Number of Franchisees	Description of Business
Addhair Technologies, Inc. (San Rafael, CA)	14	Hair replacement centers
A to Z Rental Centers (Minneapolis, MN)	63	General purpose rental stores
Barbizon International, Inc. (New York, NY)	91	Modeling and personal development schools
Budget Rent A Car Corporation (Chicago, IL)	3,230	Car and truck rental
Century 21 Real Estate Corporation (Irvine, CA)	6,500+	Real estate offices
Days Inns of America, Inc. (Atlanta, GA)	500+	Hotels and motels
Debit One, Inc. (Springfield, MO)	65	Mobile bookkeeping service
Diet Center, Inc. (Rexburg, ID)	2,200+	Weight control program
Dryclean-U.S.A., Inc. (Miami, FL)	116	Drycleaning establishments
Econo Lube n'Tune, Inc. (Newport Beach, CA)	100	Ten-minute lube and full-service auto shops
Great Clips, Inc. (Minneapolis, MN)	150	Family haircutting shops
Great Expectations (Los Angeles, CA)	17	Singles introduction service
H&R Block (Kansas City, MO)	4,000+ *	Income tax returns
Heel Quick (Marietta, GA)	17	Shoe repair operations
Jani-King, Inc (Dallas, TX)	1,100	Professional cleaning programs for commercial and industrial buildings
Jiffy Lube International, Inc. (Baltimore, MD)	532	Motor vehicle quick lubrication system
Kampgrounds of America, Inc. (Billings, MT)	650	Campgrounds for recreational vehicles

Franchisor	Number of Franchisees	Description of Business
Lawn Doctor, Inc. (Matawan, NJ)	300+	Professional automated lawn services
Lee Myles Associates Corp. (Maywood, NJ)	122	Transmission centers
Mail Boxes Etc. USA (San Diego, CA)	500	Postal and business service centers
Martin Franchises, Inc. (Cincinnati, OH)	1,016	Drycleaning establishments
Merry Maids (Omaha, NE)	450	Professional home cleaning service
Mr. Movies, Inc. (Eden Prairie, MN)	45	Video cassette rental stores
Nutri-System, Inc. (Willow Grove, PA)	731	Weight loss centers
Pearle Vision Centers (Dallas, TX)	500	Full-service optical centers
Putt-Putt Golf Courses of America, Inc. (Fayetteville, NC)	400+	Miniature golf facilities
Rainsoft Water Conditioning Company (Elk Grove Village, IL)	200+	Water treatment equipment for homes, businesses, and industry
Sanford Rose Associates International, Inc. (Akron, OH)	85	Executive recruiting offices
Sir Speedy, Inc. (LaGuna Hills, CA)	800	Printing centers
Sparks Tune-Up, Inc. (King of Prussia, PA)	155	Car tune-up service
Supercuts (San Rafael, CA)	150**	Haircut shops
The Packaging Store, Inc. (Englewood, CO)	130	Custom packaging and shipping service
Travel Agents International, Inc. (Seminole, FL)	285	Retail full-service travel agencies

* Plus 4,800 company-owned offices.
**Over 500 shops.

Source: U.S. Department of Commerce, *Franchise Opportunities Handbook* (Washington, D.C.: U.S. Government Printing Office, January 1988).

FIGURE 5–4
Checklist for evaluating a franchise

The Franchise

1. Did your lawyer approve the franchise contract you are considering after he studied it paragraph by paragraph?
2. Does the franchise call upon you to take any steps which are, according to your lawyer, unwise or illegal in your state, county, or city?
3. Does the franchise give you an exclusive territory for the length of the franchise or can the franchisor sell a second or third franchise in your territory?
4. Is the franchisor connected in any way with any other franchise company handling similar merchandise or services?
5. If the answer to the last question is "yes," what is your protection against this second franchisor organization?
6. Under what circumstances can you terminate the franchise contract and at what cost to you, if you decide for any reason at all that you wish to cancel it?
7. If you sell your franchise, will you be compensated for your good will or will the good will you have built into the business be lost by you?

The Franchisor

1. How many years has the firm offering you a franchise been in operation?
2. Has it a reputation for honesty and fair dealing among the local firms holding its franchise?
3. Has the franchisor shown you any certified figures indicating exact net profits of one or more going firms which you personally checked yourself with the franchisee?
4. Will the firm assist you with:
   (a) A management training program?
   (b) An employee training program?
   (c) A public relations program?
   (d) Capital?
   (e) Credit?
   (f) Merchandising ideas?
5. Will the firm help you find a good location for your new business?
6. Is the franchising firm adequately financed so that it can carry out its stated plan of financial assistance and expansion?
7. Is the franchisor a one-person company or a corporation with an experienced management trained in depth (so that there would always be an experienced person at its head)?
8. Exactly what can the franchisor do for you which you cannot do for yourself?
9. Has the franchisor investigated you carefully enough to assure itself that you can successfully operate one of their franchises at a profit both to them and to you?
10. Does your state have a law regulating the sale of franchises and has the franchisor complied with that law?

You—The Franchisee

1. How much equity capital will you have to have to purchase the franchise and operate it until your income equals your expenses? Where are you going to get it?

2. Are you prepared to give up some independence of action to secure the advantages offered by the franchise?

3. Do YOU really believe you have the innate ability, training, and experience to work smoothly and profitably with the franchisor, your employees, and your customers?

4. Are you ready to spend much or all of the remainder of your business life with this franchisor, offering its product or service to your public?

Your Market

1. Have you made any study to determine whether the product or service which you propose to sell under franchise has a market in your territory at the prices you will have to charge?

2. Will the population in the territory given you increase, remain static, or decrease over the next 5 years?

3. Will the product or service you are considering be in greater demand, about the same, or less demand 5 years from now than today?

4. What competition exists in your territory already for the product or service you contemplate selling?

(a) Nonfranchise firms?
(b) Franchise firms?

Source: U.S. Department of Commerce, *Franchise Opportunities Handbook* (Washington, D.C.: Department of Commerce, January 1988), xxiii–xxxiv.

fund. Depending on the requirements of the parent company, this percentage can range from 1 to 4 or 5 percent of sales. The money is spent on national and/or regional advertising as well as on various kinds of sales promotion.

As a general rule, too, you are permitted to sell only those products and/or services that the parent company has designated. Without the franchisor's permission, you may not introduce any other products or services, even if your local competitors are successfully selling them.

If you are unhappy with the arrangement you have, there is little you can do about it. Without the franchisor's blessing, you cannot legally sell the franchise to anyone else. Moreover, the parent company may cancel your franchise contract if your unit's sales do not meet their expectations, or if you fail to observe and follow all their rules and regulations to their complete satisfaction. As a further discouragement, the typical franchise contract contains a "buy-back" clause that gives the franchisor the right to buy back your unit at will.

STARTING A NEW SERVICE ENTERPRISE

Launching a new business will entail greater risk on your part than either buying a successful operation or opening a franchised unit. Yet, this avenue is the most challenging—and probably the most rewarding—of the three approaches. It also offers you several unique benefits.

The Benefits

A singular advantage of this avenue to entrepreneurship is that many kinds of service operations can be started at home. If the business you plan to open falls into this category, then you are indeed fortunate. Not only will you save a goodly amount of thought and effort but you will also discover that you need less capital to start off with.

If, however, you must seek some other location from which to run your business, you will find that the possibilities are practically unlimited. You can go wherever you want to go; you are not locked into any one area. Nor are you bound by space limitations that were predetermined for you by a franchisor or the former owner(s) of an established business. Ultimately, of course, your choices will depend on the amount of capital you have at your disposal. How you fill that space is completely up to you and your own creativity. You will also make your own decisions about the interior design and decor of your premises.

There are other benefits to this approach. You alone will possess the right and the authority to market whatever service(s) and/or products you want to sell. In addition, you can and should devise your own pricing approaches and procedures. Finally, all facets of promotion (advertising, personal selling, sales promotion, publicity, public relations) lie in your hands only, to do with as you see fit.

The Drawbacks

Although this conduit into the world of small business offers obvious benefits, it also presents a few disadvantages. Long before you are ready to launch your new enterprise, you will find yourself operating under a serious handicap: a severe lack of information. To gain the knowledge you need, expect to exert a considerable amount of preparatory effort. Among other things, you will need to decide who your customers will be, discover what they are like, determine how best to reach them, ascertain the latest industry trends, and generally learn as much as you can about your chief competitors.

You will also need to pursue, locate, and cultivate sources of supply: companies that will provide you with the equipment, materials, supplies, and other items you need to operate your new business.

Moreover, because your firm is new, you will be unable to draw upon past experiences to help you surmount unexpected difficulties. You will have to proceed at your own pace, learning from your mistakes as you go along. Neither can you expect a ready clientele; you will need to prospect for organizations or consumers whose needs your service(s) can fulfill.

DECIDING ON YOUR LEGAL FORM OF OPERATION

Before launching your new business, you will need to select the best legal form of operation for your particular circumstances.

Three distinct formats are available: the sole proprietorship, the partnership, and the corporation. Each, of course, offers both advantages and drawbacks. Each is also regarded in a different light by the U.S. Internal Revenue Service insofar as income tax liability is concerned.

To help you make your decision, the pros and cons of the three forms are presented in the next few pages.

The Sole Proprietorship

This is the most popular legal form. More than seven out of every ten business enterprises in the U.S. follow this approach.

The Pros—Ease of organization is an outstanding advantage of the sole proprietorship. If you intend to run the business under your own name, you simply start up the operation. However, few business owners choose to operate under their own names. If you plan to use a *tradename,* you will need to file a "Certificate of Conducting Business under an Assumed (or Fictitious) Name" with the county or town clerk where your business will be situated. (See Figure 5–5 for a sample D/B/A form; the initials stand for "Doing Business As.") In some areas, you must also publish in the local newspaper your intent to carry on business under your tradename.

Start-up costs are typically insignificant. Other than the cost of filing your D/B/A certificate and paying the requisite fee, you may need to apply for a permit or two and, for certain types of business, a special license.

As sole owner, you run your operation as you see fit. You are in complete control; all decisions are up to you. Moreover, you alone keep any profit the business produces (less taxes, of course!). Because the sole proprietorship is not considered a taxable entity, it incurs no income tax liability. However, you will need to declare and pay tax on all income you earn from the business. This includes both any salary you pay yourself and any profit earned by the firm.

Should you so desire, you will find it easier to close down a sole proprietorship than to terminate either a partnership or a corporation. Providing you fulfill all outstanding obligations, you can simply lock your door and walk away from it all.

Another advantage is the fact that, of the three legal forms, the proprietorship is the one least regulated by government agencies.

FIGURE 5–5
Sample D/B/A form

Blumbergs Law Products X 201—Certificate of Conducting Business under an Assumed Name For Individual JULIUS BLUMBERG, INC., LAW BLANK PUBLISHERS

Business Certificate

I HEREBY CERTIFY *that I am conducting or transacting business under the name or designation of*

at

City or Town of *County of* *State of New York.*

*My full name is**
and I reside at

I FURTHER CERTIFY *that I am the successor in interest to*

the person or persons heretofore using such name or names to carry on or conduct or transact business.

IN WITNESS WHEREOF, *I have this* *day of* *19* *, made and signed this certificate.*

* Print or type name.
* If under 18 years of age, state "I am.............years of age".

STATE OF NEW YORK
COUNTY OF } *ss.:*

On this *day of* *19* *, before me personally appeared*

to me known and known to me to be the individual described in and who executed the foregoing certificate, and he thereupon duly acknowledged to me that he executed the same.

Source: Forms may be purchased from Julius Blumberg, Inc., NYC 10013, or any of its dealers. Reproduction prohibited.

INDEX No.

Certificate
of

....

....

....

....

CONDUCTING BUSINESS UNDER THE NAME OF

....

....

Finally, if you suffer a loss during your first year of operation, you will be permitted to deduct that loss from any salary you may have earned at another job that same year.

The Cons—The main drawback to this legal form is the owner's personal liability for business obligations. Should you be unable to repay your debts, your creditors can sue you personally to recover what you owe them.

Banks and investors are reluctant to offer capital to the sole proprietorship because the firm is directed by only one person. If you, as owner, should suffer a prolonged illness or be otherwise incapacitated, the entire operation can go down the tube. Also, since the business and its owner are practically inseparable, if you should die, the business would close down.

Another disadvantage is that your business activities would be limited by the sole set of skills you bring to it. You cannot draw upon the capabilities of others, at least not until you can afford to pay for their assistance.

Then, too, although you are entitled to any profit you earn, you may discover that there is not any profit at all. You will, however, have to bear any loss your business suffers.

The Partnership

Occasionally, entrepreneurs will seek to enter partnerships rather than start up on their own. At times, their major motivation is simply that they lack sufficient financing for the venture. Or, it may be that an individual lacks the confidence to go it alone. Another possibility is that the expected workload is too heavy for one person.

Whatever the reason for this choice, two or more people can pool their resources to form a partnership. In the business world, most partners are *general* partners. General partners invest time and effort as well as capital in the business. They participate actively in day-to-day operations.

A partnership may have one or more *limited* partners. Although these individuals invest in and own part of the operation, they do not work in the business itself.

The Pros—Start-up costs for the partnership form are modest. You need to file only one document with the local government—the "Certificate of Conducting Business as Partners." (See Figure 5–6). For your own protection, though, we recommend having a "partnership agreement" drawn up. This document should also contain a "buy-sell clause." This clause outlines the procedure to be followed when disposing of a partner's share of the business.

There are two other advantages to the partnership form. Because two or more people pool their finances, the firm usually starts off with considerably more capital than does the typical sole proprietorship. Partners also bring along their individual knowledges and skills, thus expanding the talent base for the new organization to tap.

The Cons—The partnership format does have several weaknesses. Perhaps its most important drawback is that partners face the same personal liability

FIGURE 5–6
Certificate of conducting business as partners

Blumbergs Law Products X 74—Certificate of Conducting Business as Partners. Individual — Corporation.

Business Certificate for Partners

The undersigned do hereby certify that they are conducting or transacting business as members of a partnership under the name or designation of

at

in the County of , State of New York, and do further certify that the full names of all the persons conducting or transacting such partnership including the full names of all the partners with the residence address of each such person, and the age of any who may be infants, are as follows:

***NAME** Specify which are infants and state ages.*	***RESIDENCE***
....	....
....	....
....	....
....	....
....	....
....	....

***WE DO FURTHER CERTIFY** that we are the successors in interest to*

the person or persons heretofore using such name or names to carry on or conduct or transact business.

In Witness Whereof, *We have this day of 19 made and signed this certificate.*

....

....

....

....

....

....

State of New York, County of **ss.:** **INDIVIDUAL ACKNOWLEDGMENT**

On this day of 19 , before me personally appeared

to me known and known to me to be the individual described in, and who executed the foregoing certificate, and he thereupon duly acknowledged to me that he executed the same.

Source: Forms may be purchased from Julius Blumberg, Inc., NYC 10013, or any of its dealers. Reproduction prohibited.

State of New York, County of **ss.:** CORPORATE ACKNOWLEDGMENT

On this day of 19 , before me personally appeared

to me known, who being by me duly sworn, did depose and say, that he resides in

that he is the of

the corporation described in and which executed the foregoing certificate; that he knows the seal of said corporation; that the seal affixed to said certificate is such corporate seal; that it was so affixed by order of the Board of of said corporation, and that he signed h name thereto by like order.

INDEX No.

Certificate of Partners

CONDUCTING BUSINESS UNDER THE NAME OF

State of New York, County of **ss.:** INDIVIDUAL ACKNOWLEDGMENT

On this day of 19 , before me personally appeared

to me known and known to me to be the individual described in, and who executed the foregoing certificate, and he thereupon duly acknowledged to me that he executed the same.

problem as do sole proprietors. Each and every partner can be sued to collect on business debts that the firm cannot repay.

Then, too, you will need to share with your partner(s) any profits the business earns. You will also experience some loss of control since you will not be the sole decision-maker. Your partner(s) will share authority as well as duties and responsibilities. As a consequence, disagreements are bound to occur from time to time. As tensions mount, it becomes more difficult to smooth out situations. Ordinarily, just getting along with one's partners is no mean feat!

Here is something else for you to think about. An action taken by any one partner is legally binding on all partners.

Finally, like sole proprietorships, partnerships lack continuity. The business terminates upon the death of any partner. You can, though, anticipate this last situation with a well-conceived partnership agreement prepared in advance of start-up.

The Corporation

The corporate form is the most complex of the three legal formats. If you choose to incorporate your new service business, be sure to seek the aid of an attorney. You will need a lawyer not only to file the necessary documents but also to draw up a "Preincorporation Agreement" for the principals involved.

To create a corporation, you must apply for a corporate charter. To obtain the charter, you will need to file your Certificate of Incorporation with the Secretary of State of the state where your principal office is located. A check for the required fee must accompany your application. (A sample certificate of incorporation is shown in Figure 5–7.)

The Pros—This is the only legal format that can relieve you from the personal liability peril. Should your new operation fail, your debtors can seize only corporate assets.

A second benefit is that, among business formats, only the corporation enjoys a life of its own. Legally an entity, it continues to exist despite the demise of its owner(s).

Transfer of ownership is easily accomplished by selling shares in the company. Moreover, investors and lenders usually regard the corporation—with its stockholders—as less of a risk than either the sole proprietorship or partnership.

As a final thought, a corporation can often fill management slots with specialists because it employs a number of people.

The Cons—Organizing a corporation is more costly than setting up either of the other two legal forms of business. Although you could, of course, apply for a charter without legal assistance, you would be better off hiring an attorney for this task.

An unfortunate drawback to the corporate form is the fact that the firm's profits actually are taxed twice. As a taxable entity, the corporation must pay income tax on its earnings. In addition, profits that are distributed to company shareholders constitute taxable income for those individuals.

FIGURE 5–7
Certificate of Incorporation

A 234—Certificate of Incorporation
Business Corporation Law §402: 9-87

Certificate of Incorporation of

under Section 402 of the Business Corporation Law

IT IS HEREBY CERTIFIED THAT:

(1) The name of the proposed corporaton is

(2) The purpose or purposes for which this corporation is formed, are as follows, to wit:
To engage in any lawful act or activity for which corporations may be organized under the Business Corporation Law. The corporation is not formed to engage in any act or activity requiring the consent or approval of any state official, department, board, agency or other body.*

The corporation, in furtherance of its corporate purposes above set forth, shall have all of the powers enumerated in Section 202 of the Business Corporation Law, subject to any limitations provided in the Business Corporation Law or any other statute of the State of New York.

*If specific consent or approval is required delete this paragraph, insert specific purposes and obtain consent or approval prior to filing.

Source: Forms may be purchased from Julius Blumberg, Inc., NYC 10013, or any of its dealers. Reproduction prohibited.

(3) The office of the corporation is to be located in the County of
State of New York.

(4) The aggregate number of shares which the corporation shall have the authority to issue is

FIGURE 7–7
(Continued)

(5) The Secretary of State is designated as agent of the corporation upon whom process against it may be served. The post office address to which the Secretary of State shall mail a copy of any process against the corporation served upon him is

(6) A director of the corporation shall not be liable to the corporation or its shareholders for damages for any breach of duty in such capacity except for

(i) liability if a judgment or other final adjudication adverse to a director establishes that his or her acts or omissions were in bad faith or involved intentional misconduct or a knowing violation of law or that the director personally gained in fact a financial profit or other advantage to which he or she was not legally entitled or that the director's acts violated BCL § 719, or

(ii) liability for any act or omission prior to the adoption of this provision.

The undersigned incorporator, or each of them if there are more than one, is of the age of eighteen years or over.

IN WITNESS WHEREOF, this certificate has been subscribed on 19 by the undersigned who affirm(s) that the statements made herein are true under the penalties of perjury.

Type name of incorporator — Signature

Address

Type name of incorporator — Signature

Address

Type name of incorporator — Signature

Address

Certificate of Incorporation

of

under Section 402 of the Business Corporation Law

Filed By:

Office and Post Office Address

Corporations are more closely regulated than either partnerships or sole proprietorships. They are also plagued with extensive record-keeping requirements.

S Corporations—At times, it may be more beneficial for a new (or even an established) corporation to choose S corporation status rather than the customary type. S corporations do not pay income tax on earned profit. Instead, the shareholders incur income tax liability for distributed profits. (For more details about the S-corporation, see Chapter 15.)

For reference purposes, Figure 5–8 recapitulates the advantages and disadvantages of the three legal forms of business.

FIGURE 5–8
Legal forms of business operation: Advantages and disadvantages

SOLE PROPRIETORSHIP

Advantages	*Disadvantages*
Simplest legal form to set up	Personal liability for business obligations
Lowest start-up cost	Difficult to attract additional capital
Owner makes all decisions	Business may be jeopardized by owner's unexpected disability
Owner retains all profits	Owner's death terminates business
Terminating business is easy	
Greatest freedom from regulation	
Business losses may be offset against other earned income	

PARTNERSHIP

Advantages	*Disadvantages*
Simple to set up	Personal liability for business obligations
Low start-up cost	Relinquishing of some authority
More capital to start with	Difficult to attract additional capital
Additional skills/talents available	Profits must be shared
Sharing of risks and work responsibilities	Partner's decision is binding
Relatively free of government regulation	Dissolution of business upon partner's death
Business losses may be offset against other earned income	Disagreements among partners are common
	Need for a partnership agreement

CORPORATION

Advantages	*Disadvantages*
Limited liability	Most costly form to organize
Has its own legal existence: business continues after death of principal(s)	Double taxation
Ownership easily transferred	Most closely regulated form
Best form for raising additional capital	Involves considerable recordkeeping and paperwork
Possible tax advantages	
Additional skills/talents available	

YOUR SOCIAL RESPONSIBILITIES AS BUSINESS OWNER

Modern business management calls for much more than running an enterprise that produces or buys goods and/or services and then sells them, thereby earning profits. It calls for an appreciation of the firm's responsibilities toward the society within which it operates. These obligations extend from conserving our natural resources and protecting the environment to improving our quality of life. It requires an enlightened approach that strives to maintain a valid code of ethics and observe current standards of moral conduct in all dealings with its various publics, both external (customers, suppliers, competitors, government agencies) and internal (employees, stockholders). In addition, management needs to be aware of the attitudes consumers hold toward the business sphere in general and toward marketing activity in particular.

Consumerism

The twentieth century has witnessed three distinct consumer movements. The first appeared at the turn of the century. In the main, it developed as a backlash to the raw power that a few giant trusts had been exercising since the late 1800s, the manufacturing and distribution of adulterated foods and drugs, and other unfair business practices. The second grew out of the Great Depression of the 1930s and the third began early in the 1960s. In 1962, President John F. Kennedy announced these "Four Basic Rights" of consumers: the right to safety, right to be informed, right to choose, and right to be heard.

Changing socioeconomic factors set the climate for this last wave of consumerism. Among others, these included greater consumer affluence, a more relaxed work ethic, increasing self-assertiveness, and a higher level of educational attainment. The current movement was fueled by a variety of detrimental practices and, occasionally, abuses engaged in by business organizations.

Over the last several decades, consumers not only have voiced their disapproval but also have stridently objected to evidences of:

- False or misleading advertising
- Incomplete, misleading, or erroneous labeling of products
- Lack of responsiveness to consumer needs
- Misrepresentation in personal selling and in other forms of promotion
- Poor service
- Production of inferior or shoddy goods
- Incorporation of planned obsolescence in products
- Unethical pricing practices
- Unnecessarily high prices of goods and services due to excessive advertising expenditures
- Unsatisfactory resolution of customer complaints

FIGURE 5–9
Federal laws that protect the consumer

Year Enacted	Law	Intent of Law
1906	The Pure Food and Drug Act	Banned the adulteration and misbranding of food and drugs by companies engaged in interstate commerce; established the Food and Drug Administration (FDA).
1938	The Food, Drug, and Cosmetic Act	Widened the powers of the FDA; added cosmetics and therapeutics to those articles covered by the 1906 act.
1953	The Flammable Fabrics Act	Prohibited interstate shipments of clothing made from flammable fabrics. Later extended to cover home furnishings and other materials.
1958	The Automobile Information Disclosure Act	Required the full disclosure of information by new-car dealers.
1960	The Hazardous Substances Labeling Act	Ordered manufacturers to attach warning labels to bottles and other types of containers that hold dangerous or poisonous chemicals.
1956	The Fair Packaging and Labeling Act	Required that a list of the ingredients in packaged foods and other products appear on the container.
1968	The Consumer Credit Protection Act	Mandated that sellers disclose all terms and charges to customers who buy on credit.
1969	The Child Protection and Toy Safety Act	Banned the sale of unsafe toys.
1970	The Public Health Smoking Act	Mandated that cigarette packages as well as cigarette ads must display notices that warn consumers of the dangers of smoking.
1972	The Consumer Product Safety Act	Prohibited the manufacture and sale of unsafe products; established the Consumer Product Safety Commission.
1975	The Equal Credit Opportunity Act	Banned discrimination based on sex or marital status in the granting of consumer credit. Subsequently amended to include discrimination because of race, religion, national origin, and age.
1975	The Fair Credit Billing Act	Banned unfair credit practices; facilitated the questioning of billing entries by consumers.
1977	The Fair Debt Collection Practices Act	Banned the use of deceptive or abusive methods in the collection of delinquent accounts.

- Vague or ineffectual guarantees and warranties
- Willingness to manufacture and sell hazardous products

Each of the three movements led to the passage of federal legislation aimed at protecting the consumer. (See Figure 5-9 for a partial listing of consumer protection laws.) Across the country, many state and local governments instituted consumer agencies to protect the public's welfare. Some large companies have established active consumer affairs departments.

Suggestions for the Socially Responsive Company

Here are a few of the things you can and should do to establish your firm as a good neighbor and an active member of the community:

- Avoid contributing in any way to pollution of any type (air, water, noise)
- Find jobs for the handicapped
- Maintain a clean environment
- Observe civil rights legislation
- Offer complete information on all your labels
- Participate in community affairs
- Pay close attention to the ecology
- Recycle materials whenever possible
- Refuse to make or distribute unsafe products
- Resolve all customer complaints satisfactorily
- Strive to conserve essential resources
- Support urban renewal projects
- Train, if necessary, and employ the disadvantaged

FOR FURTHER INFORMATION

Books

Bond, Robert E. and Christopher E. Bond, *The Source Book of Franchise Opportunities: 1990/1991 Edition.* Homewood, Ill.: Business One Irwin, 1990.

Coltman, Michael M., *Buying and Selling a Small Business,* 2d ed. Bellingham, Wash.: Self-Counsel Press, 1990.

Dunckel, Jacqueline, *Good Ethics—Good Business: Your Plan for Success.* Bellingham, Wash.: Self-Counsel Press, 1989.

Hagendorf, Stanley, *The Complete Guide to Buying and Selling a Business,* 6th ed. Englewood Cliffs, N.J.: Prentice-Hall, 1986.

Justis, Robert T. and Richard J. Judd, *Franchising.* Cincinnati: South-Western, 1989.

Mangold, M. A., *How to Buy a Small Business,* rev. ed. New York: Pilot Books, 1987.

Pilot Books Staff and Samuel Small, *Directory of Franchising Organizations,* rev. ed. New York: Pilot Books, 1989.

Pratt, Shannon P., *Valuing a Business.* Homewood, Ill.: Business One Irwin, 1989.

Rust, Herbert, *Owning Your Own Franchise.* Englewood Cliffs, N.J.: Prentice-Hall, 1991.

Siegel, William L., *Franchising.* New York: Wiley, 1983.

Sitarz, Daniel, *The Complete Book of Small Business Legal Forms.* Carbondale, Ill.: Nova Publishing, 1991.

Business Development Publications Available from the U.S. Small Business Administration

Management and Planning

MP 25–"Selecting the Legal Structure for Your Business" ($1.00)
MP 26–"Evaluating Franchise Opportunities" ($1.00)

Booklets Available from the Superintendent of Documents

S/N 003-009-00596-5–*Franchise Opportunities Handbook, 1991*–$16.00

CHAPTER 6

GETTING ACQUAINTED WITH THE FINANCIAL SIDE

Nothing is perhaps as important to the success of a business as the efficient handling of its finances. Skilled financial management should, of course, begin long before the enterprise takes form. Undercapitalization is a major problem that afflicts many new ventures. A sizable proportion of each year's batch of aspiring entrepreneurs apparently scrape together whatever funds they can and then seem to plunge willy-nilly into the business stream. Apparently, few of them have seen fit to engage in serious financial planning.

One of the surest keys to a successful new-business launch is to formulate your initial capital requirements, using the best thinking you are capable of. A second key, equally as important, is to become thoroughly conversant with all aspects of business finance.

"But having money," admonishes the U.S. Small Business Administration, "does not guarantee making money–that is, making a profit. You not only have to have money; you have to use it well. That is why financial management is important."*

The SBA then proceeds to expand on the term "financial management":

Financial management includes the following functions:

---

*Jack Zwick, "A Handbook of Small Business Finance," 8th ed. *Small Business Management Series No. 15* (Washington, D.C.: U.S. Small Business Administration, 1975), 1.

- Seeing that the assets of the business are used in such a way as to bring the highest possible return on the money invested.
- Evaluating the need for new assets.
- Obtaining funds to finance asset additions.
- Managing both old and new assets so that each contributes its full share toward the profitable operation of the business.
- Repaying borrowed funds from profits those funds have generated.*

This chapter begins by introducing you to the two principal accounting documents: the balance sheet and the operating statement. You will become acquainted with their formats as well as the meanings of the terms used in them. (In Chapter 14, you will discover out how valuable these two documents can be in helping you run your business.) Following this introduction, we offer a useful method for determining how much capital you will need to get your new firm off to a proper start. You will also be shown how to calculate the "break-even point" for your business. To conclude the chapter, we describe a dozen possible sources of capital for your consideration.

UNDERSTANDING THE BALANCE SHEET

The balance sheet is one of the two principal accounting statements prepared at least once each year by all businesses. It is a summary of the firm's financial

FIGURE 6–1
Balance sheet for a small service firm

			Baytik Equipment **Balance** **December**
ASSETS			
CURRENT ASSETS			
Cash on hand and in bank	18,620		
Marketable securities	5,120		
Accounts receivable, less allowance for bad debts	13,560		
Merchandise inventory	8,770		
Supplies inventory	5,065		
Total current assets		$51,135	
FIXED ASSETS			
Building, less depreciation	48,300		
Machinery and equipment, less depreciation	17,890		
Furniture, less depreciation	11,460		
Van, less depreciation	9,070		
Total fixed assets		86,720	
TOTAL ASSETS			$137,855

*Ibid.

status at a given point in time. Most often, that point is the end of the firm's calendar or fiscal year. In many companies, though, balance sheets are prepared for each quarter of the year. Some firms even request them on a monthly basis.

Figure 6–1 displays an end-of-year balance sheet for a small service business. You will note that this document is divided into two halves. On the left-hand side of the page are listed the company's assets. Liabilities and net worth are shown on the right-hand side. Note also that the total amounts shown at the bottom of both sides of the balance sheet are the same–$137,855. Thus, one half "balances" the other.

Every balance sheet contains three sections: *assets, liabilities,* and *net worth.* According to the statement in Figure 6–1, the total value of all assets owned by the Baytik Equipment Rental Company–as of December 31, 1991–amounted to $137,855. At that point in time, the firm also faced liabilities of $72,250 and had a net worth (total assets – total liabilities) of $65,505.

Brief explanations of the more significant terms in the document appear below:

Assets	–	Money and other property of value that the firm owns or is due.
Current Assets	–	Assets that the company will use in its operation during the current year. (Examples: cash, bonds, stocks, accounts receivable, inventories.)

Rental Company
Sheet
31, 1991

LIABILITIES AND NET WORTH			
CURRENT LIABILITIES			
Accounts payable	$10,140		
Notes payable within one year	20,000		
Accrued taxes	2,110		
Total current liabilities		$32,250	
LONG-TERM LIABILITIES			
Note payable, due 1994	$20,000		
Note payable, due 1996	20,000		
Total long-term liabilities		40,000	
TOTAL LIABILITIES			$72,250
NET WORTH ("Owner's Equity")			65,505
TOTAL LIABILITIES AND NET WORTH			$137,855

Fixed Assets – Company property acquired for long-term use. Such items are recorded on the balance sheet at their original cost less accumulated depreciation. (Examples: buildings, machinery, equipment, furniture, cars, trucks, patents.)

Total Assets – Current assets plus fixed assets.

Liabilities – Obligations that the business must pay.

Current Liabilities – Debts owed to suppliers and other creditors that need to be repaid during the current year. (Examples: accounts payable, short-term notes, interest payable, accrued payroll, accrued taxes.)

Long-term Liabilities – Company obligations with a maturity date beyond the current year. (Examples: mortgages, bank loans, equipment loans.)

Total Liabilities – Current liabilities plus long-term liabilities.

Net worth – The amount that is left after the firm's liabilities are subtracted from its assets.

HOW TO PREPARE AN OPERATING STATEMENT

The operating statement offers a picture of the company's sales, expenses, and profit (or loss) over a specified period. Other names commonly used for this important document are income statement or profit-and-loss statement (P&L). As is true of balance sheets, operating statements should be prepared more frequently than once a year. It is especially important for the new company with limited resources. Not only will a monthly P&L show how the business is progressing but it also enables management to institute corrective measures, when needed, in a timely fashion.

An end-of-year operating statement appears in Figure 6–2.

For your information, here are the major sections of an operating statement:

Net Sales – Net revenue that flowed into the business during the period specified—for goods sold (if any) and for service(s) rendered.

Cost of Goods Sold – The total cost of all goods sold during this period.

Gross Margin – The difference remaining after subtracting the cost of goods sold from net sales.

FIGURE 6–2
Operating statement for a small service firm

BAYTIK EQUIPMENT RENTAL COMPANY
Operating Statement
For Year Ended: *December 31, 1991*

NET SALES		$211,340
–COST OF GOODS SOLD		9,280
GROSS MARGIN		$202,060
–OPERATING EXPENSES		
Salaries and wages	$83,440	
Rent	24,250	
Payroll taxes	5,830	
Depreciation	11,510	
Telephone	5,750	
Supplies	5,480	
Advertising and promotion	9,540	
Utilities	4,770	
Postage	3,800	
Maintenance	5,050	
Insurance	4,750	
Truck Expense	7,190	
Interest expense	4,385	
Dues and subscriptions	875	
Travel and entertainment	775	
Miscellaneous expenses	1,845	
Total operating expenses		– 179,180
OPERATING PROFIT		$22,880
+ OTHER INCOME		
Dividends	165	
Interest on bank account	1,010	
Total other income		1,175
Total income		$24,055
Less provision for income tax		– 6,500
NET PROFIT		$16,785

Operating Expenses – All expenses incurred while operating the enterprise during the period.

Operating Profit – The amount remaining after subtracting operating expenses from the gross margin earned.

Other Income – Income other than the net sales brought in by operating the business. (Examples: dividends on stock, interest on bank accounts.)

Net Profit (or Net Loss) – The difference between total income and the money set aside for paying income tax.

ESTIMATING HOW MUCH CAPITAL YOU WILL NEED

Undercapitalization is a common symptom among business startups. Each year, an alarming number of new enterprises run into problems paying their bills, often within a matter of months after opening. Usually, this occurs because the entrepreneurs neglected to pay as much attention to the financial end of the business as they probably devoted to all the other aspects.

Be sure to start off right. Below is a step-by-step procedure designed to help you determine the amount of financing you are likely to need to ensure a successful business start:

1. Begin by spending a few minutes glancing over Figure 6–3. As you read down the page, you will note that the worksheet is divided into two sections: (1) "Estimated Monthly Expenses" and (2) "Starting Costs You Only Have to Pay Once."
2. To begin your planning, your first challenge is to work up a realistic estimate of the sales volume you expect your new service business to produce in its first year of operation. Then, divide your expected first-year sales by 12 to derive a monthly sales estimate. Insert the monthly figure in the space indicated at the top of Column 1.
3. Proceed down Column 1, entering well-thought-through estimates of how much you will probably have to spend in the various expense categories. (Hint: First work out yearly totals for every category, then divide annual totals by 12 to arrive at your monthly figures.)
4. Now, refer to Column 3; the heading reads "What to Put in Column 2." Following the suggestions offered, enter appropriate amounts in Column 2–"Your Estimate of How Much Cash You Need to Start Your Business."
5. You are ready to tackle the second section of this form–"Starting Costs You Only Have to Pay Once." However, before you proceed, refer to Figure 6–4–"Worksheet for Furniture, Fixtures, and Equipment." Following the directions indicated in the column heads, begin estimating costs for any furniture, fixtures, and equipment you plan to use in your business. Total the last column. Transfer this total to column 2 in Figure 6–3–on the line that reads "Fixtures and Equipment."

FIGURE 6–3
Worksheet for estimating your financial needs

WORKSHEET NO. 2

ESTIMATED MONTHLY EXPENSES			
Item	Your estimate of monthly expenses based on sales of $ ______ per year	Your estimate of how much cash you need to start your business (See column 3.)	What to put in column 2 (These figures are typical for one kind of business. you will have to decide how many months to allow for in your business.)
	Column 1	Column 2	Column 3
Salary of owner-manager	$	$	2 times column 1
All other salaries and wages			3 times column 1
Rent			3 times column 1
Advertising			3 times column 1
Delivery expense			3 times column 1
Supplies			3 times column 1
Telephone and telegraph			3 times column 1
Other utilities			3 times column 1
Insurance			Payment required by insurance company
Taxes, including Social Security			4 times column 1
Interest			3 times column 1
Maintenance			3 times column 1
Legal and other professional fees			3 times column 1
Miscellaneous			3 times column 1
STARTING COSTS YOU ONLY HAVE TO PAY ONCE			Leave column 2 blank
Fixtures and equipment			Fill in worksheet 3 on page 12 and put the total here
Decorating and remodeling			Talk it over with a contractor
Installation of fixtures and equipment			Talk to suppliers from who you buy these
Starting inventory			Suppliers will probably help you estimate this
Deposits with public utilities			Find out from utilities companies
Legal and other professional fees			Lawyer, accountant, and so on
Licenses and permits			Find out from city offices what you have to have
Advertising and promotion for opening			Estimate what you'll use
Accounts receivable			What you need to buy more stock until credit customers pay
Cash			For unexpected expenses or losses, special purchases, etc.
Other			Make a separate list and enter total
TOTAL ESTIMATED CASH YOU NEED TO START WITH		$	Add up all the numbers in column 2

Source: "Checklist for Going into Business," *Small Marketers Aid No. 71* (Washington, D.C.: U.S. Small Business Administration, 1977), 6–7.

FIGURE 6–4
Worksheet for estimating your costs of furniture, fixtures, and equipment

LIST OF FURNITURE, FIXTURES, AND EQUIPMENT					
Leave out or add items to suit your business. Use separate sheets to list exactly what you need for each of the items below.	If you plan to pay cash in full, enter the full amount below and in the last column.	If you are going to pay by installments, fill out the columns below. Enter in the last column your downpayment plus at least one installment.			Estimate of the cash you need for furniture, fixtures, and equipment
		Price	Down-payment	Amount of each installment	
Counters	$	$	$	$	$
Storage shelves, cabinets					
Display stands, shelves, tables					
Cash register					
Safe					
Window display fixtures					
Special lighting					
Outside sign					
Delivery equipment if needed					
TOTAL FURNITURE, FIXTURES, AND EQUIPMENT (Enter this figure also in worksheet 2 under "Starting Costs You Only Have To Pay Once".)					$

Source: "Checklist for Going into Business," *Small Marketers Aid No. 71* (Washington, D.C.: U.S. Small Business Administration, 1977), 12.

6. Continue down column 2. Again following the suggestions noted in column 3, enter your estimates for the remaining lines in this section.
7. Total all entries you made in column 2. The sum represents the amount of capital you will need to launch your business properly.

HOW TO CALCULATE YOUR BREAK-EVEN POINT

Manufacturers use *break-even analysis* to determine selling prices for the goods they produce. Retailers rely on break-even analysis to find out the minimum markup they must maintain in order to cover all expenses they incur in the buying and resale of merchandise.

You can use the same technique to discover your new firm's *break-even point*—that point at which the revenues you have taken in will exactly equal your expenses. At that precise junction, you will have neither gained nor lost one cent. If your sales volume fails to reach that point, you will end up the year with a loss. Once you pass the break-even mark, you begin to earn profit.

Purely as a preliminary exercise, try to anticipate your probable break-even point long before you launch your new service business. As you will discover in Chapter 7, an informed entrepreneur will take pains to prepare a comprehensive business plan before starting a new enterprise. Two significant types of accounting documents—balance sheets and operating statements—form an integral and vital part of the plan. Once you have prepared these documents, you will be able to ascertain your first-year's break-even point. To work it out, you will need to take into account: (a) all the fixed costs you expect to pay, (b) how much your per-unit variable costs will total, and (c) the price you plan to charge for each service unit.

Here is a useful formula for calculating your breakeven point in terms of sales dollars:

$$\text{Break-even Point (in dollars)} = \frac{\text{Fixed Costs}}{1 - \dfrac{\text{Variable costs per unit}}{\text{Unit price}}}$$

Fixed costs are those expenses you must pay regardless of how many or how few service "units" you sell. They include executive salaries, rent, heat, maintenance, insurance, and other overhead expenses. Variable costs are those costs that vary in proportion to the number of units that are provided. Wages, payroll taxes, and packaging costs are a few examples.

An Illustration—Let us assume that you are planning to start a small music school. You plan to offer lessons in piano, guitar, and clarinet. You will give the piano lessons yourself, but you will need to employ two additional people to teach the other instruments.

You have projected first-year sales of $75,000. Your estimated fixed expenses for the year should total $28,600. You plan to charge $30 per hour for all lessons. As nearly as you can determine, your variable costs for each lesson should come to approximately $14.

To determine your break-even point in dollars, we substitute the corresponding figures for the terms in the formula and then work out the solution:

$$\text{Break-even Point (in dollars)} = \frac{\text{Fixed Costs}}{1 - \dfrac{\text{Variable costs per unit}}{\text{Unit price}}}$$

$$= \frac{\$28{,}600}{1 - \dfrac{\$14}{\$30}}$$

$$= \frac{\$28{,}600}{1 - .47}$$

$$= \frac{\$28{,}600}{.53}$$

$$= \$53{,}962.$$

Your break-even point is $53,962. Once you pass that point, your business starts earning profit.

If you would like to find out the total number of lessons that must be given at your place of business before you can reach the break-even mark, use this formula instead of the earlier one:

$$\text{Break-even Point (in units)} = \frac{\text{Fixed Costs}}{\text{Unit price} - \text{Variable costs per unit}}$$

Once more, let us fill in the proper amounts and proceed to solve the equation:

$$= \frac{\$28{,}600}{\$30 - \$14}$$

$$= \frac{\$28{,}600}{\$16}$$

$$= 1{,}787.5$$

Apparently, then, you will need to deliver 1,787.5 hourly lessons to reach your break-even point. Assuming that your place will be open for business 50 weeks a year, you will have to sell, on average, close to 36 lessons each week. That is, of course, if you are bound to the $30 per hour charge. If, instead, you decide to charge your students $35 per hour, the denominator of the fraction in the formula will change drastically—to $21, rather than $16. In this case, your break-even point occurs at 1,361.9 lessons, or an average of slightly over 27 lessons per week.

A DOZEN SOURCES OF CAPITAL FOR YOUR NEW BUSINESS

As you have already seen, many new businesses fail simply because they are launched with insufficient financing. Money, of course, is a most essential lubricant for setting a business operation in motion and keeping it running thereafter.

Here are twelve sources of funds for your service business.

1. *Tap Your Personal Savings*—You are better off by far starting your new business with your own funds, rather than relying on other people's money. Money obtained from others will always cost you more. When repaying borrowed sums, you will need to tack on a considerable amount of interest. If, instead of borrowing, you ask others to invest equity capital in your enterprise, you will have to turn over part of the ownership to them.

Be sure to put up your own personal savings for your venture. If you have not as yet been able to accumulate the amount you need, then you will have to turn to other sources of capital.

2. *Convert Personal Property into Cash*—You may be able to add other funds to your personal savings. If you own your home free and clear, consider applying for a mortgage on it. If you still have a mortgage on your house, think about refinancing it. Also, you may be able to cash in other assets, such as stocks, bonds, or jewelry. You might also think of borrowing money on the cash value accumulated in a life insurance policy you own.
3. *Appeal to Family and/or Friends*—A fairly common approach is to borrow funds from one's immediate family or close relatives. (Often, several thousands of dollars can be raised in this fashion.) If you are successful, devise a sensible loan repayment schedule, possibly on a monthly basis. Be sure to add a reasonable percentage as interest on your payments.
4. *Apply for a Bank Loan*—Banks are understandably reluctant to extend loans to an individual who is planning to start a business. They are more interested in lending money to established, profitable enterprises. Such firms would be more likely to have collateral to put up against the loan: premises, accounts receivable, equipment, and so forth. You may, however, be able to secure a loan on your savings account passbook.
5. *Shelter Some of Your Own Capital by Leasing*—Instead of purchasing any machinery or equipment you need for your new business, arrange to lease some or all of it. This step can free up capital for other, more important aspects of your operation.
6. *Obtain Short-Term Financial Aid from Suppliers*—If you succeed in quickly establishing a good credit standing, your suppliers will be happy to extend trade credit to you. You will not have to pay your bills for 30, 45, or even 60 days. In effect, this move will enable you to put your own funds to work for an additional month or two.
7. *Take In a Partner*—If you have exhausted all possible sources of financing and you still have not raised the amount of capital you need to ensure success, consider asking another person (or two) to enter into partnership with you.
8. *Sell stock in your corporation*—If you have formed a corporation, you might try to interest family members, friends, acquaintances, neighbors, or former work associates in purchasing shares of stock in your new company.
9. *Approach a Finance Company*—Should you find yourself in need of additional operating capital after you have been in business for some time, you might consider borrowing from a finance company. You will probably have to put up your accounts receivable and/or your inventory as

collateral. However, loans from such companies typically carry a high interest rate.

10. *Check with the Small Business Administration*—Despite the fact that the SBA has come under rather sharp criticism in recent years, it still maintains some lending programs. Because of the customary unavailability of funds, however, direct loans from this agency are not at all likely.

    Before you think of approaching the SBA, try to secure a bank loan for your proposed business. Make certain that a well-conceived and well-developed formal business plan accompanies your loan application. Should your application be denied by two banks, visit the nearest SBA field office to discuss your financial problem with a loan officer. There is always the possibility that the agency may be willing to endorse a bank loan by guaranteeing most of the borrowed principal.

11. *Seek Venture Capital*—The term *venture capitalist* is applied to both individuals and organizations interested in providing capital to business operations. Generally, though, they shy away from contributing to business startups. Their interest lies in healthy, growing organizations. In return for their infusion of capital, they will ask for part ownership of your business.

    You may want to consider this source of financing at some future date, long after you have successfully launched your new business.

12. *Contact an SBIC or MESBIC*—These organizations are similar to the above-mentioned venture capitalists. They are licensed by the government to provide financial assistance to small business operations—for modernization, expansion, and other reasons. If interested, they may invest capital in return for equity in your business.

    The first set of initials stands for Small Business Investment Company; the second, for Minority Enterprise Small Business Investment Company.

FOR FURTHER INFORMATION

Books

Coltman, Michael M., *Understanding Financial Information: The Non-Financial Manager's Guide,* 2d ed. Bellingham, Wash.: Self-Counsel Press, 1990.

Donnahoe, Alan S., *What Every Manager Should Know about Financial Analysis.* New York: Simon & Schuster, 1989.

Gaston, Robert J., *Finding Private Venture Capital for Your Firm: A Complete Guide.* New York: Wiley, 1989.

Glau, Gregory R., *The Small Business Financial Planner.* New York: Wiley, 1989.

Hayes, Rick Stephan, *Business Loans: A Guide to Money Sources and How to Approach Them,* rev ed. New York: Wiley, 1989.

Horngren, Charles T. and G. Sundem, *Introduction to Management Accounting,* 8th ed. Englewood Cliffs, N.J.: Prentice-Hall, 1990.

Neveu, Raymond P., *Fundamentals of Managerial Finance,* 3d ed. Cincinnati: South-Western, 1988.

O'Hara, Patrick D., *SBA Loans: A Step-by-Step Guide.* New York: Wiley, 1989.

Silver, A. David, *Venture Capital: The Complete Guide for Investors.* New York: Wiley, 1985.

Van Horne, James C., *Fundamentals of Financial Management,* 7th ed. Englewood Cliffs, N.J.: Prentice-Hall, 1989.

Business Development Publications Available from the U.S. Small Business Administration

Financial Management

FM 1–"ABC's of Borrowing" ($1.00)
FM 3–"Basic Budgets for Profit Planning" ($1.00)
FM 5–"A Venture Capital Primer for Small Business" ($.50)
FM 6–"Accounting Services for Small Service Firms" ($.50)
FM 8–"Budgeting in a Small Business Firm" ($.50)
FM 9–"Sound Cash Management and Borrowing" ($.50)

CHAPTER 7

CREATING AN EFFECTIVE BUSINESS PLAN

In this final chapter of Part II, you are introduced to the planning function. You will discover what planning entails and why it can be so important to your success in business. We then offer a helpful outline that will guide you through the creation of a solid, comprehensive plan for your new enterprise. As you develop your plan, you will find yourself thinking like a seasoned professional. You will be compelled to choose both long- and short-term goals to shoot for and you will need to determine, well in advance, the necessary steps to take to attain your objectives. Once you have completed your business plan, you should be ready to tackle Part III of this book, "Activating Your Plan."

WHY THOROUGH PLANNING IS ESSENTIAL

If you go back and look at Figure 1–1 in the first chapter of this book, you would observe this fact: nearly one out of every three service businesses that failed during 1990 was less than three years old. Analysis of Figure 1–2 in that same chapter would reveal that financial problems had plagued 38.4 percent of failed companies of *all* types. Insufficient capital and burdensome debt were the finance factors most often cited by those firms.

As you must now realize, the odds for succeeding in any new venture are not all that favorable. To increase your chances of establishing a profitable operation, you will need to devote lots of time, thought, and energy to planning.

Thorough and competent planning will enable you to anticipate much of what may come to pass. It will help you to devise the kinds of strategies and tactics you may need to institute in order to deal advantageously with alternative future eventualities. It will lend purpose and direction to your new-business launch and, thereafter, to the day-to-day activities that will insure your success.

Planning, of course, is never easy on the planner, as the following quotation explains:

> Like inventive genius, serious planning is about 1 percent inspiration and 99 percent perspiration. Planning requires thinking—and thinking requires intense concentration. Planning also demands an extraordinary amount of self-discipline. Yet, so many would-be entrepreneurs neglect this essential activity. For many entrepreneurs, the creation of a business is so intoxicating that they feel an almost irrepressible compulsion to plunge headlong into the venture without doing much sensible planning at all. The entrepreneurial personality is more action-oriented than analytical and deliberative. Further, since most entrepreneurs instinctively realize that the future is largely unpredictable, they tend to shy away from "wasting" their time and energy on what they perceive to be sheer speculation. Moreover, the average person has had little practice at planning.*

REVIEWING THE PLANNING PROCESS

Planning involves the future. We never plan for the past or the present, only the future. We look forward to some event, some happening, some state of affairs taking place at a future date.

For safety's sake, be sure to begin planning actively and creatively months in advance of the tentative date you may have targeted for launching your new enterprise. In preparing your comprehensive business plan, try not only to anticipate a successful start-up but also to give due consideration to, as an absolute minimum, your first three years of operation.

A helpful procedure for you to follow thereafter, when contemplating any major move, is suggested in Figure 7–1.

HOW TO WRITE YOUR BUSINESS PLAN

Many entrepreneurs will devise a business plan for the sole purpose of attracting outside capital. Such plans, known as *venture proposals,* are destined for submission to one or more venture capitalists. These are individuals or firms seeking to invest in established, profitable companies that need additional funds for further growth or expansion. In return for their investment, venture capitalists ask for

---

***From:** *Run Your Own Store, Second Edition* by Irving Burstiner, Ph.D. © 1989 by Irving Burstiner. Reprinted by permission of the publisher, Prentice Hall Press, A Division of Simon & Schuster, New York, NY.

FIGURE 7–1
Long-range planning: A procedure to follow

1. **Clarify your present situation**—Start by determining the current state of the economy and where the economy may be heading. Search for significant trends by analyzing your records. Review your financial resources. Know who your customers are, what they are like, and what their needs may be. Analyze your competitors' strengths and weaknesses. Scout the environment for new opportunities.

2. **Spell out the major objectives you would like to attain**—Be certain, however, that these goals are reasonably attainable. Steer clear of generalized statements of your objectives such as "to make a lot of money," "to get rich," "to expand rapidly," and the like. Such vague statements are of no value whatsoever to your planning. Specify and even try to quantify your goals.

3. **Select an approximate target date for accomplishing your objectives.**

4. **Try to anticipate the kind of economic scenario you will most likely encounter on that future date**—Will you find prosperity, a disquieting recessionary trend, or a full-blown depression? To gain insights into the future and uncover significant trends, be sure to peruse business journals, trade magazines. Also check with your suppliers, your customers, and your trade association.

5. **Divide each objective into two or more subobjectives**—This will make it easier for you to spell out all those events and activities that will probably take place between today and your targeted date.

6. **Work up all details of those strategies and tactics you will need to institute to reach your objectives.**

7. **Prioritize the steps you must take and set up a detailed timetable for accomplishing your goals.**

8. **Install controls for monitoring plan outcomes.**

9. **Make any needed adjustments to keep your plans on track.**

part ownership of the business. They are not at all likely to show interest in any newly formed firm. (See Figure 7–2 for the elements contained in a typical venture proposal.)

The plan you are about to create is of a different sort. It is not designed to help you raise capital. You will be preparing it for your own use alone. Once you have completed the plan, it should serve as a valuable guide for you to follow in starting your own successful service business.

Keep in mind, though, that you are not locked into this plan forever. No plan of any type is immutable. You can and should alter it as you need to, even as it unfolds.

As outlined, your new business plan should contain the following eight sections:

- Preliminary Details
- What My Customers Are Like

FIGURE 7–2
Elements of a venture proposal

Purpose and Objectives—a summary of the what and why of the project.

Proposed Financing—the amount of money you'll need from the beginning to the maturity of the project proposed, how the proceeds will be used, how you plan to structure the financing, and why the amount designated is required.

Marketing—a description of the market segment you've got or plan to get, the competition, the characteristics of the market, and your plans (with costs) for getting or holding the market segment you're aiming at.

History of the Firm—a summary of significant financial and organizational milestones, description of employees and employee relations, explanations of banking relationships, recounting of major services or products your firm has offered during its existence, and the like.

Description of the Product or Service—a full description of the product (process) or service offered by the firm and the costs associated with it in detail.

Financial Statements—both for the past few years and pro forma projections (balance sheets, income statements, and cash flows) for the next 3–5 years, showing the effect anticipated if the project is undertaken and if the financing is secured (This should include an analysis of key variables affecting financial performance, showing what could happen if the projected level of revenue is not attained.).

Capitalization—a list of shareholders, how much is invested to date, and in what form (equity/debt).

Biographical Sketches—the work histories and qualifications of key owners/employees.

Principal Suppliers and Customers.

Problems Anticipated and Other Pertinent Information—a candid discussion of any contingent liabilities, pending litigation, tax or patent difficulties, and any other contingencies that might affect the project you're proposing.

Advantages—a discussion of what's special about your product, service, marketing plans or channels that gives your project unique leverage.

Source: LaRue Tone Hosmer, "A Venture Capital Primer for Small Business," *Management Aids No. 235* (Washington, D.C.: U.S. Small Business Administration, 1978), 3.

- My Competitors
- My Place of Business
- My Financial Plan
- My Service/Product Plan
- My Promotion Plan
- My Management Plan

Use the outline offered in Figure 7–3.

FIGURE 7–3
Business plan for my service enterprise

PART I: PRELIMINARY DETAILS

A. My firm's name, address, and telephone number:

B. Brief description of my business:

C. My legal form of operation is:

D. These are the major goals I have set for my:

1. First year of operation:

2. Second and third years:

3. Fourth and fifth years:

PART II: WHAT MY CUSTOMERS ARE LIKE

(Note: Complete A or B below, depending on your decision as to the type of customer you choose to target. You may, of course, elect to sell to both groups.)

A. I plan to sell to consumers. Here is a rough profile of what my targeted prospects are like:

1. Demographic aspects:

a. Sex:

b. Marital status:

c. Age range:

d. Size of family:

e. Level of education:

f. Type of residence:

g. Type of car:

FIGURE 7–3
Continued

2. Other characteristics:
   a. Hobbies:

   b. Sports:

   c. Other recreational activities:

   d. Personal likes:

   e. Personal dislikes:

B. I plan to sell to organizations. In this marketplace, prospective buyers most likely reflect many of the following characteristics:
   1. Type of organization:

   2. Size of organization:

   3. Annual sales volume:

   4. Organizational needs to be satisfied:

   5. Likely titles of people to contact:

   6. Personal likes of these individuals:

   7. Personal dislikes of these individuals:

PART III: MY COMPETITORS

A. Here are the major competitors I need to face, along with their strengths and weaknesses:
   1. Name and address:

      a. Strengths:

      b. Weaknesses:

2. Name and address:

    a. Strengths:

    b. Weaknesses:

3. Name and address:

    a. Strengths:

    b. Weaknesses:

PART IV: MY PLACE OF BUSINESS

A. Here are my immediate needs regarding my place of business:

1. Total selling space required:

2. Total workroom space required:

3. Licenses and permits required:

4. Needed construction/redecorating/remodeling:

    a. Front:

    b. Interior decor:

    c. Layout:

    d. Other details:

        -1. Ceilings:

        -2. Flooring:

        -3. Lighting:

        -4. Painting:

        -5. Plumbing:

        -6. Shelving:

FIGURE 7–3
Continued

–7. Wall coverings:

–8. Other necessary work:

5. Required equipment/furniture/supplies:
   a. Air conditioning:

   b. Heating:

   c. Furniture:

   d. Equipment:

   e. Fixtures:

   f. Supplies:

PART V: MY FINANCIAL PLAN

A. Projected sales for my first year of business operation are:

1st quarter:

2nd quarter:

3rd quarter:

4th quarter:

Total for Year:

B. Initial capital needed:

C. I will need to borrow:

D. My break-even point is:

E. I plan to do my business banking at:
   Name of bank:

   Address:

   Telephone Number:

F. Proforma P&L statement for my first year:
   (See attached.)

G. Proforma balance sheet for my first year:
   (See attached.)

H. Cash flow projections for my first year:
   (See attached.)

I. I plan to institute this credit extension program:

J. My expected tax obligations (and due dates) are:
   1. Federal:
   2. State:
   3. Local:

K. My planned insurance program follows:

PART VI: MY SERVICE/PRODUCT PLAN

A. Service(s) I plan to offer:

B. Product(s) I plan to offer:

C. Approximate selling prices for these offerings:
   1. Service(s):
   2. Product(s):

D. These are my major suppliers (names, addresses, terms of sale, credit and delivery policies, etc.):
   1.
   2.
   3.
   4.
   5.

FIGURE 7–3
Continued

PART VII: MY PROMOTION PLAN

A. Description of the kind of "company image" I plan to project:

B. Promotional plans for my first year of business:
   1. Amounts budgeted for promotion:
      a. Personal selling:

      b. Sales promotion:

      c. Advertising:

      d. Publicity:

      e. Public relations:

   2. Advertising media to be used:

   3. Scheduled direct marketing efforts:

   4. Cooperative advertising efforts:

PART VIII: MY MANAGEMENT PLAN

A. Here are the names, addresses, and telephone numbers of the professionals I plan to work with:
   1. Accountant:

   2. Attorney:

   3. Insurance representative:

B. Personnel administration:
   1. This is a chart of my planned organization for my first two years of operation.
      (See attached.)
   2. I shall need people to fill the following positions:

3. Here are job descriptions for all positions:

   (See attached.)

4. This is my basic pay plan for my employees:

5. I plan to offer the following employee benefits:

FOR FURTHER INFORMATION

Books

McGarty, Terrence P., *Business Plans That Win Venture Capital.* New York: Wiley, 1989.

Mancuso, J., *How to Write a Winning Business Plan.* Englewood Cliffs, N.J.: Prentice-Hall, 1985.

O'Hara, Patrick D., *The Total Business Plan.* New York: Wiley, 1990.

Stoner, Charles R. and Fred L. Fry, *Strategic Planning in Small Business.* Cincinnati: South-Western, 1987.

Touchie, Rodger, *Preparing a Successful Business Plan: A Practical Guide for Small Business.* Bellingham, Wash.: Self-Counsel Press, 1989.

Business Development Publications Available from the U.S. Small Business Administration

FINANCIAL MANAGEMENT

FM 3–"Basic Budgets for Profit Planning" ($1.00)

FM 8–"Budgeting in a Small Service Firm" ($.50)

MANAGEMENT AND PLANNING

MP 11–"Business Plan for Small Service Firms" ($.50)

MP 21–"Developing a Strategic Business Plan" ($1.00)

Part Three

ACTIVATING YOUR PLAN

CHAPTER 8

CHOOSING YOUR PLACE OF BUSINESS

If you intend to launch a brand-new business, you will need to find a suitable location for the enterprise before you can activate your business plan. Avoid being influenced by the convenience factor. So many new entrepreneurs err by choosing sites that lie well within the neighborhoods where they live. Or at least close by, perhaps no more than a fifteen-minute drive from home at the most.

Of one thing you can be certain: many other areas—indeed, other cities, counties, or even states—may offer greater opportunities for succeeding in your own business. Take your time. Approach your location decision slowly. Think carefully about the kind of place you really need. Bear in mind that signing a lease boxes you into a long-term commitment. Buying your own building may prove a costly and often unnecessary move. Consider how much capital you have to work with—and if and where you can get more financing, should you need to. Take into consideration, too, your personal preferences as to the type of area you would like to move to, the local climate, the quality of life you would lead in that location, and so on.

SOME SERVICE ENTERPRISES MAY BE STARTED AT HOME

Searching for a location may not be at all essential when you first start up your operation. These days, many new businesses are launched from people's homes. Cottage industries have been burgeoning all across the country.

In an informative booklet on homebased business, the U.S. Small Business Administration writes:

> Homework has taken on new meaning for more than 10 million Americans. The drive for economic self-sufficiency has motivated large numbers of persons to market their skills and talents for profit from home. . . . Our increasingly service oriented economy offers a widening spectrum of opportunities for customized and personalized small business growth.*

Many types of service enterprises can easily be started at home. Here are just a few of them:

- bookkeeping
- carpet cleaning
- clipping bureau
- clock/watch repair
- consulting
- correspondence courses
- desktop publishing
- engraving
- gardening
- home cleaning
- house/apartment painting
- lawn care
- letter remailing
- maid service
- music instruction
- personal shopping
- pool cleaning
- resume writing
- secretarial/typing service
- tutoring

You will, of course, need to check into such aspects of running a homebased business as zoning regulations, deed or lease restrictions, and the necessary permits and licenses.** You also need to think about how your neighbors may react to having a business next to or near them. Also, be sure to check into tax regulations regarding conducting a business from home. (*Note:* Request a copy of Publication 587–"Business Use of Your Home" from the U.S. Internal Revenue Service.)

A PROCEDURE FOR SELECTING THE RIGHT LOCATION

Many businesses cannot be started at home. Some require unusual premises and/or special equipment; auto painting shops, bowling alleys, car washes, drycleaning establishments and laundries, hotels and motels, medical and dental laboratories, slenderizing salons, and theaters are examples. Others, like advertising agencies, architectural and engineering services, dance studios, employment agencies, schools, travel agencies, and videotape rental firms require attractive, well-furnished premises that are easy to get to and offer ample parking facilities.

Finding a suitable location for a new business is never an easy task. At this point, it might be worth your while to pause and turn your attention to Figure 8–1 for a few minutes. Knowing the kinds of questions that businesspeople typ-

*Carol Eliason, "The Business Plan for Homebased Business," *Management Aids No. 2.028* (Washington, D.C.: U.S. Small Business Administration, n.d.), 2.

**Ibid, 5.

FIGURE 8–1
Questions to ask before making a location decision

- Is the location convenient to public transportation?
- Are parking facilities sufficient for your needs?
- Is the location close to the market(s) you will be selling to?
- Will your operating costs at the location be within reason?
- Do the community's demographics match those of your target customers?
- Is the volume of traffic passing by the location heavy, moderate, or light?
- Are the premises physically suitable for your needs and in good condition?
- Is there room for future expansion?
- If you need store premises, how compatible will the neighboring stores be with your service enterprise? How far will your trading area (the area from which you will draw most of your customers) extend?
- What are your nearby competitors like? What are their strengths and weaknesses?
- Is there a local labor pool you can draw from?
- How favorable are the "quality of life" factors in the area, such as the climate, caliber of the schools, quality of police and fire services, recreational facilities, houses of worship, and so on?

ically ask about the sites they are considering should prove a useful introduction to the location-hunting procedure we recommend:

Here is the procedure:

1. Start with the premise that there are probably dozens, if not hundreds, of sites you would find suitable for your new service enterprise.
2. Work up a detailed description of the type and size of premises you will need.
3. Expand your horizons. Spend some time preparing a list of places where you believe you would enjoy living—and where your new business would most likely flourish. Be sure to consider other towns or cities, besides the one in which you reside, and even places in other states.
4. Review your list carefully. Select the 5 or 6 areas that appeal to you most.
5. Now, do your homework. Visit your public library to discover whatever you can about the places you have chosen. Write away for information to the appropriate chambers of commerce, city planning commissions, and state development agencies. Find out whether each area's population is growing or contracting, the annual per-capita income of its residents, if more businesses are moving in than moving out, what the quality of community services is like, and so on. In-person visits to local banks and interviews with local business owners in the area should also prove profitable.

6. After you have completed your research, look over the rating chart in Figure 8–2. As you can see, the child-care firm employed a set of nine criteria in evaluating the four sites under consideration.

To evaluate the places you have investigated, you will need to devise your own set of criteria. Feel free to use or discard any of those listed in Figure 8–2. Add others of your own choosing. List as many as you like, even as many as 15 or 20.

7. To rate your five or six locations on the criteria you select, use the same simple numerical rating scale employed by the child-care center:

0 = Poor
1 = Fair
2 = Good
3 = Very good
4 = Excellent

8. Working across the chart, rate all locations on the first criterion. Continue with the second and succeeding criteria in the same way until you finish filling out your chart.

9. As you no doubt suspected, the criteria you picked are not all equally important to you. You will need to assign weights to how significant you

FIGURE 8–2
Rating chart (unweighted) for a child care center

	Alternative Locations			
Criteria	A	B	C	D
Accessibility to transportation	1	2	3	2
Attractiveness of neighborhood	3	1	1	2
Community demographics	2	2	2	4
Condition of premises	1	3	2	2
Cost factors	3	4	0	3
Parking facilities	2	3	1	1
Quality of life for owner(s)	3	3	2	3
Quality of local services	3	2	2	3
Space for future expansion	2	3	3	2
Total Scores:	20	23	16	22

perceive them to be. Use a weight of 1 for any that you feel are only of slight importance. Assign a weight of 2 for those you judge twice as important. Continue along the same lines, giving weights of 3, 4, and perhaps 5, if necessary, until you have finished.

10. Multiply every rating by the weight assigned to the criterion. Total all columns for the alternative locations.

11. Check off the place with the highest rating. This is where you probably ought to go. However, the runner-up on your list may have earned only 1 to 3 points fewer than the leader. If this is the case, you might also consider this second location.*

According to the second chart, their best bet would be Location D—and Location B finished a strong second.

FIGURE 8–3
Weighted rating sheet for a child care center

		Locations			
Criteria	**Weights**	A	B	C	D
Accessibility to transportation	2	2	4	6	4
Attractiveness of neighborhood	4	12	4	4	8
Community demographics	4	8	8	8	16
Condition of premises	3	3	9	6	6
Cost factors	4	12	16	0	12
Parking facilities	2	4	6	2	2
Quality of life for owner(s)	5	15	15	10	15
Quality of local services	3	9	6	6	9
Space for future expansion	2	4	6	6	4
Total Scores:		69	74	48	76

*Note that in the unweighted chart in Figure 8–2, Location B earned the highest rating (23 points). Location D scored in second place, with a rating of 22. However, the firm's management realized they had erred in treating all nine criteria as equally important. "Community demographics," "cost factors," and "quality of life for owner(s)" were certainly more crucial to them than "parking facilities" or "space for future expansion." After considerable discussion, they decided to assign weights (of 2 to 5 points) to all criteria. Multiplying their earlier ratings by the weights, they prepared the chart displayed in Figure 8–3.

THE BUSINESS STRUCTURE OF A TYPICAL CITY

In most cities and towns across the United States, two categories of business areas can be readily identified. There is the older, largely unplanned business structure whose roots can be traced back to the earliest years of area development. Then there is the newer, planned business structure: shopping centers, commercial and industrial parks, medical centers, and other installations.

The Older Business Structure

Five types of older business areas can be readily identified:

- The central business district ("downtown")
- Secondary business districts
- Neighborhood business districts
- Clusters
- Freestanding properties

The Central Business District—At the core of the city's older structure is the central business district, or CBD. Residents call this area *downtown*. Frequently, the main thoroughfare that cuts through the CBD is named Main Street or Broadway.

In many cities, warehouses and factories may still be found in the oldest part of the downtown area. Distributed throughout the CBD are office buildings, large units of chain store organizations, manufacturers' and wholesalers' showrooms, retail shops that offer a wide spectrum of merchandise, banks, restaurants, theaters, and many other types of service firms.

Soon after the end of World War II, the once-bustling economic activity in many CBDs began to slow down. About that time, masses of middle-income city dwellers started relocating to the suburbs. Gradually, lower-income consumers replaced the former residents. Retailers followed their more affluent customers, opening branch stores along the city's rapidly-expanding perimeter and in the suburbs. Many service companies joined in the exodus. New shopping centers were erected. Seeking more room and lower land costs, manufacturers and wholesalers built new plants and warehouses outside city limits.

However, the CBD still is an extremely active place in many cities. Rents for offices, buildings, and stores are traditionally higher here than in most other areas. So are real estate taxes.

Across the country, the reconstruction and revitalization of CBDs has been going on for many years. In some instances, streets have been closed off and converted to pedestrian malls. In other cases, former warehouses, factories, office buildings, and other facilities have been torn down, remodeled, or converted to business centers that attract people from many miles away.

Secondary Business Districts—Cities with populations exceeding 100,000 may contain as many as three or four of these. Chicago, New York, and other major metropolitan areas can boast of double or triple that number. The typical district of this type developed over decades along the main roads leading out of the CBD toward the city's outer limits.

Office buildings, bank branches, drugstores, theaters, and other retail and service establishments are usually smaller than their downtown counterparts. Rents are lower than those in the CBD but still rather high.

Neighborhood Business Districts—Located close to residential areas, these sections may vary in length from a single city block up to as many as 8 or more. The buildings that provide office space are usually small, two- or three-story "taxpayers" that offer store premises at street level. Proportionately more convenience-goods retailers and service operations can be found here than in the CBD or secondary business districts. Among those types more likely to be seen are neighborhood bars, groceries, bakeries, fruit stands, hardware stores, pharmacies, shoe stores, beauty salons, drycleaning establishments, fast-food restaurants, and laundromats.

Locating in a neighborhood business district can be an excellent move for the new small business. Traffic, both pedestrian and vehicular, is often brisk—and rents are well below those in the larger business areas.

Clusters and Freestanding Properties—Small clusters of convenience-goods stores and/or service operations can be found in and around the residential sections of the city. Along the major thoroughfares, newer and much larger "strip" clusters may be seen: long rows of car dealerships, fast-food places, or other business types that can run for many city blocks.

Freestanding properties, many with their own parking facilities, are also common. These structures are often positioned at a major intersection in town, at a corner of a block, or along a highway. Among the many business types represented in this category are ice-cream shops, restaurants, service stations, used-car lots, clinics and other buildings occupied by health professionals, and private schools.

The Newer Business Structure

A new and distinctive type of business structure popped up during the late 1940s: the planned shopping center. Over the decades that followed, Americans witnessed a sharp acceleration in the construction and development of these new areas. By the 1980s, many thousands of them had appeared across the country. They took away business from the CBDs, and from the secondary and neighborhood business districts as well. They changed the shopping habits and patterns of consumers.

Other new types of planned business groupings have followed the appearance of the shopping center. Industrial centers, commercial parks, and cooperative as well as condominium-type medical and office buildings are examples.

Grouped by their size and the extent of their trading areas, most planned shopping centers fall into one of three categories: the neighborhood, community, or regional shopping center.

Neighborhood Shopping Centers—Smallest and most common of the planned shopping centers, this type is designed to serve the immediate neighborhood in which it is located. The typical center contains a dozen or so stores, all erected by the same builder. Most often, the shops are aligned in a row and offer a limited number of parking spaces in front of a common sidewalk. It is often referred to as a "strip center," to distinguish it from others that are laid out in the shape of an L or a U.

Usually, the center's main, or anchor, store is a supermarket or a drugstore. Among other retailers commonly seen in these centers are bars, beauty salons, women's wear shops, drycleaners, laundromats, shoe stores, coffee shops, and hardware stores.

Rents here are, of course, substantially lower than those asked in the larger—and typically much busier—planned shopping centers.

Community Shopping Centers—These larger developments generally cover between 8 and 12 acres and contain as many as 25 or 35 stores. Several hundred cars can be accommodated in the parking areas. These complexes have rather extensive trading areas; people come from as far away as a 20-minute drive. Frequently, such retail giants as Wal-Mart, K mart, Sears, and Sam's Wholesale Club are the anchor stores. Generally, there are more shopping- and specialty-goods retailers and service firms than in the neighborhood centers.

Renting space in a center that is situated in an area where the population is growing can prove profitable for many kinds of retail and service businesses. Although rents may be moderate to high, the volume of sales created by the heavy traffic attracted to the center generally more than compensates the renter.

Regional Shopping Centers—Largest of the planned business areas, these complexes were built on sites that range from 30 to more than 70 acres, with room for up to 150 or more stores. In addition to one or several department stores, the regional holds a wide-ranging mix of retail and service types. Among these are apparel shops and shoe stores for men, women, and children, restaurants and food courts, variety and drug stores, confectionery shops, banks, office buildings, movie theaters and other entertainment facilities, dental clinics, meeting rooms, a hotel, and even a branch of the U.S. Postal Service.

These enclosed, climate-controlled centers offer leisurely, all-day, all-weather shopping for consumers who arrive by car or public transportation from as far away as 40 or 45 miles.

A few of the newest regional centers are so huge that they have been labeled *superregionals* or *supermalls.* Two examples are the Forest Fair Mall in Cincinnati and the Mall of America in Bloomington, Minnesota. An exciting place, this latter superregional holds, in addition to more than 4,000,000 square feet of leasable space, an entire entertainment complex.

WHICH IS BEST FOR YOU: RENTING, BUYING, OR BUILDING YOUR PREMISES?

Even after you have selected what you believe is the best spot for your new service operation, you may still be bothered with an additional location quandary: Should you rent, buy, or build your place of business? Each alternative offers both advantages and disadvantages.

Renting Your Premises

Of the three choices, this is the least threatening to your company treasury. It is by far the decision preferred by entrepreneurs whose capital is limited. If you decide to rent, rather than buy or build, your place of business, you will avoid having to pay real estate taxes or buying insurance on the property. With a favorable lease, heating, air conditioning, restrooms, and other amenities will be provided. Lessors, of course, usually require renters to post a security deposit on the premises and pay one to three months' rent in advance.

There is one disturbing disadvantage to renting. When your lease is about to expire, the building's owner(s) may (a) request a substantial increase in your rent before agreeing to renew the lease or (b) decide to lease the premises to someone else. If the latter situation occurs, you will lose not only the location but also the lucrative trade you may have built up over the term of your occupancy.

Buying Your Premises

One way to avoid losing your premises or paying a higher rent upon renewing your lease is to purchase the property. While such a move might initially deliver a severe blow to your limited finances, you might be better off in the long run. You can benefit financially by depreciating this new asset over many years, thereby saving on your income tax liabilities. For another, you can also deduct from your company's earnings the real estate taxes and interest paid each year on any mortgage you take out on the building.

Some day, too, you might be able to enjoy a healthy capital gain by selling the building for considerably more than you paid for it.

The major disadvantages to buying are: the sizable down payment you may have to make, the real estate taxes you will have to pay (which will most likely increase as the years go by), and the expenses associated with both insuring and maintaining the property.

Building Your Premises

If you have sufficient financing in back of you to do so, your ideal choice would be to arrange for the construction of a building that answers all your present needs and that contains sufficient additional space to accommodate growth. Just as you are able to do with any premises that you buy, you can curtail your income tax liability by depreciating the value of the property over many years. You can also mortgage the place should you ever want to improve your cash position. A final benefit for you to think about is the promise of a long-term capital gain in your future.

YOUR PLACE OF BUSINESS: LAYOUT AND DECOR

Whatever your premises may look like, they will have a direct effect on your company's image. For the sake of your employees and possible visitors, they should always look presentable. If, in your type of service business, your customers must come to you (rather than you go to them), the layout and decor of your premises become even more important.

Naturally, the building's facade and entrance(s) should always look inviting. Keep them spotlessly clean and in excellent repair.

Inside Your Premises–Some Construction Aspects

Many new business owners share a common problem with regard to their premises. They must decide what to do with those basic construction elements: floors, walls, ceilings, and lighting. A few suggestions on the subject follow:

Floors–Before you arrive at any decisions about this element, give due consideration to these three qualities of floors: their load-bearing capability, durability, and maintenance requirements. If you plan to carry on any manufacturing activity and require the installation of heavy machinery, you will need to make certain that the floor underneath this equipment can support its weight.

The durability factor becomes a serious concern if your floors are subjected to heavy foot traffic by customers and visitors. As for the maintenance aspect, whatever floor coverings you choose should be easy and inexpensive to clean and able to resist loss of luster or fading (for example, from the use of cleaning compounds).

If attractive, some floors can be left bare. In most cases, however, you will want to select some type of floor covering. Carpeting, asphalt or vinyl tiles, and linoleum are popular choices.

Walls–You can have the interior walls painted or you can choose to have them covered with any of a wide selection of materials including wallpaper, paneling, vinyl, mirrors, and cork. For an occasional decorative touch, add a mural or two. Another useful idea is to affix shelves to one or more walls (or partitions) and set up attractive displays on them.

Ceilings–Conceal unsightly electrical cables, pipes, and ductwork under a dropped ceiling made of plasterboard or some other material (subsequently painted neatly in a pleasant color). Consider putting up acoustic tiles. Keep in mind the fact that a high ceiling imparts a sense of roominess while a low ceiling seems confining and may actually hamper employee productivity.

Lighting—To ensure the proper level of illumination inside your premises, you will most likely need to use a combination of fluorescent and incandescent lighting. Fluorescent lamps last longer, consume less electricity, and emit far less heat than incandescent lamps. Under fluorescents, though, colors often do not look the same; consequently, incandescent lamps are preferred for showing and highlighting goods on display.

Layout and Decor of Your Premises

A practical approach to designing the workplace is: "Let form follow function." To a large extent, the functions that are to be performed on the premises should dictate their arrangement. Requirements for interior layout, design, and decor may, of course, vary widely from one type of service enterprise to the next. Some businesses need to introduce partitions to section off areas for certain kinds of activities. Others call for the installation of machinery, equipment, and shelving for their supplies. Still others must meet special plumbing or electrical requirements.

For the sake of illustrating this point, spend a few moments speculating about some of the special needs of the following types of service enterprises:

- auto repair shops
- beauty salons
- bowling alleys
- car washes
- check-cashing agencies
- dental laboratories
- drycleaning establishments
- health clubs
- laundromats
- limousine services
- motels
- music schools
- nursing care facilities
- plant rental services
- telephone answering services
- truck rental services

Bear in mind, though, that facilitating all necessary work activity is not your only aim. Your premises should also be aesthetically pleasing. Strive to create the kind of environment your customers and your employees expect to find—and the special atmosphere you would like to project so that people can differentiate between your company and those of your competitors. All elements—walls, floors, and ceilings; lighting; furniture and fixtures; departments and offices; color schemes; and so on—need to be coordinated into one attractive, unified whole. You would do well to seek professional assistance with respect to this coordination.

If you occupy store premises, the greater part of your store interior will most likely be devoted to selling activity. You will need lots of room for shopper traffic, behind-the-counter aisles that are wide enough for your employees to pass through with ease, window and interior displays, storage bins, a workroom, and restrooms.

Both the grid and freeform layouts are popular designs with today's retailers. Typical of supermarkets, many drugstores, and other retail types, the grid (or "gridiron") layout offers maximum exposure to the store's merchandise. However, it constrains shoppers to proceed along straight aisles and make 90-degree turns at the end of each aisle. More aesthetically interesting, the free-form layout is based on arcs, curves, and circles rather than on straight lines. After they enter the store, shoppers go in whatever direction they please. Some stores combine the grid and freeform approaches.

If you engage in any manufacturing on your premises, arrange your machines and equipment so as to minimize the flow of materials through the production area. Consider your production flow pattern and whether you plan to employ job, batch, or mass production methods. In addition, you will require an office, storage facilities, and, perhaps, a maintenance shop. You may also need sections (and perhaps truck bays) for receiving incoming deliveries and sending out shipments.

FOR FURTHER INFORMATION

Books

Francis, Richard L. and John A. White, *Facility Layout and Location: An Analytical Approach.* Englewood Cliffs, N.J.: Prentice-Hall, 1974.

Ghosh, Avijit and Sara L. McLafferty, *Location Strategies for Retail and Service Firms.* Lexington, Mass.: Lexington Books, 1987.

Tompkins, James A. and John A. White, *Facilities Planning.* New York: Wiley, 1984.

Business Development Publications Available from the U.S. Small Business Administration

MANAGEMENT AND PLANNING

MP 2–"Locating or Relocating Your Business" ($1.00)

CHAPTER 9

MANAGING YOUR EMPLOYEES

Employees play significant roles in all but the smallest, one-person business. In the service enterprise, they can be crucial to the operation's success or failure. Because services are intangible, customers tend to ascribe far more importance to the service firm's personnel than they would to the employees of companies that are engaged in the marketing of goods.

Like most new business owners, you are probably determined not to hire your first full-time worker until you can really afford the move. You are quick to realize that, even if you were to pay your employee the minimum wage, you would be adding upwards of $12,000 annually to your operating expenses (after taking into account FICA and FUTA taxes, along with a few employee benefits.)

Ask yourself how much more in sales you will need to take in to regain that additional labor cost. As you can see, managing your personnel effectively does present a real challenge!

In this chapter, you are first introduced to the four managerial functions: planning, organizing, directing, and controlling. You will then see how business organizations are developed and learn what organizational charts look like. Among the topics that are subsequently discussed are staffing procedures, labor legislation, and employee compensation plans. Tips on training and motivating workers conclude the chapter.

HOW TO IMPROVE YOUR MANAGEMENT SKILLS

Management has been defined as "the process of planning, organizing, leading, and controlling an enterprise's financial, physical, human, and information resources in order to achieve the organization's goals of supplying various products and services."*

Rather than conjecture interminably about the kinds of characteristics that are required to manage an organization's personnel effectively, it seems reasonable to assume that effective managers:

- are able communicators
- are adept at prioritizing tasks
- clarify their instructions
- demonstrate a sense of fair play
- have a good grasp of human psychology
- have drive and perseverance
- know how to motivate people
- listen attentively to what their employees have to say
- maintain an open mind
- show consideration for others
- use good judgment
- are resourceful
- are willing to make decisions

Just about every activity a manager performs can be classified under one of four functions: planning, organizing, directing, and controlling. (See Figure 9–1.) These managerial functions are explained below:

Planning–This is disciplined thinking that attempts to bridge the gap between present and future. Planning begins with envisioning a future state of affairs and continues by trying to anticipate everything that will need to be done before that future state can be realized. It calls for setting objectives, breaking down those objectives into smaller, more readily attainable goals, establishing policies that will serve as guides for action, and devising strategies designed to reach the goals.

Organizing–The process of organizing encompasses such aspects of management as (a) determining all the work that must be performed if the firm is to accomplish its objectives, (b) breaking down the total workload into specific tasks, (c) consigning each task to the proper job title, and (d) choosing the right people to fill those positions. Out of all this activity emerges the company's organization.

When linked to the planning function, organizing consists of gathering all those components needed to get a plan off the ground: the materials,

*Ricky E. Griffin and Ronald J. Ebert, *Business* (Englewood Cliffs, N.J.: Prentice Hall, 1989), 103.

FIGURE 9–1
The four managerial functions

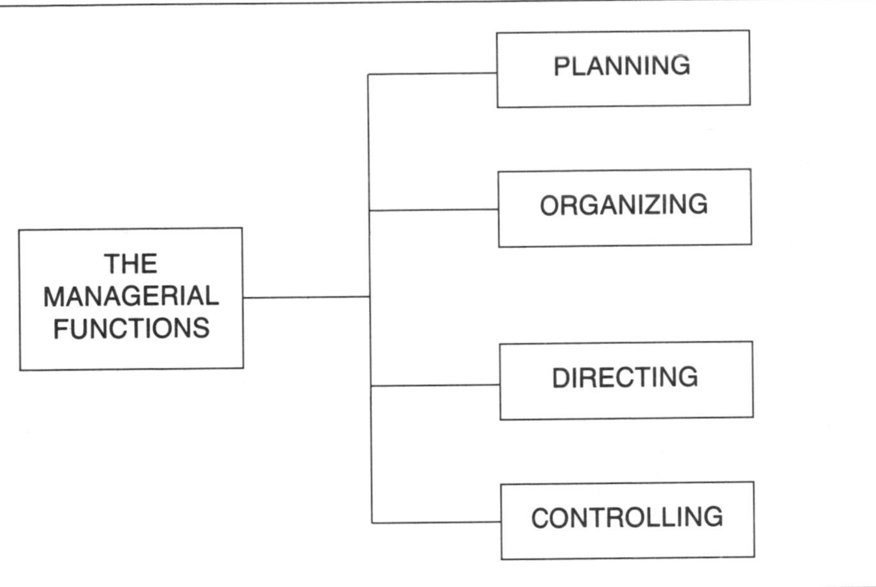

methods, procedures, equipment, people, and, of course, the financial wherewithal.

Directing—This function comes into play after the plan has been prepared, all the necessary elements have been set into place, or organized, and the plan is initiated. The manager then directs and oversees all activity as the plan starts to unfold.

Controlling—This function calls for monitoring all aspects of a plan. It requires analyzing what is going on, evaluating all aspects (methods, procedures, activities, outcomes), and taking measures to correct deviations from plan.

HOW TO DEVELOP AN ORGANIZATION PLAN

As Figure 9–2 indicates, the field of personnel management embraces five distinct areas of activity: staffing, pay administration, training and development, employee relations, and record-keeping. To make it easier for you to manage your organization later on, prepare and institute policies in all five areas long before you think of hiring your first employee. To tackle the policy-making challenge, though, you will need to: (1) determine and list all work that must be performed in order for your operation to run properly, and (2) assign each task you have listed to the particular category, or function, where it logically belongs.

In the typical service business, most work activities can be categorized according to one or another of four functions: selling, buying, operations manage-

FIGURE 9–2
Personnel management

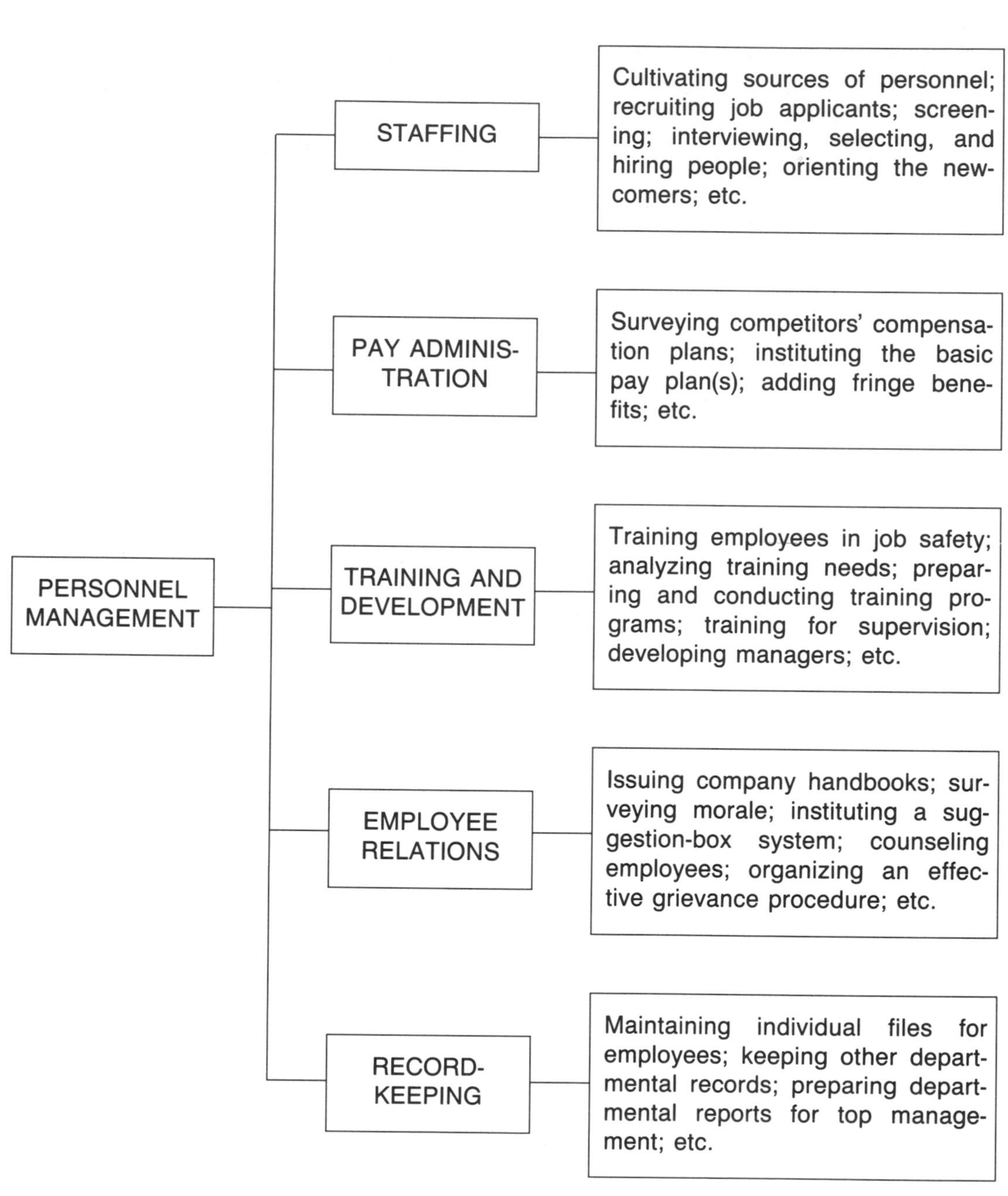

ment, or financial control. Once you have concluded this job of organizing all tasks, you can then begin preparing job descriptions for all four functions. In addition to outlining the duties and responsibilities of each position, indicate in the description to whom the person who holds that particular position is to report and the extent of authority that individual is to exercise.

If you have set up a sole proprietorship, your organizational chart will resemble that of the tool-rental firm displayed in Figure 9–3. You will, of course, need to revise the chart as you add people to your organization. Two or three years down the pike, it may begin to approximate the chart of the small commercial art supply company that appears in Figure 9–4.

Advance planning can help you have the proper organization in place whenever you need it. To get started, set your target for a date three years from today. Try to think of how many more employees you will need—and in what positions—by that time to handle your anticipated sales volume. Will you have to hire new employees for all positions, or can you train some of your present personnel to

FIGURE 9–3
Organizational chart for a tool-rental firm (sole proprietorship)

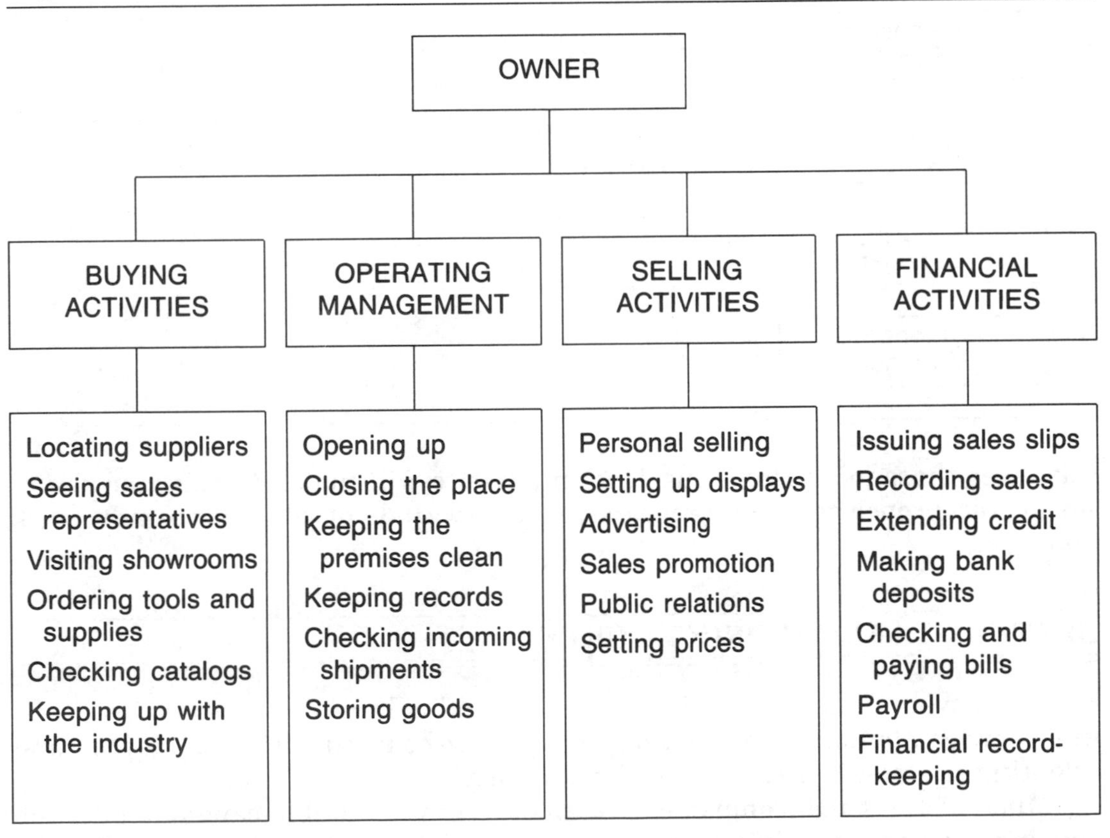

FIGURE 9–4
Organizational chart for a commercial art supply company

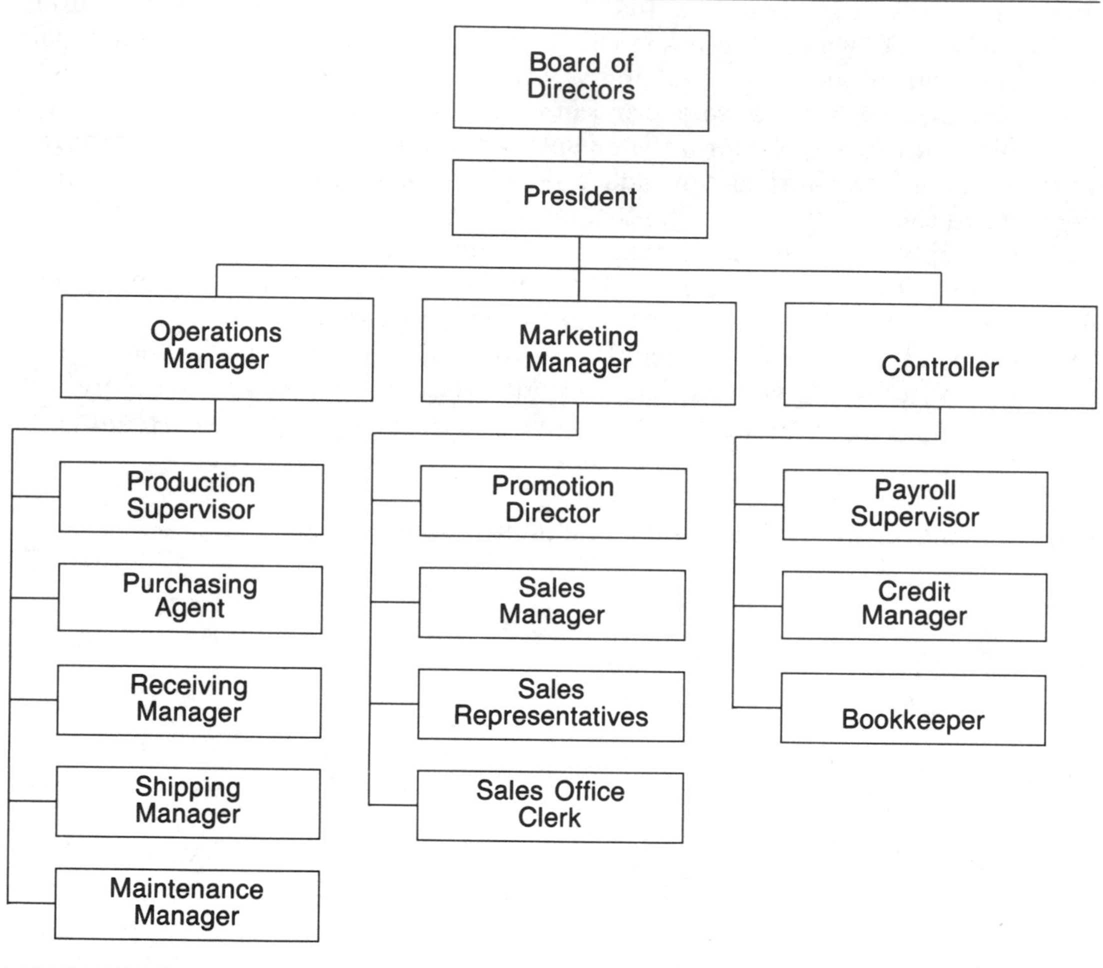

take over those jobs? Preparing long in advance will make it easier for you to set up the proper training programs, hire the kinds of people you may need, and so on.

BETTER STAFFING PROCEDURES

Staffing involves such activities as finding and cultivating personnel sources, interviewing applicants for positions that need to be filled, hiring employees, and orienting the newly hired to both job and firm.

Much of the time, companies are able to locate suitable candidates for job openings simply by relying on: (1) recommendations (from friends, relatives, suppliers, and their own employees), (2) "write-ins"—people who submit unsolicited letters of application, and (3) "walk-ins"–jobseekers who pay unexpected visits to the place of business.

To help fulfill all your staffing needs, you should also consider turning to these additional sources:

- "help-wanted" signs (on bulletin boards, walls, or windows)
- newspaper advertisements (display and classified ads)
- local high schools (especially valuable for hiring part-time workers)
- state employment agencies
- private employment agencies
- temporary help services
- placement offices at nearby colleges and universities
- on-campus interviews
- trade associations
- professional organizations

The Selection Process

Before you start setting up your selection procedure, review the federal legislation listed in Figure 9–5. These laws were designed to protect the rights of employees. Learn as much as you can about them. Check with your attorney for additional details so that you may more fully understand your legal responsibilities with regard to personnel management.

As for the selection process itself, the tools at your disposal should be familiar to you: the employment application form, the employment interview, a reference-checking procedure, and the initial trial, or probationary, period for a new employee. For positions in your firm that require specific skills, for example: word-processor, lab technician, or lathe operator, testing may also be recommended.

The Employment Application–Ask each jobseeker to fill out an employment application. The completed form is useful for screening out applicants who fail to meet the minimum requirements outlined in the job specifications for the particular position. More importantly, it will serve you well as a point of departure for the subsequent employment interview. You can purchase standard employment application blanks from any business stationery retailer.

The Employment Interview–Most valuable of all selection tools, this two-way exchange can help you to:

- learn more about the jobseeker than can be discerned solely from the information entered on that person's employment application.
- clarify and expand further upon some of the details that appear on the form.

FIGURE 9–5
Significant federal legislation pertaining to employees

Date	Federal Law	Major Thrust of Law
1935	National Labor Relations Act	Established workers' right to organize and engage in collective bargaining.
1938	Fair Labor Standards Act	Established the minimum hourly wage, provided for overtime pay, and imposed constraints on the employment of minors.
1963	Equal Pay Act	Banned pay discrimination among employees on the basis of sex. Called for equal pay for men and women doing the same work.
1964	Civil Rights Act	Barred discrimination in a firm's hiring practices on the basis of race, color, sex, national origin, or religion.
1967	Age Discrimination in Employment Act	Prohibited discrimination in the employment process on the basis of age.
1970	Occupational Health and Safety Act	Mandated that companies maintain safe working conditions for their employees.
1972	Equal Employment Opportunity Act	Amended the Civil Rights Act to cover firms employing 15 or more people, local and state governments, educational institutions, and other organizations.
1973	Vocational Rehabilitation Act	Outlawed discrimination in employment against handicapped people who are capable of doing their assigned work.
1974	Employee Retirement Income Security Act	Assured the safety of employee pension rights (including vesting rights).
1978	Mandatory Retirement Act	Barred organizations from requiring that their employees retire at age 65.
1983	Job Training Partnership Act	Facilitated federal grants to states for the training of economically disadvantaged persons.

- appraise the applicant's appearance, poise, communication skills, self-control, and various other traits and capabilities.
- gain insights into the depth of knowledge and breadth of experience that the applicant offers.
- tell the applicant about the company and the job.

To improve your employment decisions—which job applicants ought to be hired and which ones should be rejected—we suggest that you develop and use an objective interview rating form.

References—Follow up on all references submitted by applicants you would like to employ. Check these by mail or by telephone. Question them about the length of time the applicant worked for the organization, how they would rate that person's performance, why he or she left the job, and so on.

Testing—Mindful of the many laws against bias and discrimination in the workplace, many companies avoid testing job applicants altogether. If tests are applied, they are usually limited to assessing an applicant's manual dexterity, skill at mathematics, knowledge of machinery or specialized equipment, typing accuracy and speed, or other aspects and capabilities that are essential to the position.

Probationary Period—After a new employee has been through an orientation program, that person's work performance should be observed carefully for another four to six weeks. This trial period should provide ample opportunities for evaluation and for deciding whether or not to retain the worker. Appointing an experienced employee to coach the newcomer during that period would be helpful.

In this context, a well-prepared employee handbook can also be of value in orienting new employees to their surroundings. The "Sample Table of Contents" in Figure 9–6 presents a range of topics for you to consider including in your firm's handbook.

DEVISING A PAY PLAN THAT MEETS YOUR NEEDS

Devote much thought and considerable time to setting up an effective compensation plan for your employees long before you get ready to hire your very first worker. An understanding of what employees want will help you in this undertaking. So will a studied appraisal of your needs and some knowledge of the pay plans that are prevalent in commerce and industry.

Most employees would like:

- a pleasant and safe work environment
- just compensation for their work
- fair and effective supervision
- opportunities for promotion
- an occasional pay increase
- to enjoy a sense of security
- recognition for their contributions

Most employers would like:

- a fair return on their investment in labor
- a knowledgeable personnel
- employees who are attentive and courteous to customers
- fewer absences and even fewer late arrivals

FIGURE 9–6
Suggested table of contents for an employee handbook

Welcome Message
History of the Company
This Is Our Business
You and Your Future
What You Will Need to Know
- Working Hours
- Reporting to Work
- "Time Clock"
- Rest Periods
- Absence from Work
- Reporting Absences
- Employment Record
- Pay Period
- Shift Premiums
- Safety and Accident Prevention
- Use of Telephones
- How to Air Complaints

These Are Your Benefits
- Vacations
- Holidays
- Group Insurance
- Hospitalization and Surgical Benefits
- Free Parking
- Training Program
- Christmas Bonus
- Savings Plan
- Profit-Sharing Plan
- Suggestion Awards
- Jury Duty
- Military Leave
- U.S. Old Age Benefits
- Unemployment Compensation
- Equal Employment Opportunity

These Special Services Are For You
- Credit Union
- Education Plans
- Medical Dispansary
- Employee Purchases
- Company Cafeteria
- Monthly Magazine
- Annual Outing
- Bowling League
- Baseball Team

Index

Source: "Pointers on Preparing an Employee Handbook," *Management Aids No. 197* (Washington, D.C.: U.S. Small Business Administration, 1975), 3.

- to retain exceptional workers, rather than lose them to competitors or other employers

To compensate workers for their labor, most companies depend on one of three approaches: the straight salary plan, the straight commission plan, or some type of combination plan.

The Straight Salary Plan—This is the simplest of all compensation plans from management's point of view. The company can anticipate its labor costs and devise its budgets accordingly. As for the employees, receiving a regular salary every payday reinforces their sense of security.

This is usually the best method for compensating nonselling personnel. An oft-heard complaint, though, is that the plan provides no incentive whatsoever for a worker to put forth extra effort. This is not as bad as it sounds. Effective supervisors are capable of motivating their subordinates and increasing productivity.

Under this arrangement, management establishes a pay range for each job title in the company. Minimum and maximum salaries are fixed according to the type of work and level of responsibility involved. Occasional raises are granted (up to the maximum), usually following satisfactory performance evaluations.

The Straight Commission Plan—For the most part, this compensation approach is reserved for sales personnel. Its most important advantage to a company is that salespeople are not paid unless and until they consummate sales. The straight commission plan is a top motivator; it encourages sales employees to push harder in promoting sales and to "trade up" customers to higher-priced alternative products or services. A major drawback to this approach is that the firm cannot know its sales costs beforehand. When budgets are prepared, management must build in likely, rather than actual, labor costs. Another disadvantage is that this pay plan often encourages aggressive, high-pressure tactics by sales representatives that can damage the company's image.

Combination Plans—Several types of pay plans fall into this category, for example: the salary-plus-commission, the salary-plus-bonus, and the draw-against-commission plans. Under the salary-plus-commission plan, the company pays its sales representatives a fixed salary designed to cover their immediate needs. It then adds a commission, usually based on a small percentage of the sales each individual has generated. The salary-plus-bonus plan is somewhat similar. In addition to receiving a regular salary, those salespeople who demonstrate exceptional selling capability are rewarded with a bonus. A management that institutes the draw-against-commission plan seeks to accomplish two goals: (1) provide in advance for the salesperson's day-to-day expenses and (2) stimulate greater selling effort. Salespeople are offered a "draw"—a specified amount of commission dollars granted, most often on a weekly basis, *in advance of* any sales they may consummate. At the end of each month, the individual "drawing accounts" are tallied. All sales commissions earned are credited to the account; monies advanced to, or "drawn out" of the account are debited; and the remaining balance is then issued to the salesperson.

Take Care of the Fringes, Too!

Today, certain benefits granted to employees are no longer looked upon as "fringe benefits" but as integral elements in a company's compensation plan, regardless of the size of the firm. You will need to work up your own list of fringe benefits to incorporate into your compensation plan. Naturally, you will want to keep tight reins on the list until your business is well established. However, a few particular benefits are granted by almost all companies and your employees will expect you to provide them. As an example, workers are accustomed to staying home—without losing any pay—on certain holidays. If your business demands that you bring employees in on one of these holidays, be sure to offer them twice as much (at the very least!) as they would earn on a typical work day.

Here are two other benefits that workers regard as essential:

Vacations—All employees want, and most certainly need, an annual vacation. It should come as no surprise that they fully expect their employers to pay for the vacation period. You will need to establish your own company policy on paid vacations. A common approach is to (1) grant one week of vacation time (with pay of course!) to employees who have been with the firm for one or two years, (2) two weeks for those with the organization for three to five years, and (3) three weeks for the longer-termers.

Sick days—No worker wants to lose a day's pay because of illness. Consider granting the sick employee three days off with pay during the year providing that person has been working for you for at least six months. Anyone with you longer than one year deserves, as a minimum, a full week of sick days.

A year or two down the road, you may want to think about tacking on several other fringe benefits to your compensation package. Some of the more popular "extras" are:

accident insurance
company car
employee discounts
employee lunchroom
health insurance
life insurance
performance bonuses
profit-sharing plan
retirement plan
recreational activities
severance pay
social events

TIPS ON TRAINING AND MOTIVATING YOUR STAFF

Even as you begin to savor the first sweet taste of success in your new enterprise, you should begin thinking about the people you will need to help you with your growing workload. How customers perceive your company will be strongly influenced by their contacts with your employees. This is especially true in the service sector, for to customers, the employees who serve them ARE the company.

The Importance of Effective Training

In a service operation, half the job of motivating workers is accomplished with the proper initial training. Training, however, should be ongoing. If you provide continuous training, your employees will feel that you are interested in them and that they can look forward to a bright future with your organization.

Among other benefits, effective training will help you to:

- cut down on waste
- increase productivity
- inspire and motivate workers
- lift employee morale
- lower your costs
- promote teamwork
- raise work efficiency

You may find the checklist in Figure 9–7 of value when you need to teach employees new tasks.

FIGURE 9–7
Checklist for instructing a worker

Four steps are necessary for giving employees proper instructions about new tasks:

1. *Prepare them* by:
   Putting them at ease
   Telling them what you are going to teach them
   Getting them interested in learning
   Finding out what they already know
   Giving them credit for what they already know
2. *Present each task to be learned* by:
   Giving them one step at a time
   Telling them how to do the task
   Showing them how the task is done
   Stressing key points of the task
   Presenting no more than they can master
3. *Let the learners do the task under supervision* by:
   Having them explain the task
   Having them show you how the task is done
   Correcting their mistakes
4. *Test the learners* by:
   Asking them for information about the task
   Checking on their performance and speed
   Checking on their quality
   Correcting mistakes—reteaching the points they may have missed
   Being sure that they can do the task without help

Source: Adapted from William B. Logan, "Training the Technical Serviceman," *Small Marketers Aid No. 117* (Washington, D.C.: U.S. Small Business Administration, 1973), 3.

Most training activity in the small business falls into the category of "on-the-job training." It is usually assigned to a more experienced employee or the worker's immediate supervisor. Yet it is never too early to begin making plans for more professional training programs, especially those that aim at preparing people for higher-level positions in your organization as business continues to expand. Developing your own supervisors and managers is always less costly than hiring them from outside the company.

As a first step toward coordinating all training efforts, conduct a needs analysis of your current organization. Follow immediately with a second needs analysis, this time of the organization you have projected for five years from today. (See Figure 9–8 for a helpful procedure to follow when you are ready to develop training programs.)

You may use any or all of these popular instructional approaches in your training programs:

- case analysis
- college courses
- in-basket exercises
- job rotation
- lectures
- management games
- programmed instruction
- role playing
- small-group discussions

Motivating Employees

All employers would like to get top-notch performance from their employees. To know how to motivate workers so that they apply their best efforts to their work requires a working knowledge of both adult and social psychology as well as

FIGURE 9–8
A procedure for developing effective training programs

1. Analyze the training needs of your employees.
2. Based on your analysis, list the subject areas that should be covered by your training efforts.
3. Outline each subject area, specifying the more important topics and subtopics to be treated.
4. For each training program, clearly identify the objective(s) you hope to attain.
5. Work up a suitable budget for each program. Be sure that you have allocated sufficient funds to insure that you reach your objective(s).
6. Prepare a time schedule for conducting the training.
7. Select the most appropriate instructional methods for accomplishing your purpose.
8. Choose the right person(s) to train your employees.
9. Begin the training program.
10. Evaluate the results of the training: did you accomplish your objective(s)?

motivation theory. You may already be familiar with such famous sources as Abraham Maslow ("Hierarchy of human needs"), Douglas McGregor ("Theory X" and "Theory Y"), and Frederick Herzberg ("Hygiene needs and satisfiers"). You can, of course, enhance your present grasp of these and other significant contributions by reading some of the books on management and supervision that are listed at the end of this chapter.

Even without digging more deeply into this extensive body of knowledge and supposition about human motivation, you will find yourself on the right track by realizing that your employees' satisfaction at work and morale are directly affected by:

- being granted more responsibility
- capable and fair supervision
- good working conditions
- job enhancement and job rotation
- on-the-job growth through training
- opportunities for advancement
- participation in decision making
- receiving just compensation for their work
- recognition by management for their accomplishments

Some useful thoughts for fostering good human relations in your organization appear in Figure 9–9.

FIGURE 9–9
Ideas for better human relations in your service firm

1. Improve your own general understanding of human behavior.
2. Accept the fact that others do not always see things as you do.
3. In any differences of opinion, consider the possibility that you may not have the right answer.
4. Show your employees that you are interested in them and that you want their ideas on how conditions can be improved.
5. Treat your employees as individuals; never deal with them impersonally.
6. Respect differences of opinion.
7. Insofar as possible, give explanations for management actions.
8. Provide information and guidance on matters affecting employees' security.
9. Make reasonable efforts to keep jobs interesting.
10. Encourage promotion from within.
11. Express appreciation publicly for jobs well done.
12. Offer criticism privately, in the form of constructive suggestions for improvement.
13. Train supervisors to be concerned about the people they supervise, the same as they would be about merchandise or materials or equipment.
14. Keep your staff up-to-date on matters that affect them.
15. Quell false rumors, and provide correct information.
16. Be fair!

Source: Martin M. Bruce, "Human Relations in Small Business," *Small Business Management Series No. 3,* 3rd ed. (Washington, D.C.: U.S. Small Business Administration, 1969), 14–15.

FOR FURTHER INFORMATION

Books

Adelstein, Michael E. and W. Keats Sparrow, *Business Communications,* 2d ed. San Diego, Calif.: Harcourt Brace Jovanovich, 1990.

Aldag, Ramon J. and Timothy M. Stearns, *Management,* 2d ed. Cincinnati: South-Western, 1991.

Beach, Dale S., *Personnel: The Management of People at Work,* 6th ed. New York: Macmillan, 1991.

Halloran, Jack and George Frunzi, *Supervision: The Art of Management,* 2d ed. Englewood Cliffs, N.J.: Prentice-Hall, 1986.

Harcourt, Jules and A. C. "Buddy" Krizan, *Business Communication,* 2d ed. Cincinnati: South-Western, 1991.

Hilgert, Raymond and Theo Haimann, *Supervision: Concepts and Practices of Management,* 5th ed. Cincinnati: South-Western, 1991.

Hodgetts, Richard M. and Donald F. Kuratko, *Management,* 3rd ed. San Diego, Calif.: Harcourt Brace Jovanovich, 1991.

Ivancevich, John M. and William F. Glueck, *Foundations of Personnel: Human Resource Management.* Homewood, Ill.: Irwin, 1989.

——— et al., *Management,* 4th ed. Homewood, Ill.: Irwin, 1989.

Mosley, Donald C. et al., *Supervisory Management: The Art of Working With and Through People,* 2d ed. Cincinnati: South-Western, 1988.

Newman, Ruth and Marie Danziger, *Communication in Business Today.* Lexington, Mass.: D.C. Heath, 1987.

Portnoy, Robert A., *Leadership: What Every Leader Should Know about People.* Englewood Cliffs, N.J.: Prentice-Hall, 1986.

Reece, Barry L. and Rhonda G. Brandt, *Effective Human Relations in Organizations,* 3rd ed. Boston: Houghton Mifflin, 1986.

Sherman, Arthur W., George W. Bohlander, and Herbert J. Chruden, *Managing Human Resources,* 8th ed. Cincinnati: South-Western, 1988.

Stoner, James and R. Edward Freeman, *Management,* 4th ed. Englewood Cliffs, N.J.: Prentice-Hall, 1989.

Stout, Vickie J. and Edward A. Perkins, Jr., *Practical Management Communication.* Cincinnati: South-Western, 1987.

Twomey, David P., *Equal Employment Opportunity Law,* 2d ed. Cincinnati: South-Western, 1990.

Williams, J. Clifton and George P. Huber, *Human Behavior in Organizations,* 3rd ed. Cincinnati: South-Western, 1986.

Wolf, Morris Philip and Shirley Kuiper, *Effective Communication in Business,* 9th ed. Cincinnati: South-Western, 1989.

Business Development Publications Available from the U.S. Small Business Administration

MANAGEMENT AND PLANNING

MP 1–"Effective Business Communications: ($.50)

PERSONNEL MANAGEMENT

PM 1–"Checklist for Evaluating a Training Program" ($.50)

PM 2–"Employees: How to Find and Pay Them" ($1.00)

PM 3–"Managing Employee Benefits: ($1.00)

Part Four

MARKETING YOUR SERVICE(S)

CHAPTER 10

PRICING YOUR SERVICE(S) FOR PROFIT

In this chapter, you will come to understand the need for ensuring the viability of your new service enterprise by instituting proper pricing procedures. You will become acquainted with a number of pricing approaches and practices commonly used in business. We then identify and provide insights into several promotional pricing techniques. A discussion of discounts concludes the chapter.

PROPER PRICING IS CRUCIAL TO SUCCESS

Pricing is a vital component of your firm's marketing mix. Improper pricing approaches can prove catastrophic. If you set your selling prices lower than you should, the amount of year-end profit you will earn may be disappointing to you. Perhaps you will not realize any profit at all, but suffer a loss. You may even be forced out of business. On the other hand, if you set prices that are too high, you may discover that your sales revenues are insufficient to support your operation—and you are compelled to shut it down.

How, then, can you play it safe? What is the right way to go about pricing your service(s)?

By way of introduction to the problem, read through the following statements. Then, keep them in mind as you begin to develop your pricing strategies and tactics.

- The prices of goods and services respond to the interaction between supply and demand.
- Prices tend to rise as demand increases for a product or service and to fall as demand decreases.
- Setting prices on goods and services facilitates both buying and selling.
- The selling prices you establish for your product and service offerings can affect your revenues (and profits) favorably or adversely.
- You may have to modify your own pricing approaches in response to the pricing strategies and tactics of competitors.
- Regard price not only as a promotional tool but also as a formidable competitive weapon.
- If you plan to sell your service(s) through distributors, you will need to build these intermediaries into the picture when setting your prices and discount structure.

EFFECTIVE PRICE-SETTING APPROACHES

As a cautionary note, be sure to consider all of the following aspects before you start to work on pricing your service(s):

- *The state of the economy*—How is it faring at the present time? What should it be like next year—and the year after that?
- *The demand for the service(s)*—Is the demand of a seasonal nature? What is its current level? Do you expect the demand level to be higher, lower, or about the same six months from now?
- *Your competitors*—Should you price your service(s) higher than, lower than, or about on the same level with the prices of your competitors?
- *Your distribution plans*—What marketing channels, if any, are you planning to use?
- *The location of your business.*
- *Your costs.*
- *The net profit percentage of sales you would like to earn.*
- *The public's perception of the relationship between price and quality.*
- *Your plans for using promotional pricing methods.*

Choose Your Objectives First!

Demand, sales, competition, and cost are all legitimate bases for price-setting. A company with demand-oriented pricing objectives in place will plan to vary the selling prices of its products and/or services as changes in demand level occur. It may raise its prices as demand increases and, of course, lower them as demand diminishes. Sales-based objectives will lead an organization to specify the level of sales (either in units or in dollars) that it wants to reach and then set prices that will enable them to reach that goal.

Firms that choose competition-oriented objectives take under consideration their competitors' pricing strategies and tactics. Depending on how they want to position their firms with relation to the competition, they will set prices that are above, below, or on the same level as the others. In the event that a competitor decides to change its prices, the company will alter its prices accordingly.

Finally, organizations with cost-oriented objectives first total all applicable costs (fixed and variable) and then add a desired profit margin to arrive at their selling prices. Fixed costs are those expenses that tend to remain unchanged despite variations in the quantity produced or sales revenues generated. Rent, insurance, and executive salaries are examples. Costs that increase or decrease in tandem with changes in production output are variable costs. Some examples are the costs of raw materials and components, production wages, sales commissions, and packaging expenses.

Pricing Goals

Across all of industry, three of the more popular pricing goals are: (1) to secure a specific return on investment (ROI), (2) to increase sales, and (3) to maximize profits.

In the first situation, company management decides on the amount of profit it would like to earn—expressed as a percentage of the sum invested—and then builds that percentage into its selling prices. In the second, management targets a set percentage increase in sales during a particular period, and reduces prices sufficiently to produce the desired increase. Finally, a management that desires profit maximization will deliberately raise its selling prices to a high level to bring in as many gross margin dollars as it can without slowing down sales appreciably.

Cost-plus Pricing

Cost-plus pricing is the general norm in all business sectors. Manufacturers seek to recover all expenditures incurred in producing their goods and earn some profit in addition. Thus, they will build into their pricing structure the costs of raw materials, semifinished goods, and/or components required for the manufacturing process; direct labor costs; packaging and cartonning expenses; a proportionate share of the firm's administrative and selling expenses; and the profit margin management would like to earn.

Wholesalers and retailers also rely on cost-plus pricing. These distributors incorporate into their selling prices: (1) all expenses associated with the purchasing, receiving, storage, handling, and distribution of the merchandise they offer for resale, (2) an allocated percentage of their administrative and selling costs, and (3) a reasonable profit margin.

Service companies approach price administration just a bit differently. Of course, if any merchandise is offered for sale (as, for example, the shampoos, hair colorings, and other products that are frequently sold in beauty salons), the selling prices are set by following a procedure similar to that used by retailers. Most service firms, however, do not sell goods. Often, direct labor is their most significant expense factor. To arrive at its selling prices, the service company will add to its labor costs: (1) all expenses incurred in producing and delivering the service(s)–including those indirect costs traceable to its investment in machinery and equipment, (2) an appropriate share of the administrative overhead, and (3) the desired profit.

PROMOTIONAL PRICING TECHNIQUES

In marketing their goods and/or services, companies are able to choose from an array of promotional pricing approaches. Unfortunately, several of the techniques designed to tempt prospective buyers are deceptive or illegal. Nine of the more common methods are briefly described below:

1. *Bait pricing*–A deceptive and inherently illegal practice used by some shady operators. To attract potential customers, the firm will deliberately promote a popular product or service at a surprisingly low price. Despite having made the offer, the company has made no plans to sell the "bait." When prospective buyers arrive, the firm's salespeople try to persuade them to purchase another, more expensive product or service.

2. *Comparative pricing*–This is another attempt to defraud customers. In one commonly-seen version of this promotional ploy, the seller attaches a price ticket to an article. Several successively lowered selling prices are displayed on the ticket. All but the last price has been crossed out. This tactic leads shoppers to believe that the item has been marked down two or three times–and that the final price indicates a real bargain.

   In another variation, the firm makes the claim (in its advertising or on price tags) that its prices are well below those asked by competitors for the identical good or service. Such claims may be worded in this manner: "Regularly sold by the X Company for $89.95; our price is only $55.00." Or: "Our competitor offers this item for $150; we sell it at less than half their price–for $69.95."

3. *Flexible pricing*–Most retail and service organizations in the United States diligently adhere to a one-price policy; they charge all buyers the same price for a particular article or service. Some, however, adopt a flexible, or variable, pricing policy. Anticipating that buyers may resort to bargaining, these firms may "adjust" the price of an item to what the traffic will bear. Retailers of antiques and used car dealers are examples.

4. *Leader pricing*–This popular promotional approach is perfectly legal. In a typical case, the firm selects a popular product or service and offers it at a

reduced price through media advertising and/or sales promotion methods. The selling prices of these "leaders" are established by applying a lower-than-usual markup so that they represent real "buys" for the customers.

5. *Multiple pricing*—Companies that employ this technique offer two or more units of a product or service at a lower price than buyers would normally have to pay if they were to purchase the items individually. A combination offer for admission to three forthcoming plays, a season ticket at the ball park, and a six-pack of Budweiser are examples.

6. *Odd- or even-pricing*—This is a pricing policy with psychological overtones. Some business organizations end all their selling prices in odd numbers, for example: $49.99 and $169.95. This approach is based on the belief that buyers will associate odd-price endings with special sales and bargain offers. (Of course, research findings on price endings have never supported this belief!) Other companies are inclined toward the use of even-price endings, such as $17.50 and $30.00. Rounded selling prices are often favored by more conservative firms, especially those anxious to generate a quality image.

7. *Prestige pricing*—Another technique with psychological ramifications, this is favored by organizations that covet a prestige image. They set prices for their goods and/or services that are higher than those of their competitors. Consumers tend to equate higher prices with higher quality. Top tour operators, fine restaurants, and expensive apparel shops are examples of enterprises that practice prestige pricing.

8. *Rebates*—Occasionally, distributors will offer printed rebate slips to purchasers of certain items. These forms are usually contributed by the manufacturers or other producers. The customer is asked to complete the form and mail it away according to the directions on the slip. Subsequently, the buyer receives a check in the amount of the announced rebate.

9. *Trade-ins*—This promotional approach is popular with used car dealers, tire distributors, retailers of large appliances, and some other types of merchandise retailers. The seller will offer a trade-in allowance—a small amount of money in exchange for an old item turned in if a new one of the same type is purchased. Effectively, this reduces the buyer's purchase price.

UNDERSTANDING DISCOUNTS

Discounts are amounts deducted from the regular selling prices of goods or services. These reductions may be expressed either in dollars and cents or, more commonly, as a percentage of the price.

Seven types of discounts are commonly seen in business: cash, early-bird, employee, introductory, quantity, seasonal, and trade discounts. All are described below:

Cash discounts–Offered to encourage the early payment of invoices. The percentage allowed for a cash discount usually appears on the face of the invoice, next to the "Terms of Sale." For example, the terms indicated on an invoice may read "3%/10, N30." The first entry "3%/10" is interpreted as an offer by the supplier to grant a cash discount of 3 percent of the face amount shown on the bill *IF* the bill is paid in full within ten days of the date of the invoice. The "N30" that appears after the comma means that the customer has 30 days after the invoice date to pay the bill in full. No discount is given if the bill is paid after the tenth day.

Early-bird discounts–Granted to encourage early buying. For example, a restaurant may offer an "early-bird discount" to consumers who arrive before dinnertime, say between 4 P.M. and 6 P.M. By so doing, the restaurant picks up additional business during a slow period of the day and relieves the strain on its facilities caused by the regular dinner crowd.

Employee discounts–Many firms offer their employees 5 to 30 percent off the regular selling prices of their products and/or services as an employee benefit.

Introductory discounts–Generally, companies offer these for one or both of two reasons: (1) to induce other marketing channel members (wholesalers, retailers) to carry a new product, product line, or service, or (2) to introduce new items or services to consumers.

Quantity discounts–Granted to customers (organizational buyers or consumers) to induce them to purchase large quantities of goods or services.

Seasonal discounts–A promotional tactic often employed by manufacturers and distributors to generate immediate cash or to clear out excessive stocks. Customers willing to buy early–in advance of an upcoming season–may be granted discounts of up to 5 percent or even more.

Trade discounts–Offered by one channel participant to others in order to compensate them for performing their ordinary functions in the distribution of goods and/or services. Thus, the manufacturer's, wholesaler's, and retailer's selling prices will all differ.

FOR FURTHER INFORMATION

Books

Hirshleifer, Jack and M. Sproul, *Price Theory and Applications,* 4th ed. Englewood Cliffs, N.J.: Prentice-Hall, 1988.

Marshall, A., *More Profitable Pricing.* New York: McGraw-Hill, 1980.

Montgomery, Stephen L., *Profitable Pricing Strategies.* New York: McGraw-Hill, 1988.

Nagle, Thomas T., *The Strategy and Tactics of Pricing: A Guide to Profitable Decision Making.* Englewood Cliffs, N.J.: Prentice-Hall, 1987.

Oxenfeldt, Alfred R., *Pricing Strategies.* New York: AMACOM, 1982.

Symonds, Curtis W., *Pricing for Profit.* New York: AMACOM, 1982.

Business Development Publications Available from the U.S. Small Business Administration

FINANCIAL MANAGEMENT

FM 12–"A Pricing Checklist for Small Retailers" ($1.00)

FM 13–"Pricing Your Products and Services Profitably" ($1.00)

CHAPTER 11

THE PROMOTION MIX: TELLING YOUR STORY AND SELLING YOUR SERVICE(S)

In this first of three chapters on the role of promotion in a firm's marketing activity, we begin by defining the term. You will then be introduced to the five components of the "promotion mix." You will learn how company management strives to apportion its promotion dollars beneficially among these components. Subsequently, we stress the importance of choosing appropriate objectives before setting out to plan any kind of promotional effort. The chapter ends with a discussion of the more popular methods companies use to develop their advertising budgets.

ELEMENTS OF THE PROMOTION MIX

Promotion may be defined rather simply as purposeful communications from a source to other people. In your case the source is your new service company. Your promotional efforts will aim at conveying information to prospective buyers; arousing their interest in knowing more about your company and its products and services; building desire on their part to acquire what you offer for sale; and persuading them to buy from you.

Promotion, or rather the "promotion mix," is one of the four major components of a firm's marketing mix. The other three are the products-and-services mix, pricing, and distribution. Marketing entails selecting the right products and services to offer for sale, pricing them sensibly, promoting them, and arranging for their distribution to consumers and/or organizations.

The promotion mix contains five elements: personal selling, advertising, sales promotion, public relations, and publicity. (See Figure 11–1.) Each firm prepares its own mix, assigning a different proportion of its total budget for promotion to each ingredient according to the task it is expected to perform.

The five components are briefly defined below:

Personal selling–Promotion through oral communication on a person-to-person basis (one or more salespeople making a presentation).

Advertising–Nonpersonal promotional communication aimed at prospective buyers that is paid for by an identified sponsor.

Sales promotion–A term that encompasses various types of promotional methods useful for rounding out and supplementing both advertising and personal selling. (Examples: coupons, demonstrations, displays, premiums, sampling.)

Public relations–Two-way communication between an organization and its various publics, generally to help the company's image.

FIGURE 11–1
The promotion mix

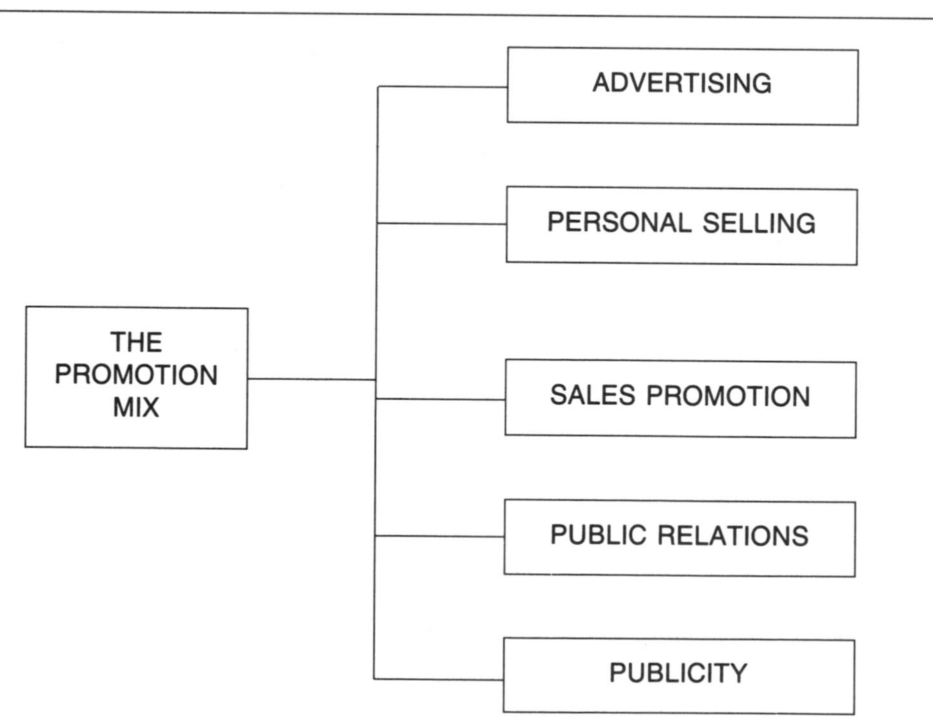

Publicity—Nonpersonal communication from an organization that is offered through the media at no cost to the organization.

Carefully select and then study the promotional objectives you hope to attain. This should provide some useful insights into how to apportion your promotion budget effectively. To put it another way, try to get the biggest possible return on your promotion dollars.

Typical promotion mixes for different types of service operations appear in Figures 11–2 and 11–3. These show the percentages of the total promotion budget assigned by the firm's management to the various mix components.

SELECTING PROMOTIONAL OBJECTIVES

As you discovered in Chapter 7, you would be wise not to begin planning of any kind without first choosing one or more objectives for you to pursue. Keep this in mind when you are about ready to tackle your promotion plans for the coming quarter, six-month season, or year. Be sure to select and clarify the objective(s) you would like to attain.

Here are some of the more popular promotional objectives used by business organizations of all sizes and descriptions:

- To attract new buyers
- To build strong ties between your firm and the community
- To cultivate customer loyalty
- To differentiate your firm from those of competitors
- To enhance your company's reputation
- To extend your firm's trading area
- To generate excitement about a forthcoming promotion
- To increase sales
- To inform prospective buyers about your company and the service(s) you offer
- To introduce a new service
- To keep old customers
- To keep your firm's name in the public's mind
- To open new territories
- To persuade people to try your service(s)
- To support your sales staff

General objectives are okay—for a start. To extract the maximum value from them in your planning, get more specific. Strive to quantify your objectives. Assume, for the sake of illustration, that you are starting in early January on

FIGURE 11–2
Promotion mixes for two consumer-service companies

A slenderizing salon:

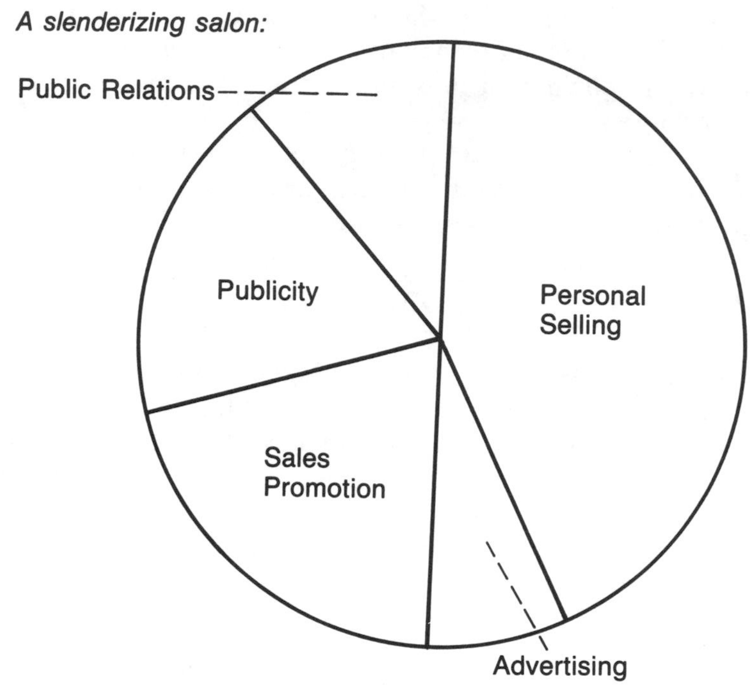

A real estate agency:

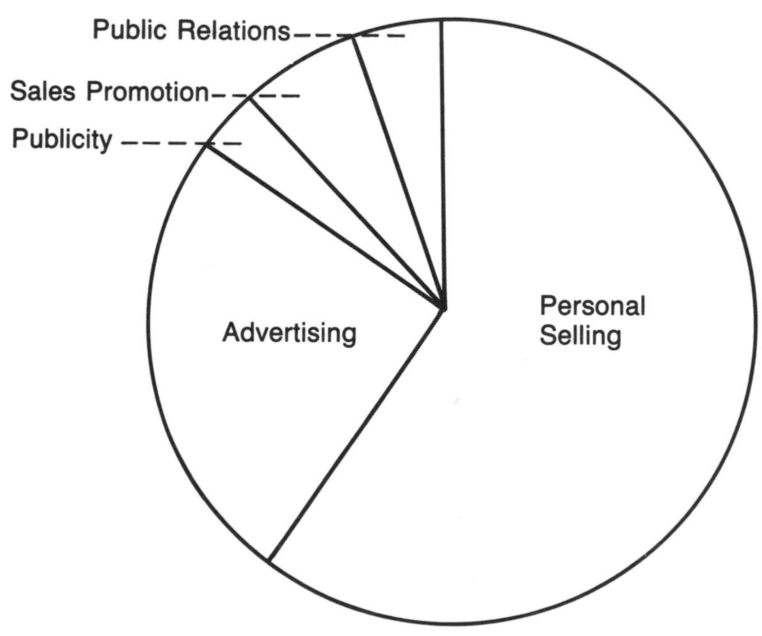

FIGURE 11–3
Promotion mixes for two business-service companies

A business machines repair firm:

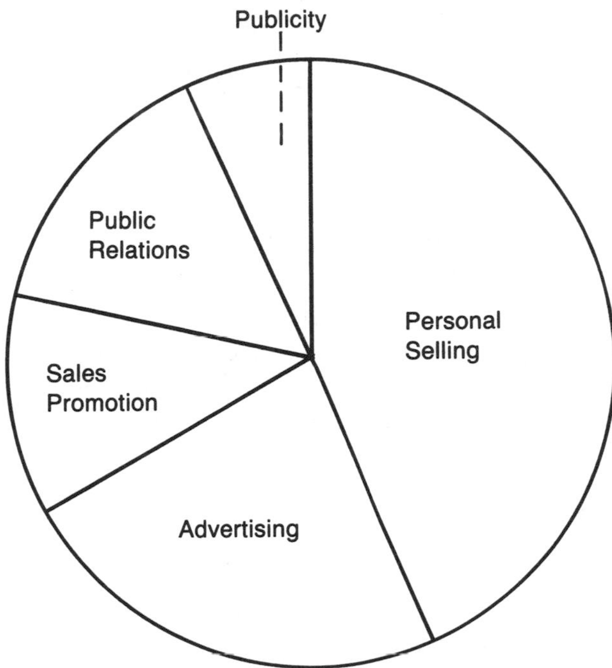

A management consulting organization:

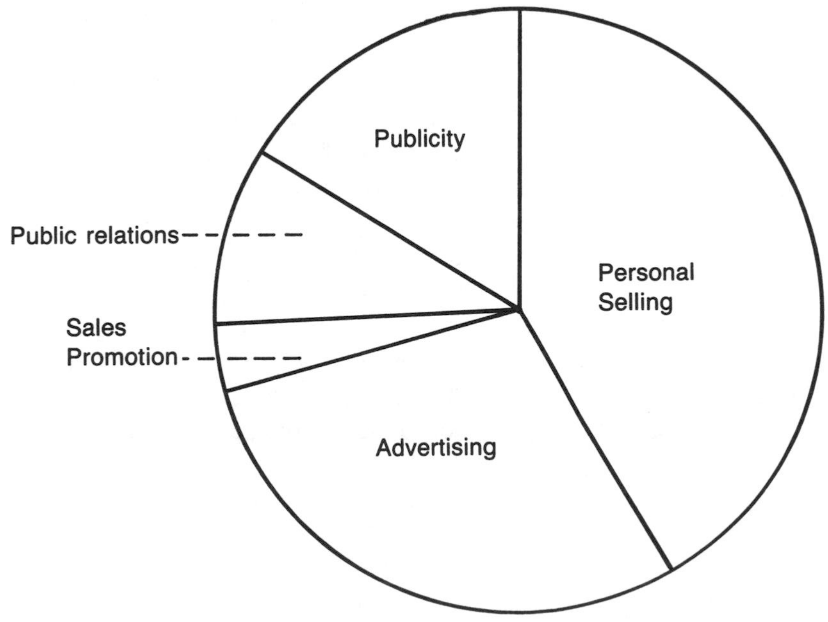

your promotion planning for the third quarter of the year. Consider the first item on the above list of objectives: "To attract new customers." Change this to: "to attract 150 new customers in the third quarter of this year." Or, better still: "To sell our service to a minimum of 50 new customers per month during the months of July, August, and September."

Again, rather than settling for the objective "to increase sales," set up a more specific target, such as "to increase sales in the third quarter by 18 percent over the same quarter last year."

DETERMINING HOW–AND HOW MUCH–TO BUDGET FOR ADVERTISING

Every year, company management faces the difficult chore of preparing an advertising budget. Central to this problem is the decision about the amount of money to be spent on advertising. Different strategies may be employed to arrive at the decision. Five of the more popular approaches are:

- The "Keep the Status-Quo" approach
- The "We'll Spend What We Can Afford" method
- The "Let's Meet our Competition" technique
- The "Objective-and-Task" method
- The "Percentage-of-Sales" approach

Business managers who lack confidence in the value of advertising tend to follow one of the first two approaches in the above-mentioned list. An owner who adheres to a "Keep the Status-Quo" position will allocate to the new ad budget precisely the same number of dollars that the firm spent on advertising during the prior year. A company that follows the "We'll Spend What We Can Afford" method will (a) estimate its probable revenues for the entire year, (b) deduct from this projected sales figure the amount it will need to cover all operating expenses other than advertising, (c) subtract the net profit it would like to earn, and (d) allot what is then left over to the ad budget.

The "Let's Meet Our Competition" Technique–This involves matching your competitor's ad budget. If it proves too difficult for you to determine the size of that budget from the competitive firm's advertising, try contacting the local media and/or your trade association for the information.

As you suspect, though, this method is based on fallacious reasoning. For one thing, your competition may not know what it is doing. For another, its management may be relying on the same technique, basing their budget on what they think you are spending (or intend to spend).

The "Objective and Task" Method–In using this approach, company management specifies the objective(s) it would like to attain and then prepares an estimate of how much must be spent on advertising to achieve its goal(s).

This technique makes more sense than all the others mentioned thus far. It is a logical approach based on the belief that advertising brings in, or causes, sales. You simply set a specific sales target and then spend what you need to reach that goal.

Despite the logic behind the concept, this approach is difficult to put into effect. The problem is that judgment alone must be relied on to determine what level of advertising expenditures is needed to attain the sales goal.

The "Percentage of Sales" Approach—Of the five methods, this one offers the most pragmatic route to the preparation of an ad budget. It is also the most popular technique of all. It involves relating your advertising expenses to your net sales.

To do this, you will need two figures from your end-of-year operating statement: (1) the amount you spent on advertising and (2) your net sales for the year. Divide the first figure by the second and then multiply the result by 100 percent. This will yield your advertising-to-sales ratio for last year.

Here is the formula for calculating the ratio:

$$\text{Advertising-to-Sales Ratio} = \frac{\text{Advertising Expense for Year}}{\text{Sales for Year}} \times 100\%$$

To illustrate the procedure, assume that you are reviewing your operating statement for the year just ended. You note that your net sales came to $165,000 and your total expenditures for advertising totaled $5,600. Here is how you would develop your advertising-to-sales ratio for last year:

$$\text{Advertising-to-Sales Ratio} = \frac{\text{Advertising Expense for Year}}{\text{Sales for Year}} \times 100\%$$

$$= \frac{\$5{,}600}{\$165{,}000} \times 100\%$$

$$= .034 \times 100\%$$

$$= 3.4\%$$

As you have just determined, you spend 3.4 percent of last year's sales on advertising. To arrive at a decision about how much to allocate to your ad budget for the coming year, you would need to (1) estimate the amount of revenue you expect your firm to receive during the year and (2) multiply this sales projection by 3.4 percent.

A brand-new business may encounter a slight problem in using this approach. There is no previous history; therefore, no operating statement is available from which to derive the figures you need to compute your advertising-to-sales ratio. If, however, you did prepare proforma accounting documents (as was recommended in Chapter 7), you would have anticipated both your first-year's revenues and your advertising expense. Moreover, if you worked diligently on your business plan, you probably contacted your trade association early in the game to ascertain how much the average firm of your type and size spent on advertising.

One caution is in order: you would be making a serious mistake if you were to allocate approximately the same percentage of sales to your advertising as other similar firms do. In your new enterprise, you face a far greater communication challenge than do companies that are well established. So few prospective customers know you, your company, or what you have to sell. For best results, we recommend that you at least *double* your advertising-to-sales ratio for your first two or three years in business.

Determining Your Monthly Advertising Expenditures

How do you decide on how much you ought to spend each month on your advertising? Certainly not by dividing your annual appropriation by 12! Your sales can vary substantially from one month to the next. In fact, for many types of businesses, just two months (November and December) can account for 30 to 45 percent or more of annual sales. On the other hand, January, February, July, or August may each contribute no more than 3 to 6 percent of the year's revenues. (Unless, of course, you own an ice cream parlor!)

If your business is more than one year old, you should have some idea of what percentage of annual sales each month contributes. If it is not, your trade association may be able to help you with this information.

To demonstrate the procedure for determining monthly outlays for advertising, assume that you have projected the following percentages for the coming year:

January	7%	July	6%
February	7%	August	6%
March	8%	September	8%
April	9%	October	9%
May	8%	November	11%
June	6%	December	15%
1st half –	45%	2nd half –	55%

According to the above table, you should take in 45 percent of next year's sales during the first six months and 55 percent over the second half of the year.

Now, let us suppose that you have decided to spend $9,000 on advertising for the year. Begin applying the monthly percentages shown above. To work out the amount to spend during January, multiply $9,000 by .07 (for 7 percent). This comes to $630. Continue your calculations in the same manner all the way through December.

This is how your table of monthly expenditures should look when completed:

January	$630	July	$540
February	$630	August	$540
March	$720	September	$720

April	$810	October	$810
May	$720	November	$990
June	$540	December	$1,350
1st half –	$4,050	2nd half –	$4,950

One last thought about the percentage-of-sales approach is in order at this point. You need not adhere slavishly to the concept should you decide to use it. Many entrepreneurs prefer to advertise more heavily during those months that people ordinarily are more interested in buying their products or services. They feel that their advertising will produce better results because of the timing. On the other hand, there are many who will spend proportionately more during the slower periods of the year to beef up their sales volume.

FOR FURTHER INFORMATION

Books

Davidson, Jeffrey P., *Marketing on a Shoestring.* New York: Wiley, 1988.

Govoni, N. et al, *Promotional Management.* Englewood Cliffs, N.J.: Prentice-Hall, 1986.

Johnson, Eugene M., Eberhard E. Scheuing, and Kathleen A. Gaida, *Profitable Service Marketing.* Homewood, Ill.: Business One Irwin, 1986.

Putman, Anthony O., *Marketing Your Services: A Step-by-Step Guide for Small Businesses and Professionals.* New York: Wiley, 1989.

Ross, Marilyn and Thomas Ross, *Big Marketing Ideas for Small Service Businesses.* Homewood, Ill.: Dow Jones-Irwin, 1990.

Slutsky, Jeff, *Streetsmart Marketing.* New York: Wiley, 1989.

Withers, Jean and Carol Vipperman, *Marketing Your Service: A Planning Guide for Small Business.* Bellingham, Wash.: Self-Counsel Press, 1987.

Business Development Publications Available from the U.S. Small Business Administration

MANAGEMENT AND PLANNING

MP 11–"Business Plan for Small Service Firms" ($.50)

MARKETING

MT 2–"Marketing for Small Business: An Overview" ($1.00)

MT 4–"Marketing Checklist for Small Retailers" ($1.00)

CHAPTER 12

ADVERTISING, SALES PROMOTION, PUBLIC RELATIONS, AND PUBLICITY

In the previous chapter, you were introduced to the promotion mix and its various components. After stressing the importance of developing an appropriate mix for your service firm, we surveyed the more popular methods that companies use to determine how much to budget for promotion.

We begin this chapter by examining four of the five mix elements: advertising, sales promotion, public relations, and publicity. Treatment of the fifth component, personal selling, has been deliberately omitted. Because personal selling is often the principal promotional approach used by many service companies, a separate chapter (Chapter 13) has been devoted entirely to the subject.

Later on, we review the major advertising media, pointing out the advantages and disadvantages that each offers the advertiser. Some recommendations are offered that can help you create effective advertising. You are then introduced to a wide range of sales promotion techniques. Finally, you are shown how to maintain good relations with your various publics and how to generate valuable publicity for your company.

Effective promotion management requires attention to such specifics as selecting and then researching market segments; setting advertising objectives; conceptualizing plans; constructing messages and designing ads; and choosing the best media for conveying your messages to your targeted audiences. In selecting your media, be sure to follow this basic principle: try to reach as many prospects as you can at as low a cost as possible.

Bear in mind, though, that it will be difficult–if not almost impossible–to assess the effectiveness of your firm's media advertising. Mail order advertising and direct mail are exceptions; often, these efforts can be evaluated through the use of keying or couponing.

WHY YOU NEED TO MAXIMIZE YOUR ADVERTISING DOLLARS

Careful planning is the key to extracting the biggest return for the money you invest in advertising. Yes, advertising is expensive, and you should try to make every cent count. Typically, small firms spend next to nothing on media advertising. For some, a boldface listing or a small display ad in the Yellow Pages suffices for the year.

Perhaps this is so because many small business owners regard advertising as just another, perhaps unnecessary, expense–one that they cannot readily evaluate in terms of its effectiveness in increasing their sales.

According to records compiled by trade sources, most companies annually spend on media advertising an amount equal to between two and four percent of their yearly sales volume. Thus, the small service firm with annual sales of, say, $400,000 is likely to allocate $8,000 to $16,000 to its advertising budget. If its management were to spread this total evenly over the year, the firm would be spending between $667 and $1,333 each month.

What can such a small sum buy in the media? Here are a few likely possibilities:

- In a metropolitan daily newspaper: A small, one column × 3″ (or, perhaps, 4″) display ad–or a lengthy 1-column classified ad
- On radio: 10–20 one-minute spot announcements
- On TV: 1–3 one-minute commercials (production costs included)
- By direct mail: 1,000–2,000 mailing pieces (stamped and delivered to the post office)

Sales, however, are never the same from one month to the next. In most industries, the majority of companies expend considerably less than one-half of their annual advertising budgets during the first six months of the year. In fact, for many kinds of businesses, the last quarter traditionally accounts for 40 to 70 percent of the year's sales.

HOW TO CHOOSE THE RIGHT MEDIA

No matter what the size of your firm, take care to dispense your media dollars with a stern sense of frugality. Always try to extract the greatest return for the money you invest.

Those vehicles that carry advertising messages to large numbers of prospective buyers are known as "the mass media." The three most widely used mass media classifications are: (1) the *print media*–newspapers and magazines, (2) the *broadcast media*–radio and TV, and (3) *direct mail*. Other media types, used less frequently in the business world, are the *position media* (examples: billboards, posters, car cards) and the *supplemental media* (examples: matchbook covers, skywriting).

There are at least six questions to ask yourself before committing one dollar of your advertising budget to the media:

1. Who are the people who are most likely to buy my service(s)?
2. Are these prospects final consumers (who buy for themselves) or do they represent and purchase for organizations?
3. What specific needs do my prospects have that my service(s) may be able to fulfill?
4. In my media advertising, how can I demonstrate that my service(s) will indeed fulfill those needs?
5. Through which medium or media will I be able to reach these potential buyers most effectively with my offers?
6. How can I choose the best media buys, thereby earning the maximum return on my advertising expenditures?

The major advertising media are discussed in the next few pages. Each one, of course, has its advantages and its disadvantages for advertisers. These are summarized in Figure 12–1.

Newspapers

Newspapers and magazines constitute the print media. American business spends more money each year on advertising in newspapers than in any other medium. Ads placed by local retailers and service companies represent the bulk of this advertising.

Newspapers find their way into most homes across the nation. Some 1,600 different newspapers are published each weekday. Another 7,000-plus appear on a weekly basis. Also available each week are hundreds of pennysavers, shopping guides, and other types.

Advantages–This medium offers advertisers a number of benefits.

Newspapers offer extreme geographic selectivity. For all practical purposes, advertisers can access almost any American city, town, or village. Furthermore, a substantial proportion of the residents in most areas read their local paper regularly.

When compared to the other media on a per-reader basis, newspaper advertising is relatively inexpensive. So are production costs. Moreover, local service and

FIGURE 12–1
The media: Major advantages and disadvantages for advertisers

Medium	Advantages	Disadvantages
Newspapers	Market selectivity Intensive coverage of the area Fast results Low cost per reader Short lead time Flexibility Modest production costs Availability of special position	Waste circulation Clutter Short life of message
Magazines	Market selectivity Long life of message Good reproduction of photographs Availability of color Multiple readership Reader loyalty Beneficial to firm's image	Higher cost per thousand readers than newspapers Slow results Waste circulation Long lead time Lack of flexibility
Radio	Universality Market selectivity Fast results Low cost per listener Short lead time Flexibility Substantial audience loyalty	Fragmentation of audience Short life of message Appeals to only one sense Audience easily distracted
Television	Extensive reach Appeals to two senses Impact Fast results Flexibility Beneficial to firm's image	High cost of air time High production costs for commercials Short life of message Considerable waste Tendency for viewers to "tune out" commercials
Direct Mail	Versatility Most persuasive medium of all Control of promotional effort "Uncluttered" Results can be measured	High cost per reader Tendency to discard "junk mail" without reading Slow results Long lead time needed for production
Position Media	High frequency Fast results Modest cost per viewer	Messages must be short Substantial lead time needed for production Lack of flexibility Appeals to only one sense Waste circulation

retail firms are usually charged lower rates than national companies are required to pay.

Reaction to a newspaper advertisement is quick. The ad you place in one morning's paper often brings in sales by the afternoon—and even the same morning. In fact, it is common to register from 50 to 70 percent of the sales resulting from one newspaper ad within one week after the ad's publication.

Another benefit is the ultra-short "lead time"—the amount of time that elapses between the ad insertion order and the date the readership is exposed to the ad. Once you have prepared an ad, you can run it over to the paper and see it in print the very next day. Newspapers also offer great flexibility; you can modify the ad—art, headline(s), and/or copy—and have it printed the next morning with all the changes you indicated.

Bear in mind, too, that newspaper circulation figures do not take into account secondary, and perhaps tertiary, readers. In many homes, both spouses read the paper. So may one or more children. Then there are those people who read newspapers in waiting rooms and at libraries. You may also benefit by the fact that, often, readers will clip out an ad and hold it for future use. Some firms take advantage of this occasionally by offering coupons in their ads.

Disadvantages—There are four major drawbacks to the newspaper for the advertiser:

1. Much Waste Circulation—Many of the readers of any newspaper are neither potential users nor prospective buyers of a particular product or service. These readers often constitute a sizable percentage of the paper's announced total circulation—and the copies purchased by those people can be considered as just so much "waste."
2. Excessive Clutter—Typically, each issue of a newspaper is packed with ads that promote other companies' goods and services. There are also many news items that grab the reader's attention. Any ad you place will have to compete with all this "clutter."
3. Short Message Life—Most readers discard their newspapers just as soon as they have finished reading them. Any message you advertise, then, is quickly lost—often within minutes after exposure.
4. Poor Reproduction of Photographs—In preparing halftones of photographs for publication, newspapers use rather coarse screens. Consequently, any photograph you use in an ad may appear blurred or indistinct when reproduced.

Buying Newspaper Space—Newspapers sell advertising display space by column inches. Costs are tied to circulation figures. In a large metropolitan daily, with a circulation of, say, 400,000, a small 6-inch ad (3 inches by 2 columns) may cost you as much as $700 or $800—and, in some instances, even more. An identical ad placed in a small-town paper may run you less than $100.

For single insertions, you pay the "open rate." This entitles you to "run-of-paper" (ROP) placement; the newspaper decides where to place your ad. You can, though, request a special position—in the entertainment or sports section, on a specific page, at the top right hand corner of a page, and so on. If this can be done, you will be asked to pay a small additional charge for the service.

If you plan to advertise frequently, consider signing a bulk-rate contract. The more space you use in total, the lower the rate you will earn. Combination rates are also available for firms that advertise in both weekday and Sunday papers or in successive issues.

Most retailers and service firms pay the local rate; this usually runs some 40 to 50 percent below the paper's national rate.

Space in the classified section is offered on a per agate line basis; there are 14 agate lines to one column inch.

Magazines

Well over 10,000 magazines of all types and descriptions are available to advertisers. Most are monthly publications. Some are issued on a weekly or bimonthly basis.

Most magazines can be classified under one of five major categories:

- *Business, trade, and professional magazines*—(Examples: *Antiques Dealer, Architectural Digest, Builder and Contractor, Business Week, Forbes, Fortune, Lodging Hospitality, National Jeweler, Nation's Business, Sales & Marketing Management)*
- *Farm magazines*—(Examples: *American Fruit Grower, Farm Journal, Ohio Farmer, Progressive Farmer, Rural Missouri, Texas Agriculture)*
- *General consumer magazines*—(Examples: *Cosmopolitan, Esquire, Family Circle, Glamour, Good Housekeeping, House Beautiful, Redbook, Self, Vogue*)
- *Special interest magazines*—(Examples: *Baby Talk, Camping Magazine, Cats Magazine, Ceramic Arts and Crafts, Family Health, High Fidelity, Popular Photography, Popular Science, Trailer Life*)
- *Sports magazines*—(Examples: *Field & Stream, Golf Magazine, National Racquetball, Skiing Magazine, Sports Illustrated, World Tennis*)

Advantages—As an advertising medium, magazines outperform newspapers in a number of ways. A magazine ad enjoys a longer life than a newspaper ad. Magazines may be kept around the house—or in the office, waiting room, or library—for several weeks and even longer. Secondary, or passalong, readership is common; often a few different individuals will read the same copy.

Magazines also employ much finer screens than newspaper do when they prepare photographs for reproduction. Added color is also readily available for enhancement purposes.

Then, too, magazine readers are an extraordinarily loyal group. Most avidly devour each and every issue of their favorite publications. Moreover, all advertisements in those magazines seem to acquire, for some reason or other, the prestige of the publication itself. This factor will lend credibility to what your ads will have to say and to your firm's reputation as well.

Magazines offer one other distinct advantage: target market selectivity. By carefully choosing the right magazines, advertisers can effectively reach a broad spectrum of consumer or organization types. Among the many groups a firm can target are baseball fans, boating enthusiasts, skiers, and sporting goods dealers; collectors and hobbyists of many kinds; dairy farmers, cattle raisers, and fruit growers; golfers and tennis players; lovers of country music and soap opera fans; motorcyclists and hot-rodders; parents, children, teachers, and schools; pet owners and the pet industry; residents of New York, Los Angeles, and other metropolitan areas; small business owners, sales representatives, and purchasing agents; soap opera enthusiasts; and so on.

Disadvantages—When we compare this advertising vehicle to the newspaper, several disadvantages are obvious. For one thing, magazine space commands a considerably higher cost per thousand readers than newspaper space. For another, reader reaction to magazine advertising is typically slower than the results one can expect from a newspaper ad. Results trickle in over time—possibly over four to six months and often longer.

You may also expect that a sizable proportion of any magazine's advertised circulation figures will turn out to be waste circulation. Many of its readers will not be prime prospects for the service(s) you offer.

One of the more unfortunate drawbacks is the long lead time required. Usually, you will need to reserve space—and forward the completed camera-ready ad—months in advance of publication. The scheduled closing date for any one issue may fall as early as two to four months before the date that appears on the magazine's cover. No changes are permitted after the closing date; this fact affords the advertiser no flexibility at all.

Magazines also share the same limitation as newspapers: both appeal only to one of the five senses. However, you may occasionally come across a pleasant ad in a magazine that does appeal to the reader's sense of smell. Perhaps it advertises a famous brand of perfume—or some popular cake or confectionery item. While it is possible for newspapers to employ this technique, newspaper ads that do are rarely seen.

Buying Magazine Space—Space for advertising in magazines is sold by the column inch, fractional page, and full page. National advertisers must pay the highest rate. Book and record clubs, camps, schools, some other types of retailers and service firms, and mail order advertisers typically enjoy lower rates.

Color advertising is available at a premium. Adding another color to your full-page, black-and-white advertisement might add as much as 10 to 30 percent to your bill. A full-page, four-color ad could run you up to 70 or 75 percent more. Note, too, that the cost of a fractional-page ad in full-color is much higher, proportionately, than that of the full-page ad.

Lower contract rates for frequent advertisers are, of course, available. Some magazines publish regional editions; advertisers may purchase space in one or more of these to avoid paying for the entire circulation. Similarly, split-runs are made available by a few publications. These enable the advertiser to test two (or several) different ads at one time.

Radio

Radio and television are known as the broadcast media. There are approximately 9,000 commercial radio stations (AM and FM) currently operating in the United States. While some belong to one of the major national networks (ABC, NBC, CBS), the vast majority are independents. Most radio advertising is local in nature.

Advantages—Radio's primary advantage is that it is a universal medium. Radios can be found wherever people can be found: in apartments and homes, in cars and trucks, at the workplace, on small boats and ocean liners, and in countless other locations.

Radio offers excellent market selectivity and loyal audiences. It enables advertisers to reach specific target groups: followers of all kinds of sports, people who enjoy listening to talk shows, others who favor all-news stations, lovers of classical music, jazz buffs, country music fans, young people, blacks, Hispanics, Orientals, and so on.

Other benefits offered by this medium include:

- Speedy audience reaction to broadcast messages
- Relatively low cost per listener
- Short lead time
- Extraordinary flexibility

Disadvantages—A major drawback of radio is the so-called "fragmentation" of its audiences. In any one area of the country, as many as five or more stations may be on the air at the same moment. Many people will be listening to some other station at the very time your message is broadcast. Even for those who are tuned in to the station airing your announcements, a myriad of distractions may interfere with the receipt of your messages.

Another disadvantage is that the radio announcement has a short life. Most radio announcements are only one minute in length. Some are even shorter, taking no more than 10 or 30 seconds to broadcast. Listeners cannot refer to and mull over the radio message as they are able to do with a newspaper or magazine ad.

A final drawback is that radio suffers from the same limitation as the print media do: it appeals to only one sense. To promote their products and/or services, advertisers have to rely entirely on words, music, and possibly sound effects.

Buying Air Time on Radio—Radio stations charge their accounts rates that vary according to the size of the audience and the choice of "dayparts" during which the messages are to be aired. The most costly daypart is the period that runs from 6 to 10 A.M. on weekdays. It is also referred to as "morning drive time" or "AAA" time. Far less expensive, of course, is the daypart that embraces the hours from midnight to 6 A.M.

Television

Although the newspaper still ranks as the #1 medium in the amount of advertising dollars spent annually, TV runs a close second. Nearly 1,000 commercial TV stations service American consumers. One or more TV sets are found in almost every residence. Cable TV has been installed in more than half the homes. Each day, millions of viewers watch stations like CNN, ESPN, HBO, and MTV.

Advantages—Television is the most powerful advertising medium of all. Its reach is extensive; network TV can carry a message simultaneously to millions of people. Local TV can reach many thousands. TV appeals to the sense of sight as well as that of hearing. Both color and movement add tremendously to its strong impact on the viewer.

Viewer reaction to TV commercials is fast, as so many direct marketing companies can readily attest. Moreover, the medium's flexibility is fairly good in that broadcast schedules can be rearranged and new commercials aired without much difficulty. TV also enhances the advertising firm's public image.

Disadvantages—Despite its obvious advantages, TV advertising does have a few drawbacks. Air time is costly; a one-minute commercial on a small rural station can run as high as several hundred dollars. You may have to pay two, three, or four times that amount in a metropolitan area. Furthermore, production expenses for TV commercials are typically quite high.

Like the radio announcement, the TV message is short-lived. (Unless, of course, it has been recorded on your VCR!) There is also the omnipresent waste factor; many viewers will not be prospective users of your service(s).

Another disadvantage of TV is that, occasionally, your messages may fall on deaf ears. Many consumers make use of the time it takes to broadcast a string of commercials to perform a quick chore, get a snack, or converse with another person in the room.

Buying Air Time on TV—As is the case with radio advertising, air time on TV is also sold by audience size and daypart. Generally, weekday evenings from 7:30 P.M. to 11 P.M. command the highest rates. Post-midnight hours are usually offered at near-bargain rates.

Direct Mail

Advantages—Direct mail is the most pervasive, selective, and versatile of all advertising media. It can be used to blanket a single town or village or cover an entire county or region. It can be used to home in on specific target groups of any kind all across the country: architects, interior designers, or construction companies; teachers of math, science, or social studies; art, coin, or stamp dealers; physicians or physicists; manufacturers of ski equipment, home furnishings, or sporting goods; distributors of food products, toys, or office supplies; two- or four-year colleges; private or public hospitals; ad infinitum.

Of all media, direct mail offers you the greatest degree of control over your advertising messages. You are able to convey the complete story quite readily in your mailing piece; this is something you often cannot afford to do in the print media or on radio or TV. Moreover, direct mail arrives at the targeted addresses unhampered by the surrounding clutter of competitive advertising.

Disadvantages—The major drawbacks to direct mail advertising are:

- the high cost per reader (when contrasted with all other media)
- the fact that many recipients automatically discard so-called "junk mail" without reading it
- the long lead time required to prepare and have printed the necessary materials, collate the pieces, insert them into envelopes, add postage, and deposit the finished mail at the post office
- the tendency for replies to straggle in over a long period of time

Position Media

This category includes two major media types: (1) **outdoor advertising** (billboards, illuminated signs) and (2) **transit advertising** (posters in airports, railroads, subways; car cards in taxis, busses).

Advantages—Because these media are placed in high-traffic locations, advertising costs run quite low in terms of the numbers of passersby who are likely to read the messages they carry. Frequency of exposure is high; many ads are seen day after day as workers, for example, travel to and from their places of employment.

Disadvantages—Some of the drawbacks to advertising in the position media are:

- Long lead time
- High production costs
- Comparatively inflexible when contrasted with the other media; copy and art cannot be changed easily
- Appeals to only one of five senses
- Message length is necessarily limited
- Many people pass by too quickly to get the complete message

CREATING ADVERTISEMENTS THAT REALLY PULL

Direct, or product/service, advertising is designed to attract the attention of prospective buyers, arouse their interest, generate desire on their part to acquire what is being offered for sale, and get action in the form of a sale. Indirect, or institutional, advertising is used to inform people about an organization or, perhaps, an entire industry.

Most of your advertising will be of the direct type. Write the best possible copy for each ad–copy that will be effective in selling whatever offer you make. Regardless of the medium, or media, you choose to convey your messages, make sure that each offer comes through loud and clear.

Here are some suggestions for generating good copy:

Keep your target audience firmly in mind as you write copy
Base your message strategy on the advertising objective(s) you have selected
Try to evoke immediate audience interest
Use language that your audience can readily understand
Make every word count
Avoid passive verbs; be sure to use only active, power-packed verbs
Appeal to your prospects' needs and wants
Build credibility into your copy
Stress the benefits your product/service offers the buyer
Give the major selling points of your product/service
Try to integrate an emotional appeal
Specify any guarantee
State the selling price
Add an inducement to buy
Identify your firm; give its name, address, and telephone number

Headlines, Artwork, and Layout in Print Advertising

If you plan to advertise in newspapers or magazines, or via direct mail, you will need to learn more about other essential elements of the print ad, such as headlines, artwork, and layout. Headlines are used primarily to grab the reader's attention. Both artwork (illustrations, photographs) and layout complement and reinforce the ad message.

Here are a few final thoughts on print advertising for you to ponder over:

1. While doubling the size of an ad may give it greater impact, this does NOT lead to the ad being read by twice as many people.
2. Generally, a series of smaller ads yields better results than a single large ad. (Reinforcement through multiple exposure of the message!)
3. Readership of an ad can be increased by using a photograph (halftone) or illustration. Artwork will also enhance the reader's understanding of the message.

4. Other techniques can be used to attract more attention: heavy or unusual borders around the ad, printing in reverse (white letters against a black background), unusual typefaces, wide margins surrounding the ad, headlines (or art) in a different color (in direct mail pieces), and so on.

A useful checklist for mail order advertisers appears in Figure 12–2.

FIGURE 12–2
Checklist for mail order advertising copy

Headline

- Does the headline appeal to self-interest, offer exciting news, or arouse interest?
- Is the headline positive, rather than negative?
- Does the headline suggest that the reader can obtain something easily and quickly?
- Does the headline make use of the powerful words of mail order advertising?
- Does the headline stress the most important benefit to the product?
- Does the headline stop the reader and cause him or her to read further?
- Is the headline believable?
- Does the headline tie in with the copy?

The Offer

Are all the elements of the offer present in the copy?

Product	Price
Terms	Guarantee
Options	Additional Inducements to buy
Dates	Places

- Do you gain interest at once by use of a story, or startling or unusual statement, a quote, or news?
- Do you show benefits and advantages that appeal to emotional needs so that your offer is irresistible?
- Do you establish credibility with your reader through the use of testimonials, statements, by your accountant, or some other means?
- Do you encourage immediate action by listing a reason to order now, i.e., limited quantities, time limit on offer, etc.?

Copy Quality

- Is the copy written in a conversational tone?
- Does your copy move right along?
- Do you use short words, short sentences, and short paragraphs?
- Do you use several subheadings throughout your copy?

Source: William A. Cohen, "Selling by Mail Order," *Management Aid* 4.023 (Washington, D.C.: U.S. Small Business Administration, n.d.), 6.

EFFECTIVE SALES PROMOTION TECHNIQUES

To attain their promotional objectives, many small service enterprises place far more emphasis on sales promotion methods than on media advertising.

If you run your service business from a retail store, you enjoy a definite advantage. You are able to use your storefront beneficially—to project your company's image, inform passersby about the kind of business you are in, what you stand for, your pricing approaches, and so on. Window and interior displays, along with an effective layout and attractive decor, will help "sell" your firm and its service(s).

Many of the more popular techniques of sales promotion are described below:

Advertising Specialties—These are useful, typically inexpensive items imprinted with the company's name and/or a short message. Examples include balloons, calendars, key chains, and pencils. Distributing "ad specialties" is as popular with consumer-oriented firms as it is with companies that sell to organizations.

Audiovisuals—This category includes TV monitors, film and slide projectors, tape recorders, and similar types of equipment, including the slides, films, and other accessories, materials, and supplies needed to operate the equipment. Audiovisuals are effective for demonstrating products and/or services in action, showing prospective buyers how to use or handle them, and explaining their more significant selling points.

Brochures and Other Printed Pieces—Printed materials are valuable for informing prospects about a company's offerings, promoting merchandise and service(s), offering instructions, and persuading people to buy. In addition to brochures, this classification includes broadsides, catalogs, flyers, handbills, instruction sheets, package enclosures, and other types of printed items.

Contests and Games—Business organizations use various types of contests and games to promote sales. Among the more popular ones are "Bingo," "Count-the-Jelly Beans-in-the-Jar," jingle-writing, "Lotto," mini-compositions ("In 50 words or less, tell us why you like our company/product/service,"), "Name the New Product/Service," "Prettiest Baby Photo," and sweepstakes.

Prizes may take the form of cash awards, gifts of merchandise or services, theater tickets, and even vacations. (Note: in-house contests and games are also valuable for stimulating selling effort.)

Coupons—An extremely popular sales promotion device, coupons offer buyers a chance to purchase something at a savings. They are effective for introducing a new service or persuading people to switch to another brand or company. They are readily distributed through printed flyers and circulars, in newspaper advertisements, or through cooperative mailings.

Demonstrations—Whether carried out in-house or outside the business premises, demonstrations that show a product or service in action are effective in securing the attention of passersby and arousing their interest.

Displays–Attractive displays capture attention, arouse viewer interest, create excitement, and generally help convince prospects to buy. Thus, they serve as "silent salespeople."

Exhibits and Shows–When creatively conceived and professionally produced, most of these can be exciting affairs that generate a great deal of interest. Exhibits or shows of antiques, bric-a-brac, clothing, giftware, handicrafts, paintings, or rustic furniture are among the more popular types.

Premiums–These are items that (1) are distributed free, or (2) sold at reduced prices to customers who purchase other goods or services. Companies offer premiums to increase their overall sales volume, to encourage repeat patronage, and, generally, to foster goodwill for the firm.

Promotional Pricing Approaches–These are price-related techniques occasionally used by firms to promote sales. Three in particular are worthy of mention here: leader pricing, multiple pricing, and trade-in allowances. In applying leader pricing, the company advertises a popular article/service at a sharply reduced price to attract customers. Multiple pricing involves offering customers a price break when they purchase two or more units of a particular product/service. Firms that promote trade-in allowances give customers credit for an old, used article when they purchase a new one.

Push Money (PMs)–This term refers to special awards of modest sums of money designed to stimulate additional selling effort. Also known as "spiffs," PMs may be used to encourage "trading up" the customer (from a less expensive to a more expensive article), to induce salespeople to employ suggestion selling (attempting to sell the customer another item in addition to the one purchased), or to get the salesperson to push overstocked or slow-moving goods.

Publicity Events–Forthcoming events planned by a company are often of sufficient interest to the general public that the local media may be more than willing to publicize them. Examples of such events include special exhibits or shows, the grand opening celebration, an appearance of the Easter Bunny or Santa Claus, anniversary promotions, ribbon-cutting ceremonies, neighborhood sales days, cooperative promotions, celebrity appearances, and lectures on topics of general interest.

Special Sales Events–Each year, most retailers and many service firms offer special promotions tailored to various holidays. Valentine's Day, Easter, Thanksgiving, and Christmas are examples. Many other themes can be adopted to help promote sales, especially during slower periods: anniversary promotions, Summer or Fall previews, pre- and post-holiday sales, early-bird or midnight madness events, buyers' (or assistant buyers') sales, and the like.

Sampling–A tried and proven promotion technique for inducing people to try something new, sampling has long been favored at bakeries, confectionery stores, cheese shops, and food stores in general. Perhaps, with the exercise of a bit of creativity by management, some service operations may be able to put the sampling concept to work for them.

FIGURE 12–3
Useful sales promotion tools

Advertising specialties
Audiovisuals
Brochures, catalogs, and other printed pieces
Contests and games
Coupons
Demonstrations
Displays
Exhibits and shows
Premiums
Promotional pricing approaches
Push money ("spiffs")
Publicity events
Sampling
Special sales events
Tie-in promotions
Trading stamps
Trade-in promotions

Tie-in Promotions–These events are planned, organized, and set into motion by two or more companies. Characteristically, the participants share the costs as well as the benefits.

Trading Stamps–These can be considered a type of premium. On making a purchase, the buyer receives a number of gummed stamps. These may be of several different denominations; the total amount of stamps received is tied to the dollar amount of the purchase. The customer saves the stamps, pasting them on special sheets or in booklets. When enough have been accumulated, the completed sheets or booklets can be redeemed for merchandise or services.

Trade-in Promotions–This promotional approach is more often used in the marketing of products rather than of services. Customers are encouraged to bring in an old article of merchandise when they are ready to buy a new one of the same type. For trading in the old item, the firm offers the buyer an "allowance" toward the purchase of the new article.

For ready reference, a list of the foregoing sales promotion techniques appears in Figure 12–3.

PREPARING YOUR PUBLIC RELATIONS PROGRAMS

A broad, and often highly effective, component of the promotion mix, public relations (PR) strives to facilitate meaningful, two-way communication between an organization and its publics. Yes, we deliberately use the plural "publics," rather than the singular version, because PR activities involve a number of different groups. We can assign each group to one or another of two classifications: (1) *internal publics*—those within the company, or (2) *external publics*—those outside the company. Employees, top managers, and stockholders are all internal publics. Among the firm's external publics are its customers, suppliers, competitors, and government agencies at all levels (federal, state, and local).

All organizations are involved in public relations activity, even those that have never exerted conscious effort along these lines. Many business firms neglect this area completely.

When used effectively, your public relations programs will enhance goodwill toward your firm. Over time, they will lead to increasing sales and higher profits. For each of your publics, develop a separate PR program of at least six months duration. Careful planning and organization will result in programs that can deliver a great deal in exchange for a modest investment.

Effective PR begins at the top, with a company management that firmly believes in:

1. Selling the right merchandise and/or services at fair prices
2. Guaranteeing customer satisfaction
3. Maintaining open, two-way communication with its various publics
4. Acting responsibly (ethically, morally) in conducting business
5. Treating all equitably
6. Responding promptly to complaints
7. Standing behind its products/services

TIPS FOR GETTING LOTS OF FREE PUBLICITY

Generally speaking, people are more likely to believe information about an organization presented as news by the media than they are willing to accept the veracity of any statement offered in a paid advertisement.

Publicity is a valuable asset that every firm, large or small, can and should cultivate. Properly programmed, publicity can help you build the kind of public image you want your company to have. Its cost is never more than nominal, yet the eventual payoff can be great!

Most information about your firm can be tailored to become grist for the publicity mill. Here are some newsworthy occasions or events the media may be willing to publicize:

Anniversary celebrations	Plans for company expansion
Appearances by celebrities	Plans for plant renovation
Birthday parties	Premiums offered
Contests	Special sales and other

- Giveaways
- Management changes
- New clients
- Open house
- Participation in community-sponsored events
- promotional events
- Speaking engagements
- Sponsorship of social, cultural, and other local events
- Team sponsorship

Employees are also logical sources of useful publicity. Examples of the kinds of information that may interest others in your area with regard to your employees include:

- Achievements
- Affiliations (with civic, political, fraternal, and other types of organizations)
- Association memberships
- Attendance (at seminars, trade shows, conventions)
- Awards received
- Community participation
- Hobbies
- Publications (articles, books)
- Retirements
- Special training received
- Speeches made

Publicity Releases

Your primary tool for obtaining publicity is the publicity, or news release. By all means, do NOT try to turn a publicity release into a sales letter. Editors and station managers are not at all interested in helping you market your offerings. What they do look for are stories that they feel will interest their readers, listeners, or viewers.

In brief, treat each release as a news item. State the facts simply and clearly. Cover all angles by providing answers to every one of the "Five Ws": Who? What? Where? When? Why?

Type the publicity release on 8-½″ × 11″ sheets of quality-grade, white bond paper. Margin widths should run approximately 1-½″ on all sides of the page. Double space all text. Start the first page of the release on your company letterhead. Several lines below the name and address, at the left hand margin, give the name, title, address, and telephone number of the person to be contacted if the reader should desire additional details. Skip four additional lines and then type, in capital letters, the words "FOR IMMEDIATE RELEASE." Occasionally, you may want the reader to defer publicizing the information until a later date. In such cases, substitute the phrase "HOLD FOR RELEASE ON:," followed by the date desired and, when necessary, the actual hour for releasing the story.

Center the page number at the bottom of each page. At the end of your story, type the number "30"–or the symbol "#"–below the last line of text.

Duplicate the release, then send copies to all newspapers, radio stations, and TV stations in your area.

FOR FURTHER INFORMATION

Books

Bacon, Mark S., *Do-It-Yourself Direct Marketing.* New York: Wiley, 1991.

Baker, Kim and Sunny Baker, *How to Promote, Publicize, and Advertise Your Growing Business.* New York: Wiley, 1991.

Burstiner, Irving, *Mail Order Selling,* 2nd ed. New York: Prentice Hall Press, 1989.

Caples, John, *Tested Advertising Methods,* 4th ed. Englewood Cliffs, N.J.: Prentice-Hall, 1986.

Cohen, William, *Direct Response Marketing.* New York: Wiley, 1984.

Connor, Richard A., and Jeffrey P. Davidson, *Getting New Clients.*

———, *Marketing Your Consulting and Professional Services.* New York: Wiley, 1985.

Davidson, Jeffrey P., *Marketing on a Shoestring.* New York: Wiley, 1988.

Dennison, Dell and Linda Tobey, *The Advertising Handbook.* Bellingham, Wash.: Self-Counsel Press, 1991.

Fletcher, Tana and Julia Rockler, *Getting Publicity.* Bellingham, Wash.: Self-Counsel Press, 1990.

Govoni, N. et al, *Promotional Management.* Englewood Cliffs, N.J.: Prentice-Hall, 1986.

Gray, Ernest A., *Profitable Methods for Small Business Advertising.* New York: Wiley, 1984.

Johnson, Eugene M., Eberhard E. Scheuing, and Kathleen A. Gaida, *Profitable Service Marketing.* Homewood, Ill.: Business One Irwin, 1986.

Jugenheimer, Donald W. and Gordon E. White, *Basic Advertising.* Cincinnati, Ohio: South-Western, 1991.

Kotler, Philip and Paul Bloom, *Marketing Professional Services.* Englewood Cliffs, N.J.: Prentice-Hall, 1984.

Norris, James S., *Public Relations.* Englewood Cliffs, N.J.: Prentice-Hall, 1984.

Ross, Marilyn and Tom Ross, *Big Marketing Ideas for Small Service Businesses.* Homewood, Ill.: Business One Irwin, 1989.

Slutsky, Jeff, *Streetsmart Marketing.* New York: Wiley, 1989.

Smith, Jeanette, *The Publicity Kit.* New York: Wiley, 1991.

Wheatley, Edward W., *Marketing Professional Services.* Englewood Cliffs, N.J.: Prentice-Hall, 1983.

Withers, Jean and Carol Vipperman, *Marketing Your Service: A Planning Guide for Small Business.* Bellingham, Wash.: Self-Counsel Press, 1987.

Business Development Publications Available from the U.S. Small Business Administration

MARKETING

MT 9–"Selling by Mail Order" ($1.00)

MT 11–"Advertising" ($1.00)

CHAPTER 13

GENERATING SALES THROUGH PERSONAL SELLING

Over the two preceding chapters, you were introduced to the promotion mix and its various components. Subsequently, you were made aware of the roles that advertising, sales promotion, public relations, and publicity play in a company's marketing efforts. We chose, deliberately, to defer the treatment of one other element of the promotion mix, personal selling, until this moment.

We begin this final chapter of Part Four by stressing the significance of personal selling in producing revenues. You will then become acquainted with the steps in the personal selling process. You will learn how to improve the selling skills of your sales representatives. Finally, you will learn about the potential of using the telephone to generate sales for your new enterprise.

PERSONAL SELLING MAY BE YOUR MOST IMPORTANT "PROMOTOOL"

Personal selling is the single most powerful element in the entire promotion mix. No other component is as valuable in persuading prospects to buy. Particularly because of the intangibility and inseparability features of services, personal selling can play a significant role in ensuring the success of your service enterprise. To a large extent, customer, attitudes toward—and their "image" of—a company are formed by their contacts with the firm's sales representatives.

ANALYZING THE PERSONAL SELLING PROCESS

As indicated in Figure 13–1, the personal selling process consists of seven activities, or steps, that are performed sequentially by the salesperson. The steps are:

- Prospecting for potential buyers
- Qualifying prospects
- Conducting the preapproach
- Making the sales presentation
- Meeting and overcoming objections
- Closing the sale
- Following up the sale

All seven steps are discussed over the next few pages.

Prospecting for Potential Buyers

Salespeople use the term "prospecting" to describe the activities they engage in to locate "prospects"—people, or organizations, who may become customers.

Before embarking on your search for prospects, strive to (a) acquire an understanding of what potential buyers of your service(s) are like, and (b) learn as much as you can about their buying behavior.

If you intend to sell to consumers, rather than to organizations, try to determine precisely what motivates them to make a purchase decision. What do they need or want? Are they looking for comfort? Convenience? Entertainment? Good health? Status? (See Figure 13–2 for a more extended listing of consumer wants and needs.)

If, on the other hand, you plan to enter the organizational marketplace, you will discover that purchasing agents differ from consumers in two ways: (1) as buyers, they are better trained and more professional than consumers, and (2) they are far more likely to base their purchase decisions on such motives as economy of price, quality, performance, warranties, and similar criteria.

Whether your new company will cater to consumers or to organizations, here are a few suggestions for locating prospective buyers:

From Available Print Sources: The "Yellow Pages," industrial directories (Standard & Poor's *Register,* Dun & Bradstreet's *Million Dollar Directory,* Thomas' *Register,* and others), indexes (*New York Times Index, Business Periodicals Index,* and others), trade directories, magazines (business, general, news, trade), newspapers.

Through Promotional Effort: Flyers, media advertising, cold canvassing, direct mail, telephone marketing.

FIGURE 13–1
Steps in the personal selling process

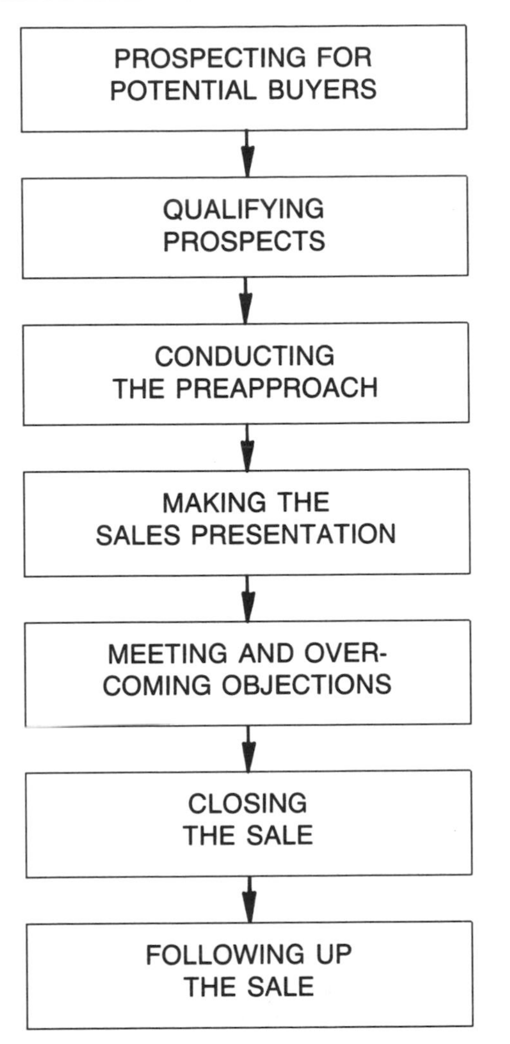

By Personal Contact: Referrals from others (customers, suppliers, trade associations), cold canvassing, finding prospects in organizations that you have joined (business, civic, fraternal, professional), meeting prospects in audiences at lectures and speeches that you have presented, locating prospects among the readers of articles or books you have written.

Qualifying Prospects

The development of a list of prospects is only the initial step in the selling process. Indeed, the list might be more appropriately referred to as a "suspect list," since you only "suspect" that the people or organizations named are prospec-

FIGURE 13–2
Some common wants and needs that buyers seek to satisfy

achievement	peace of mind
adventure	physical health
affection	pleasure
approval	popularity
care	prestige
comfort	pride
companionship	profit
convenience	recognition
ego satisfaction	romance
emulation	security
entertainment	self-actualization
esteem	self-fulfillment
excitement	self-gratification
friendship	self-improvement
fun	self-preservation
happiness	sense of belonging
hope	spiritual well-being
hunger	status
knowledge	thirst
mental health	

tive buyers. You still need to cull through the entries and discard some before you can be sure of their prospect status. You "qualify" the names by ascertaining whether or not they need your particular service(s), if they are financially sound and in a position to buy, and so on. With organizations, you would also want to determine company size, annual sales volume, who actually does the buying, location, and other aspects.

Conducting the Preapproach

In the preapproach phase, you attempt to secure as much information as you possibly can about the prospects on the list: Only after this preparation should you approach each prospect by letter or telephone and try to set up an appointment. Before you keep that appointment, you try to tailor your upcoming sales presentation in the light of what you have learned about the prospect.

Making the Sales Presentation

This is the most challenging part of the selling job. How you meet with and lead the prospect into your sales presentation is often called the "approach." (Incidentally, many textbooks on selling present a number of useful ways to handle those first few minutes with the prospect.)

As you proceed, try to build a rapport between the two of you as quickly as you can. Bear in mind that the task before you is to hold the prospect's attention, arouse interest in your service(s), build desire on that person's part to buy, and get commitment in the form of an order. Show how your service(s) will satisfy the buyer's needs and stress the benefits the customer will receive.

Meeting and Overcoming Objections

Frequently, the prospect will raise one or more objections as you are making your presentation. Make it your policy to listen carefully, without sidestepping or challenging any one of them. As you gain sales experience, you will become familiar with most types of objections. There are techniques for overcoming most of them, approaches you can learn to deliver skillfully.

Expressions of displeasure about the price of a product or service are the most common type of objection voiced by prospective buyers. Before they begin any presentation, well-trained salespeople anticipate such comments as, "We weren't planning to spend that much," "I don't think your firm offers enough value for the money," "We have already exhausted our budget," or, even more simply, "We can't afford it." When objections of this nature are raised, capable salespeople overcome them quite easily. One popular method in product sales, for example, is to (1) point out how the item will satisfy the buyer's needs over a lengthy period, and (2) then show how the cost for this long-term satisfaction would amount to no more than "x" dollars a week (or month).

Other objections that are frequently heard in the service sector may question the quality of the service, the benefits it is supposed to offer, and the qualifications of the service providers themselves.

Most books on personal selling identify and describe a number of techniques for handling objections. Three of the more familiar approaches are the "Yes, but . . . Method," the "Questioning Technique," and the "Turnaround."

The "Yes, but . . . Method"—As soon as an objection is raised, the salesperson will quickly agree with the prospect's point of view—and then move on to strengthen the sales presentation by introducing one or more, previously unmentioned, selling points.

The "Questioning Technique"—In this method of handling objections, the salesperson will attempt to change the prospective buyer's opinion by posing a few short, simple questions. These are designed to induce the prospect to realize that he or she may have erred by stating the objection. Two examples of such questions are: "Can you tell me why you think that it's too expensive?" and "Why do you feel that we would not be able to provide the quality of service you need?"

The "Turnaround"—Also known as the "Boomerang Method," this technique is usually associated with the "hard-sell" type of presentation. Upon hearing an objection, the salesperson tries to "turn it around" by attempting to persuade the prospect that the point objected to is, in reality, more of an advantage than a drawback.

Closing the Sale

Toward the end of the presentation, the salesperson will try to assess the prospect's readiness to buy through the use of one or more "trial closes." These take the form of brief questions, for example: "Which of the two would you prefer?", "When would you like to go?", and "How soon do you want us to start?" Based on the prospect's responses, the salesperson may decide that the time is ripe to "close" the sale. The close, or closing, brings the sales presentation to an end. Five of the more popular closings are the assumptive, hook, summary, SRO, and balance-sheet closes.

The Assumptive Close—This is the most commonly used technique of all. Convinced that the prospect is ready to buy, the salesperson simply takes out the salesbook and begins to write up the order.

The Hook—This closing technique is of value in situations where prospects cannot make up their minds. The salesperson attempts to sweeten the proposal with a special offer such as, for example: "If you sign up with us today, I can give you a 15 percent discount off the regular selling price."

The Summary Close—With this technique, the salesperson concludes the presentation by ticking off the benefits, one by one, that a favorable purchase decision will bring to the customer. As each point is made, the salesperson pauses to make certain that the prospect is in agreement before continuing the summary.

The SRO Close—In the SRO ("Standing Room Only") technique, the salesperson applies a bit of pressure by declaring, for example, that demand for the service(s) is so high that the company cannot promise delivery earlier than six weeks hence unless the order is placed today. Or, perhaps, pointing out that an increase in price is scheduled for the coming week.

The Balance Sheet Close—This approach is often used when prospects are reluctant to buy. In such situations, the salesperson draws a line down the center of a blank sheet of paper and notes down on the left-hand side of the page the advantages of making the purchase. To the right of the center line, the salesperson then enters the disadvantages of not buying. The completed "balance sheet" will, of course, demonstrate to the prospect that the "evidence" for an affirmative buying decision far outweighs the negative aspects.

Following Up the Sale

Getting the order does not end the selling process; the "follow up" does. In this final step, the salesperson expresses appreciation for the order, reassures the customer of the wisdom of the decision to buy, and pledges to contact the buyer later on to make certain that the service delivery has been satisfactory. The purpose of the follow up is to build a long-lasting, trusting relationship with the customer that will facilitate repeat buying.

HOW TO POLISH YOUR EMPLOYEES' SELLING SKILLS

For companies of all types, salespeople are often the main revenue generators. A well-trained and effective sales contingent will deliver a much higher volume of sales than a group of mediocre performers. Top performers easily outsell the average salesperson by as much as 300 or 400 percent or even more.

Substitutes for a Salesforce

A small manufacturing company that cannot afford to develop and maintain its own salesforce may contract with a selling agent to sell the plant's entire output. An alternative approach is to enlist the aid of manufacturers' representatives ("reps"), assign them to individual territories, and charge each with securing orders for some portion of the company's production. With either alternative, the firm can expect to generate revenues quite readily. If sales volume continues to grow, management may eventually decide to invest the necessary capital and create a salesforce of its own.

Some types of service firms find that "reps" are useful for bringing in business. However, the majority of service companies hire and train their own sales personnel.

Keys to Better Selling

If you plan to have your own selling staff, the principal key to increasing revenues is: Hire the right people at the very outset and then train them well. Here is a recommended procedure for you to follow:

- Locate and hire an effective sales manager.
- Help your new sales manager to select the best candidates for the selling job.
- Train these recruits well.
- Back them up with an efficient sales office.
- Develop and institute an effective order handling and delivery system.
- Add a top-notch credit manager to your payroll.

Because of their significance, the first three suggestions are treated in somewhat more depth over the next several paragraphs.

Locate and Hire an Effective Sales Manager—Find a capable sales manager, one with an excellent track record, preferably in the same service industry as the one you are in. What are the responsibilities of this sales executive? As indicated in Figure 13–3, the major functions of the sales management position are:

- recruiting salespeople
- structuring the sales organization
- establishing the compensation plan(s)
- training salespeople

FIGURE 13–3
Sales force management

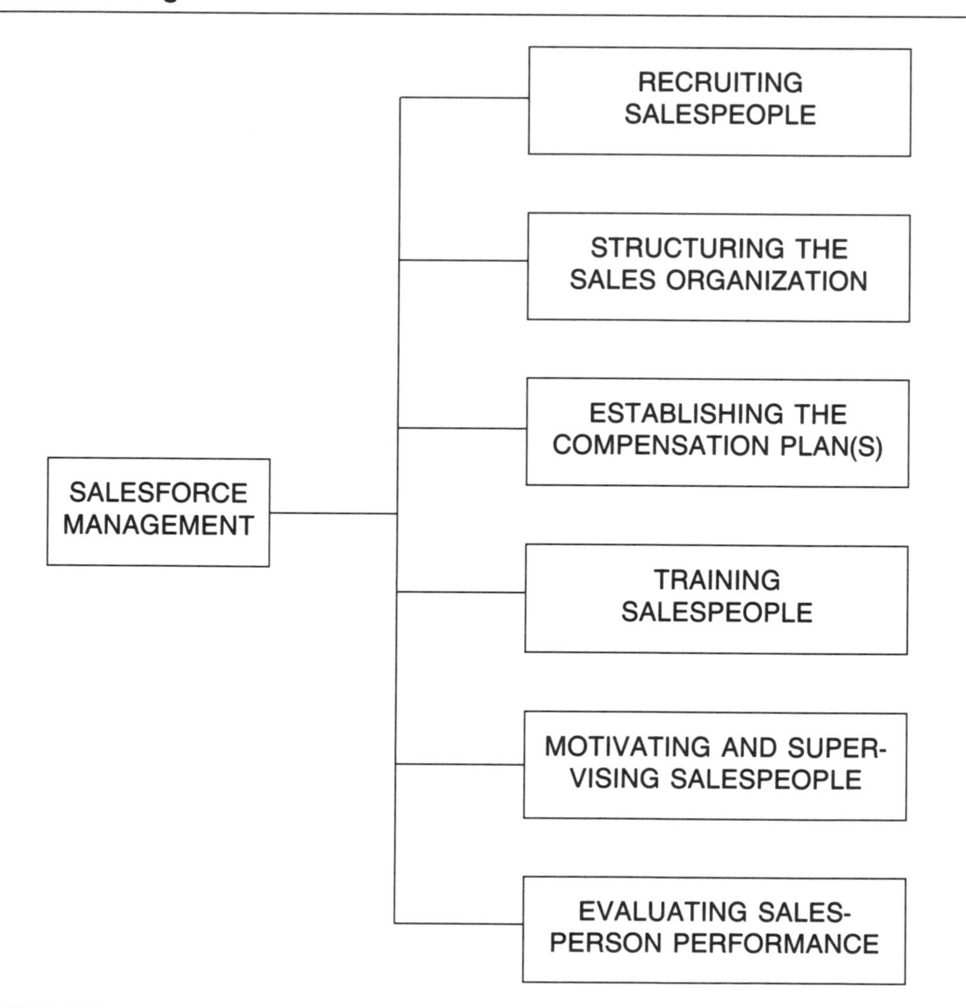

- motivating and supervising salespeople, and
- evaluating salesperson performance

Give the new executive a thorough grounding in your business: your company's mission, long-term objectives, organization, strengths and weaknesses, systems and procedures, marketing strategies and tactics, and so on. Then, grant your sales manager full authority to plan, organize, direct, and control your new salesforce.

Help Your Sales Manager to Select the Best Candidates—You will have a problem trying to hire outstanding salespeople; they are seldom unemployed. Instead, encourage your sales executive to look for, screen, and hire promising candidates for the selling job. (Note: for details on the recruitment, training, and supervision of employees, refer to Chapter 9.) Service firms need salespeople who are courteous, dependable, energetic, and well-groomed. They should also be able to communicate (and listen) well, be emotionally well-balanced, and display excellent interpersonal relations.

Train the Recruits Well—Charge your sales manager with developing and setting into place an effective training program for the new recruits. (*Note:* Follow-up and refresher training programs will need to be prepared at later dates.) Appropriate instructional approaches may be selected from among the wide variety that is available. Films, slides, videotaped sales presentations, and other audiovisual techniques; role-playing methods; programmed instruction; lectures followed by small-group discussions; and demonstrations are some of the more useful techniques.

Be sure to ask the sales manager to evaluate the results of the training and modify the program in light of this evaluation.

Here are the major topic areas the trainees will need to know about:

- The history of your company; what it is like; and what you stand for.
- Your organization's policies, procedures, and systems
- Who your customers are and what they are like: demographics, lifestyles, likes, dislikes.
- All the facts about the service(s) your company offers: descriptions, quality levels, prices, guarantees, credit arrangements, and so on.
- How your service(s) compare with those of your competitors.
- Instruction in how to sell.

Some Additional Insights into Sales Management

Among the many operational details to work out are the type of organization to build, territorial assignments, how to handle travel and entertainment expenses, the motivation of salespeople, and performance evaluation.

Type of Organizations—Salesforces may be organized on a geographical basis, by product or service, by type of customer, or by some combination of these.

Territorial Assignments—Assigning salespeople to specific territories reduces travel expenses, facilitates more intensive coverage of each assigned area, and leads to better servicing of company accounts. It also makes it easier to hold salespeople accountable. In addition, proper attention to scheduling and routing is bound to increase productivity.

Travel and Entertainment Expenses—Some companies require their field salespeople to absorb the costs of transportation, meals away from home, hotel rooms, and other travel and entertainment expenses. Usually, this is true of companies that pay their sales representatives on a commission basis. However, most firms reimburse their sales representatives for these expenses. To keep sales costs under control, the companies request that their sales personnel submit weekly (or monthly) expense reports. These are reviewed for accuracy by the sales manager.

Motivating Salespeople—To do an effective job of motivating their representatives, management first needs to evaluate—and then seek to improve—those general factors that have a direct bearing on salesforce morale, such as:

- working conditions
- company rules and regulations
- the compensation plan (including benefits offered)
- opportunities for promotion
- the nature and quality of the supervision

Bonuses, contests, and other incentives may be offered occasionally to stimulate sales over the short term. For further details about motivation, see the section on "Tips on Training and Motivating Your Staff" in Chapter 9.

Assessing Performance—Evaluations, performed periodically, are designed primarily to improve salesforce productivity over an extended period of time. To be able to judge effectively the performance of its sales representatives, the company needs to collect, examine, and compare data on each individual. Both objective and subjective measures are used for this purpose. Examples of subjective data include the salesperson's personal grooming and proper attire, work habits, and level of knowledge (of the firm, its competitors, and the industry). Among the more frequently seen objective criteria are: the number of sales calls made per week or per month, the number of new accounts opened in relation to the number of existing accounts, the average sales volume per order, order accuracy, and the ratio of travel expenses to the total sales volume brought in.

MAKING SALES OVER THE TELEPHONE

You have a veritable gold mine on your premises—your business telephone. Learn to use it properly, and often. It can offer you these twin benefits: (1) it can bring more revenue into your firm's treasury, and (2) it can lower your operating expenses.

As the costs of in-person sales presentations burgeoned over the 1980s, to the point where the average cost of a sales call passed the $200 mark in many industries, companies have increasingly been turning to the telephone. They discovered that it is truly a wonderful instrument with many, many uses.

In your service business, your telephone can help you to:

- arouse the interest of prospective buyers
- arrange for delivery of your service(s)
- generate leads
- get new business
- hold down your selling costs
- notify customers of special promotions, price changes, or a new service
- obtain orders from areas that are not covered by your salespeople
- "presell" prospects before your sales representatives visit them
- qualify prospects
- receive and process orders
- research customer attitudes, opinions, needs
- revive closed accounts
- sell more to your present clientele
- set up appointments for your salespeople
- solicit reorders

The modern term for all this marketing activity by phone is, of course, *telemarketing.* To find out more about the opportunities that telemarketing offers the business organization, check with your local telephone company. You may be surprised to learn that they may offer sales training, at no cost to you, to your telemarketing employees.

For a productive telephone salesforce, you will need people who:

- communicate easily and well
- can relate to and establish rapport rapidly with others
- have pleasant speaking voices
- demonstrate enthusiasm in selling
- are quick to understand prospects' needs
- know how to build trust
- have above-average patience
- are not easily discouraged

Having several WATS lines installed (the initials stand for Wide Area Telephone Service) can be of immeasurable value. In time, you may consider adding automatic dialing equipment; this will enable you to reach large numbers of prospective buyers at relatively low cost.

FOR FURTHER INFORMATION

Books

Bencin, Richard L., *Strategic Telemarketing.* Philadelphia: Swansea Press, 1987.

Coppett, John I. and William A. Staples, *Professional Selling: A Relationship Management Process.* Cincinnati: South-Western, 1990.

Cummings, Richard, *Contemporary Selling.* San Diego: Harcourt Brace Jovanovich, 1987.

Dalrymple, Douglas J., *Sales Management: Concepts and Cases,* 3d ed. New York: Wiley, 1988.

Futrell, Charles M., *ABC's of Selling,* 2d ed. Homewood, Ill.: Irwin, 1988.

Hair, Joseph F., Francis L. Notturno, and Frederick A. Russ, *Effective Selling,* 8th ed. Cincinnati: South-Western, 1991.

Johnson, H. Webster and Anthony J. Faria, *Creative Selling,* 4th ed. Cincinnati: South-Western, 1987.

Johnston, Karen and Jean Withers, *Selling Strategies for Service Businesses.* Bellingham, Wash.: Self-Counsel Press, 1988.

Kordahl, Eugene, *Telemarketing for Business.* Englewood Cliffs, N.J.: Prentice-Hall, 1984.

McHatton, Robert J., *Total Telemarketing.* New York: Wiley, 1988.

Masser, Barry and William M. Leeds, *Power Selling by Telephone.* Englewood Cliffs, N.J.: Prentice-Hall, 1983.

Pederson, Carlton A. et al, *Selling: Principles and Methods,* 9th ed. Homewood, Ill.: Irwin, 1987.

Pesce, Vince, *A Complete Manual of Professional Selling.* New York: Prentice Hall Press, 1989.

Putman, Anthony O., *Marketing Your Services: A Step-by-Step Guide for Small Businesses and Professionals.* New York: Wiley, 1989.

Roman, Ernan, *Integrated Direct Marketing: Techniques and Strategies for Success.* New York: McGraw-Hill, 1988.

Slutsky, Jeff, *Streetsmart Marketing.* New York: Wiley, 1989.

Withers, Jean and Carol Vipperman, *Marketing Your Service: A Planning Guide for Small Business.* Bellingham, Wash.: Self-Counsel Press, 1987.

Business Development Publications Available from the U.S. Small Business Administration

MT 1–"Creative Selling: The Competitive Edge" ($.50)

MT 2–"Marketing for Small Business: An Overview" ($1.00)

MT 3–"Is the Independent Sales Agent for You?" ($.50)

MT 9–"Selling by Mail Order" ($1.00)

Part Five

MASTERING THE FINANCIAL SIDE OF YOUR BUSINESS

CHAPTER 14

MANAGING THE COMPANY'S FINANCES—I

In Chapter 6, you were introduced to those two vital accounting documents: the balance sheet and the operating statement. To aid your recall, we now repeat our descriptions of these documents: (1) the balance sheet "summarizes the firm's financial status at a given point in time" and (2) the operating statement (or P&L) "offers a picture of the firm's sales, expenses, and profit (or loss) over a specified period."

In this first of two chapters designed to help you achieve more effective management of the financial end of your business, you will discover how ratio analysis can help you improve your operation, what records you should keep and how long to keep them, how to avoid cash-flow problems, how to maintain tight control over your expenses, what to do about capital budgeting, and how to manage credit sales.

IMPROVING YOUR OPERATION BY WATCHING YOUR RATIOS

Ratios are useful tools for monitoring, measuring, and evaluating the performance of any business. Ratios are readily determined with the aid of a pocket calculator by juxtaposing entries from either or both of the major accounting statements. Formulas for the more useful ratios are offered in the following sections. They can keep you posted as to how you are doing every step of the way. Not only can they reveal your firm's weaknesses and strengths but they can also help you spot trends in time to enable you to take advantage of them.

To grasp the significance of your present ratios, compare them with those calculated from last year's statements. If you have been in business longer than one year, check them against ratios you produced two and three years ago. You should also try to evaluate your firm's performance in the light of ratios obtained from businesses similar to your own. Often, this can be accomplished by referring to information provided by your trade association, by Dun & Bradstreet's, or through your business bank. (Usually, bank officers have access to the "Annual Statement Studies" compiled by Robert Morris Associates, of Philadelphia.)

The more significant ratios fall into three categories: (1) liquidity, (2) profitability, and (3) activity ratios.

Liquidity Ratios

These ratios are obtained from data on the company's balance sheet. They assess the firm's liquidity. In essence, they answer the question, "Will the company be able to pay all debts that fall due?" Generally, the higher these figures the better. The two most important liquidity measures are the current and quick ratios.

FIGURE 14–1
Balance sheet for a small service firm

			Baytik Equipment Balance December
ASSETS			
CURRENT ASSETS			
Cash on hand and in bank	18,620		
Marketable securities	5,120		
Accounts receivable, less allowance for bad debts	13,560		
Merchandise inventory	8,770		
Supplies inventory	5,065		
Total current assets		$51,135	
FIXED ASSETS			
Building, less depreciation	48,300		
Machinery and equipment, less depreciation	17,890		
Furniture, less depreciation	11,460		
Van, less depreciation	9,070		
Total fixed assets		86,720	
TOTAL ASSETS			$137,855

Current Ratio–This ratio tells you whether or not the firm possesses enough current assets to pay off its current liabilities in full. The formula to use is:

$$\text{Current Ratio} = \frac{\text{Current Assets}}{\text{Current Liabilities}}$$

For your convenience and better understanding, we have reproduced the balance sheet and operating statement for the Baytik Equipment Rental Company that originally appeared in Chapter 6. They appear here as Figures 14–1 and 14–2.

Refer now to Figure 14-1. According to this balance sheet (for the year ended December 31, 1991), the company had "total current assets" at that time of $51,135. "Total current liabilities" came to $32,250. We enter those figures into the formula and then proceed to calculate the firm's current ratio:

$$\text{Current Ratio} = \frac{\text{Current Assets}}{\text{Current Liabilities}}$$

$$= \frac{\$51{,}135}{\$32{,}250}$$

$$= 1.59$$

Rental Company
Sheet
31, 1991

LIABILITIES AND NET WORTH

CURRENT LIABILITIES			
Accounts payable	$10,140		
Notes payable within one year	20,000		
Accrued taxes	2,110		
Total current liabilities		$32,250	
LONG-TERM LIABILITIES			
Note payable, due 1994	$20,000		
Note payable, due 1996	20,000		
Total long-term liabilities		40,000	
TOTAL LIABILITIES			$72,250
NET WORTH ("Owner's Equity")			65,505
TOTAL LIABILITIES AND NET WORTH			$137,855

FIGURE 14–2
Operating statement for a small service firm

Baytik Equipment Rental Company
Operating Statement
For Year Ended: *December 31, 1991*

NET SALES		$211,340
– COST OF GOODS SOLD		9,280
GROSS MARGIN		$202,060
– OPERATING EXPENSES		
Salaries and wages	$83,440	
Rent	24,250	
Payroll taxes	5,830	
Depreciation	11,510	
Telephone	5,750	
Supplies	5,480	
Advertising and promotion	9,540	
Utilities	4,770	
Postage	3,800	
Maintenance	5,050	
Insurance	4,750	
Truck Expense	7,190	
Interest expense	4,385	
Dues and subscriptions	875	
Travel and entertainment	775	
Miscellaneous expenses	1,845	
Total operating expenses		–179,180
OPERATING PROFIT		$22,880
+ OTHER INCOME		
Dividends	165	
Interest on bank account	1,010	
Total other income		1,175
Total income		$24,055
Less provision for income tax		–6,500
NET PROFIT		$16,785

We read Baytik's current ratio as 1.59 to 1. In brief, the value of the firm's current assets amounts to 1.59 times its total current liabilities. If it had to, Baytik could pay off its current debts completely and still have some assets left.

As a general rule, a ratio of 2 to 1 is considered acceptable for most types of businesses. This lower figure of 1.59 to 1 would seem to indicate that Baytik may be running up too much debt or else has less than it should have in current assets. A check of trade sources, however, reveals that other equipment rental companies typically show current ratios of between 1.6 and 1.9. For Baytik's management, then, the current ratio may not be too worrisome.

There are, of course, several ways for Baytik's management to improve its current ratio before the next balance sheet is drawn up. It can reduce the denominator of the fraction by paying off some of its current liabilities. Or, the firm might consider beefing up the numerator by adding cash and/or securities in the form of either equity or long-term loan capital.

Quick Ratio–A similar, but considerably more precise measure of a company's liquidity is the quick, or acid-test, ratio. We use nearly the same formula as the current ratio's, with one exception: the value of all inventory is dropped from the numerator of the fraction. The thought behind this is that only "quick" assets should be used–cash or other current assets that can be readily turned into cash. It may be difficult to "liquidate" inventory easily.

The new formula then becomes:

$$\text{Quick Ratio} = \frac{\text{Cash} + \text{Marketable Securities} + \text{Accounts Receivable}}{\text{Current Liabilities}}$$

Again, we enter the appropriate figures from Figure 14-1 in the formula:

$$\text{Quick Ratio} = \frac{\$18{,}620 + \$5{,}120 + \$13{,}560}{\$32{,}250}$$

$$\text{Quick Ratio} = \frac{\$37{,}300}{\$32{,}250}$$

$$= 1.16$$

Baytik's quick ratio is 1.16 to 1.

Ordinarily, a quick ratio of 1 to 1 is considered satisfactory. If, however, accounts receivable constitute a substantial percentage of the firm's quick assets and collections are slow, then the quick ratio should be somewhat greater than 1 to 1.

Profitability Ratios

Information on the firm's operating statement as well as its balance sheet is used to determine whether or not the operation has been profitable and just how profitable it has been. Four useful ratios in this category are the cost of goods-to-sales, gross margin-to-sales, operating expenses-to-sales, and return on assets ratios. All are usually expressed as percentages.

The following are calculations for the Baytik Company's profitability ratios.

$$\text{Cost of Goods-to-Sales Ratio} = \frac{\text{Cost of Goods}}{\text{Net Sales}}$$

$$= \frac{\$9{,}280}{\$211{,}340}$$

$$= 4.4\%$$

$$\text{Gross Margin-to-Sales Ratio} = \frac{\text{Gross Margin}}{\text{Net Sales}}$$

$$= \frac{\$202{,}060}{\$211{,}340}$$

$$= 95.6\%$$

$$\text{Operating Expenses-to-Sales Ratio} = \frac{\text{Operating Expenses}}{\text{Net Sales}}$$

$$= \frac{\$179{,}180}{\$211{,}340}$$

$$= 84.8\%$$

$$\text{Return on Assets Ratio} = \frac{\text{Net Profit after Taxes}}{\text{Total Assets}}$$

$$= \frac{\$16{,}785}{\$137{,}855}$$

$$= 12.2\%$$

Activity Ratios

Computing these ratios will help you keep tabs on how your business operation has been faring. The debt-to-net worth ratio explores the relationship between your firm's obligations and its net worth. The inventory turnover ratio (also known as "stock-turn") apprises you of how fast–or how slow–your inventory has been moving.* The asset turnover ratio lets you know whether or not you have been putting your company's assets to good use.

Here are the step-by-step calculations for the Baytik Equipment Rental Company:

*To derive this ratio, you will also need to check your inventory records to ascertain the "average inventory" kept on hand during the period in question. This ratio is of much more value to wholesalers and retailers than it is to the typical service company.

$$\text{Debt-to-Net Worth Ratio} = \frac{\text{Total Debt}}{\text{Net Worth}}$$

$$= \frac{\$72{,}250}{\$65{,}505}$$

$$= 110.3\%$$

$$\text{Inventory Turnover Ratio} = \frac{\text{Net Sales}}{\text{Average Inventory*}}$$

$$= \frac{\$211{,}340}{\$10{,}000}$$

$$= 211.34\%$$

$$\text{Asset Turnover Ratio} = \frac{\text{Net Sales}}{\text{Total Assets}}$$

$$= \frac{\$211{,}340}{\$137{,}855}$$

$$= 153.3\%$$

Some of the more useful financial ratios appear in Figure 14–3.

RECORDS: WHICH SHOULD YOU HOLD–AND FOR HOW LONG?

Many new-business owners plan to handle the firm's books all by themselves, at least until they believe they are able to afford outside accounting services. If you feel as they do, visit your local business stationer's to inquire into the simplified bookkeeping systems they offer for sale. Or, ask an accountant to set up your books beforehand and then work with you on a monthly retainer.

According to the Internal Revenue Service, a business may keep its records on either the cash or the accrual basis. If, however, inventories will be playing an important part in your operation, as they usually do in the retail and wholesale trades, you must follow the accrual method in recording your sales and purchases.

If you follow a cash basis, you do not record any expense or any income in your *journals* (books of original entry) until you actually pay out or receive the money. Under the accrual method, income from a sale is entered when the transaction takes place, even though the money may not be collected until some future date. The same holds true for expenditures; these are recorded when they are incurred even though payments may not be made until later.

*For the sake of illustration, let us assume that Baytik maintained an average inventory valued at $10,000 during the period in question.

FIGURE 14–3
Some useful financial ratios

Liquidity Ratios:

Current Ratio = $\frac{\text{Current Assets}}{\text{Current Liabilities}}$

Quick (or "Acid-test") Ratio = $\frac{\text{Cash + Securities + Accounts Receivable}}{\text{Current Liabilities}}$

Profitability Ratios:

Cost of Goods-to-Sales Ratio = $\frac{\text{Cost of Goods}}{\text{Net Sales}}$

Gross Margin-to-Sales Ratio = $\frac{\text{Gross Margin}}{\text{Net Sales}}$

Operating Expenses-to-Sales Ratio = $\frac{\text{Operating Expenses}}{\text{Net Sales}}$

Return-on-Assets Ratio = $\frac{\text{Net Profit after Taxes}}{\text{Total Assets}}$

Activity Ratios:

Debt-to-Net Worth Ratio = $\frac{\text{Total Debt}}{\text{Net Worth}}$

Inventory Turnover Ratio = $\frac{\text{Net Sales}}{\text{Average Inventory}}$

Asset Turnover Ratio = $\frac{\text{Net Sales}}{\text{Total Assets}}$

What Books Should You Keep?

At the very least, you should maintain the following books of record:

Business Checkbook–This will help you keep track of those business expenses you pay by check. If the stubs are filed out properly, they will serve as a useful chronological record.

Cash Receipts Journal–Use this book to record, on a daily basis, every cash transaction.

Cash Disbursements Journal–Enter in this book each day's outlay for expenses and purchases.

General Ledger–This is used to keep track of company assets, liabilities, and capital. Record the costs of equipment, machinery, inventory, and any other assets, together with their purchase dates.

Accounts Payable Ledger–Enter here all amounts you will need to pay to your creditors as you incur these obligations.

Accounts Receivable Ledger–A book of accounts in which you record payments received and balances still due from those customers who buy from you on credit terms.

Petty Cash Record–A notebook that can provide you with a valuable record of minor cash expenditures and the reasons for these outlays.

Employees' Payroll Record Book–You will need this for recording wages paid to each employee as well as the amounts you are required to deduct for income tax withholding, social security, and so on.

Figure 14–4 offers suggestions about how long you ought to keep different types of business records.

HOW TO MAINTAIN A POSITIVE CASH FLOW AT ALL TIMES

Regardless of the industry or type of business you are engaged in, you can expect your revenue curve to reflect valleys as well as peaks during the year. At times, the cash balance you maintain may slide so abruptly that you find it difficult to pay your bills. There is no need for this to happen to you. With the proper planning, you can anticipate these cash-poor occasions and devise tactics in advance to avoid them.

Cash-flow planning is a valuable tool you should use the year round to maintain a positive cash flow. The chart in Figure 14–5 will get you started; explanations of the items to be entered appear below:

1. *Cash on hand and in bank*–For this first entry, you will need to total all the cash, checks, and money orders you have in the business. This includes not only the current balances in your firm's checking and savings account(s) but also the money in your petty cash fund. Add in, too, any "bank" you may hold overnight on your premises that you use to make change and cash large bills the next business day.
2. *Expected cash sales for month*–The total amount you believe you will take in at your premises during the month.
3. *Expected collections for month*–Payments you expect to receive during the month from customers who owe you money (your "accounts receivable").
4. *Other income expected*–Additional monies you may earn during the month–from interest on bank accounts, stock dividends, selling an old piece of equipment, and so on.
5. *Total receipts*–Add columns 2, 3, and 4 above to obtain the total for the month's receipts.
6. *Total cash and receipts*–For this item, enter the sum of columns 1 and 5.

FIGURE 14–4
How long to keep records

Type of Record	Length of Time to Hold
General ledgers	Indefinitely.
Cash receipts journals	A minimum of six years.
Cash disbursements journals	A minimum of six years
Accounts payable ledgers (including canceled checks)	On average, six years. However, this depends on your state's statute of limitations (which can range from 3 to 20 years).
Accounts receivable	Paid invoices should be kept for three to four years.
Records of sales and use taxes	Three years.
State and federal income tax returns (and back-up records)	At least six years. (*Note:* statutes of limitations may be extended if fraud has been involved.)
Legal papers: Evidences of ownership—copyrights, patents, trademark registrations—, deeds, easement records)	Indefinitely.
Contracts and leases	Six years after they expire (unless renewed annually).
Records of lawsuits	Six to 10 years after settlement.
Corporation bylaws, minutes of stockholders' meetings, annual reports	Indefinitely.
Payroll, personnel records, wages and hours information	Three years (to comply with the Fair Labor Standards Act). Hold supporting data (timecards, piecework tickets) for two years.
Records of payroll deductions for income taxes and social security	At least four years after the tax becomes due or is paid, whichever is later. (*Note:* some state and local authorities require that payroll records be kept longer than four years.)
Employee applications	Retain according to your needs.
Pension records	At least 1 year after the pensioner's death

Source: Robert A. Shiff, "Records Retention: Normal and Disaster," *Management Aid No. 210* (Washington, D.C.: U.S. Small Business Administration, September 1973 reprint).

FIGURE 14–5
Cash flow chart for first four months of year

	January	February	March	April
1. Cash on hand and in bank				
2. Expected cash sales for month				
3. Expected collections for month (accounts receivable)				
4. Other income expected				
5. Total receipts (Add 2, 3, and 4.)				
6. Total cash and receipts (Add 1 and 5.)				
7. Total disbursements for month				
8. Cash balance at end of month. (Subtract 7 from 6.)*				

*End-of-month balance is posted to line 1 of the following month.

Source: Adapted from: John F. Murphy, "Sound Cash Management and Borrowing," *Small Marketers Aid No. 147* (Washington, D.C.: U.S. Small Business Administration, 1978), 3; Jack Zwick, "A Handbook of Small Business Finance," *Small Business Management Series No. 15* (Washington, D.C.: U.S. Small Business Administration, 1975), 34–35; "Business Plan for Retailers," *Small Marketers Aid No. 150* (Washington, D.C.: U.S. Small Business Administration, 1970), 17.

7. *Total disbursements for month*—Review all of your accounts payable to determine which bills you plan to pay during the month. Add up these debts to obtain your expected total disbursements figure.

8. *Cash balance at end of month*—This is what you will have left in the kitty after subtracting item 7 from item 6.

BUDGETING: YOUR KEY TO EXPENSE CONTROL

The surest sign of a healthy company is a top management that continually monitors expenses in order to maintain them at levels that are properly proportionate to the volume of sales it enjoys.

There are, of course, a few business costs about which you can do little or nothing. Your monthly rent payment is an example. So is the interest due on any loans you may have made. You can, however, control most expenses through effective budgeting.

Preparing a budget of any kind is never an easy task. Most owners of small businesses have had little experience with budgeting procedures. Yet, budgets are immensely valuable both as planning tools and as control devices. For your own good, you should strive to make budgeting a way of life for you in your new service business.

The following short paragraph offers several insights into the value of budgeting:

> Briefly, budgeting requires you to consider your basic objectives, policies, plans, resources, and so forth. It requires you to make sure your company is properly organized. It requires you and your key people to undertake a coordinated, comprehensive, and informative effort to achieve common objectives. It helps you to assure that proper controls and evaluation procedures are established throughout your company. It encourages and motivates everyone concerned to put forth a good effort. It provides a plan so that all of you know where you are going—as well as why, how, when, and with whom. In short, the budgeting process is a valuable tool in planning for profit.*

Initiate the budgeting process by developing as accurate a forecast of next year's revenues as you possibly can. Once you have targeted your overall sales objective, you should then start preparing your sales budget. You will find that all other budgets are related to this first one. With the aid of your sales budget, you can work up budgets for production costs, administrative expenses ("overhead"), selling expenses, labor costs, promotion expenses, and other aspects of your operation. This also includes your proforma profit-and-loss statement for next year.

For even better planning and stricter control, be sure to break down your annual budgeted amounts into quarterly figures.

For the sake of demonstrating the procedure, let us assume that your company provides tape editing services to wedding videographers. You sell your basic service ("Service A") for $99.00. For that price, you edit the videocassette, make a copy, and forward both the original and duplicate tapes to the videographer. Your total cost for delivering a Service A unit amounts to $66.50. This figure takes into account your production costs, selling expenses, allocated overhead charges, and all other expenses. Your firm also offers an enhanced, deluxe edition of the videocassette ("Service B") for $145.00. This more expensive service costs you $94.00.

According to your projections for the coming year, you will most likely receive 875 orders for Service A and 340 orders for Service B.

Here is how your budget might shape up:

---

*Charles J. Woelfel, "Basic Budgets for Profit Planning," *Management Aids No. 1.004* (Washington, D.C.: U.S. Small Business Administration, n.d.), 2.

SALES BUDGET

For the Year Ended December 31, 19___.

Number of Orders

Service	First Quarter	Second Quarter	Third Quarter	Fourth Quarter	Total for Year
A	100	390	265	120	875
B	35	160	95	50	340
	135	550	360	170	1,215

Sales in Dollars

Service	First Quarter	Second Quarter	Third Quarter	Fourth Quarter	Total for Year
A	$9,900	$38,610	$26,235	$11,880	$86,625
B	5,075	23,200	13,775	7,250	49,300
	$14,975	$61,810	$40,010	$19,130	$135,925

Now, let us take a look at two expense budgets:

SELLING EXPENSES BUDGET

For the Year Ended December 31, 19___.

Expense	First Quarter	Second Quarter	Third Quarter	Fourth Quarter	Total for Year
Commissions	$580	$2,390	$1,550	$740	$5,260
Rent	1,000	1,000	1,000	1,000	4,000
Advertising	1,950	8,125	5,210	2,480	17,765
Telephone	540	2,150	1,400	680	4,770
Depreciation (Office)	720	720	720	720	2,880
All other Expenses	2,800	3,800	3,150	3,340	13,090
	$7,590	$18,185	$13,030	$8,960	$47,765

ADMINISTRATIVE EXPENSES BUDGET

For the Year Ended December 31, 19____.

Expense	First Quarter	Second Quarter	Third Quarter	Fourth Quarter	Total for Year
Salaries	$3,670	$3,670	$3,670	$3,670	$14,680
Insurance	1,225	1,225	1,225	1,225	4,900
Telephone	650	950	950	700	3,250
Supplies	1,355	2,325	1,800	1,042	6,522
Bad Debts	400	400	400	400	1,600
Other Expenses	2,600	3,080	2,950	2,800	11,430
	$9,900	$11,650	$10,995	$9,837	$42,382

SENSIBLE CAPITAL BUDGETING

In many business ventures, management commits a grievous error; it invests too heavily at the outset in capital assets. This kind of mistake in judgment often leaves the new firm with insufficient operating funds.

From time to time, though, the established company will ponder whether or not to spend a substantial amount of its precious capital for some significant reason. Perhaps it is seeking to raise its production capability or reduce its operating costs. Perhaps it hopes to increase its revenues and/or its end-of-year profit. To accomplish its objective, the firm may need to purchase new machinery or equipment, rent a warehouse, construct a second plant, or relocate the business.

How to work through problems such as these and arrive, in each instance, at the most favorable decision is the essence of the capital budgeting process. The process involves stating, weighting, and evaluating alternatives. In brief, the procedure calls for developing a different budget for each alternative and then comparing them carefully before making a decision.

Should you, some day, be faced with the challenges of capital budgeting, be sure to keep in mind the following facts:

- Like most companies, your firm does not have access to unlimited financial resources.
- Inflation, regardless of its pace, is bound to continue as the years pass by. Because of this fact, what you have in your treasury today will certainly buy more than the same amount will buy next year or any year thereafter.

- Borrowed capital is always more expensive than the funds you have on hand, because you will be asked to pay some rate of interest on the loan's principal.
- The value of today's dollar goes up each year, because you can place that same dollar in an interest-bearing savings account, or invest it in some other profitable manner.

Moreover, you should seek answers to these questions before attempting to arrive at a decision:

- How much will it cost our company to implement each alternative?
- For each alternative, how soon can we expect to reach our breakeven point? When should the inflow of funds resulting from our acquisition and use of the capital item equal our original investment, or outflow of funds?
- Can we possibly put our capital to some other use that may lead to greater profits than any of the alternatives now under consideration?

Evaluating Capital Investments

The two most common approaches used to evaluate budget alternatives are the payback period and net present value methods.

The Payback Period Method–This approach calls for determining how long it will take for the company to recover its original investment from its net earnings (after taxes) each year.

Let us assume, for example, that you are thinking of replacing one of your older tape-editing machines with a newer model. You believe that this new piece of equipment will increase your overall editing capability by more than 20 percent. The purchase price of the machine is $16,750. According to your calculations, you anticipate about $4,400 in additional profit each year because of the increase in production.

If we divide the cost of the equipment ($16,750) by your expected annual profit ($4,400), it will take you 3.8 years to recover your investment. This looks good to you, so you decide to buy the machine. However, if you had projected a net annual gain of only $2,000 annually, you might well have decided against the purchase. With a payback period of more than 8.3 years, this would not have been an attractive investment at all!

The Net Present Value Method–This approach takes into account an important fact: due to inflation, the dollar falls in value as the years pass. Because it recognizes this depreciation factor, this method is considered superior to the payback period approach. It calls for adjusting the projected annual inflow of net profit to compensate for the decreasing value of money. Value tables, arranged to compensate for different rates of inflation, are available for calculating the worth of $1 invested today over the number of payback years expected.

MANAGING CREDIT FOR YOUR SERVICE BUSINESS

Credit is a sales-stimulating tool used by companies of all kinds. Firms that extend credit to their customers regard it as a powerful strategy that not only can increase their revenues but may also give them a substantial competitive edge.

Two types of credit are seen in our economy: trade credit and consumer credit. Manufacturers, producers, and other suppliers extend trade credit to wholesalers, retailers, and service companies to facilitate the roles these entities play in the marketing and distribution of goods and services. Consumer credit is, of course, the type with which we are more familiar because we often make use of it as consumers of products and services.

The Extension of Credit

Every new business must decide whether it will require of its customers full payment in cash or to offer to sell on credit to those deemed trustworthy. Rather than initiate credit plans of their own, many service businesses prefer to arrange for the acceptance of second-party credit plans. The company that offers opportunities to buy on credit, in addition to accepting cash, will usually enjoy a greater overall sales volume. The resulting sales increase should more than offset the fees charged by agencies such as MasterCard, VISA, and Discover Card.

If you sell your service(s) primarily to organizations, you will probably be expected to extend credit to many customers. Should you be interested in developing your own credit plan, rather than—or in addition to—accepting second-party plans, you might want to consider these other popular approaches:

- *Open Credit*—This type extends short-term credit to customers without requiring a down payment and without adding interest or a carrying charge to the bill. It is also referred to as "open account," "open book," or "regular" credit. A 30-day extension is the most commonly granted term.
- *Revolving Credit*—This plan sets a ceiling on the total amount of credit the company will extend to each customer. Minimum monthly payments on the account are required. The customer must pay a finance charge on any unpaid balance.
- *Option-terms Credit*—This credit plan combines features of both open and revolving credit. A buyer may charge goods and/or services up to a pre-established limit, then exercise one of two options: (1) pay the total amount due within a specified period (usually, 30 days), thus avoiding any additional charge, or (2) forward partial payment of the account. If the customer selects the second option, the firm is then entitled to add a carrying charge to the balance due.

  As these partial payments are made, credit is again released (up to the predetermined ceiling).

Granting Credit—When attempting to develop its own credit approach, a company will ordinarily follow a procedure similar to the one indicated below:

1. Set policies, including standards for evaluating each credit applicant.
2. Devise an application form to be completed by the person or firm applying for credit.
3. Check the information entered on the form by the applicant by mail and/or telephone—and with a major credit bureau or mercantile agency.
4. Evaluate each application and approve those that meet your requirements.
5. Establish a credit ceiling for each applicant.
6. Carefully monitor thereafter the applicant's credit history.
7. Set into place a sensible collection policy for delinquent accounts.

The "Three C's of Credit"—Decisions to grant credit to a client are generally based on the grantor's evaluations of the applicant according to three criteria. These are character, capacity, and capital. Credit managers call them the "three C's of credit." Brief explorations of the terms follow on page 218.

FIGURE 14–6
How to handle delinquent accounts

No matter how tightly supervised your credit activities may be, there will still be some customers who pay their bills late and others who won't pay them at all. The structuring of a good collection procedure helps to reduce "delinquency" to an appreciable degree. A working policy might include the following steps:

1. Institute some kind of "red flag" bookkeeping technique to alert you when an account is tardy in payments.
2. Mail a duplicate invoice—stamped *past due, second notice,* or some similar phrase—to the customer shortly after discovering an amount overdue.
3. After several weeks elapse without your receiving a response, send out the first in a series of form letters. (Prepare these long in advance.) The first letter should be pleasant in tone and suggest that the customer may have accidentally overlooked payment of such-and-such an amount. (You might consider placing a telephone call in between the first and second letters to find out what has been happening.)
4. If you hear nothing further, send out the other letters, each of which becomes progressively stronger. These should be spaced so that they reach the addressee about every ten days or two weeks. Your last letter in the series should emphasize the fact that you're about to turn the delinquent account over to your attorney.
5. Give the matter over to your attorney.

Source: THE SMALL BUSINESS HANDBOOK, Revised, by Irving Burstiner. © 1989. Reprinted by permission of the publisher: Prentice Hall Press/A division of Simon & Schuster, Englewood Cliffs, NJ.

- *Character*—Does the person/organization customarily pay bills early, when they fall due, or after their due dates?
- *Capacity*—Does the person/organization enjoy enough current income to be able to pay off this obligation without difficulty?
- *Capital*—Is the net worth (or accessible financial resources) of this person/organization greater than is necessary to repay this debt?

FOR FURTHER INFORMATION

Books

Bernstein, Leopold A., *Analysis of Financial Statements,* 3rd ed. Homewood, Ill.: Business One Irwin, 1990.

Coleman, Bob, *The New Small Business Survival Guide.* New York: W. W. Norton, 1991.

Kolb, Burton A. and Richard F. Demong, *Principles of Financial Management,* 2d ed. Homewood, Ill.: Irwin, 1988.

Krevolin, Nathan, *Filing and Records Management.* Englewood Cliffs, N. J.: Prentice-Hall, 1986.

Milling, Bryan E., *Cash Flow Problem Solver,* 2d ed. Radnor, Pa.: Chilton, 1984.

Neveu, Raymond F., *Fundamentals of Managerial Finance,* 3rd ed. Cincinnati: South-Western, 1989.

Perline, Neil, *The Small Business Guide to Office Automation.* Homewood, Ill.: Dow Jones-Irwin, 1990.

Scott, Gina Graham, *Positive Cash Flow: Complete Credit and Collections for the Small Business.* Holbrook, Mass.: Bob Evans, 1990.

Simini, Joseph P., *Budgeting Basics for Nonfinancial Managers.* New York: Wiley, 1989.

Van Horne, James C., *Fundamentals of Financial Management,* 7th ed. Englewood Cliffs, N. J.: Prentice-Hall, 1989.

Business Development Publications Available from the U.S. Small Business Administration

FINANCIAL MANAGEMENT

FM 1—"ABC's of Borrowing" ($1.00)

FM 3—"Basic Budgets for Profit Planning" ($.50)

FM 4—"Understanding Cash Flow" ($1.00)

FM 5—"A Venture Capital Primer for Small Business" ($.50)

FM 6—"Accounting Services for Small Service Firms" ($.50)

FM 7–"Analyze Your Records to Reduce Costs" ($.50)

FM 8–"Budgeting in a Small Service Firm" ($.50)

FM 9–"Sound Cash Management and Borrowing" ($.50)

FM 10–"Recordkeeping in a Small Business" ($1.00)

MANAGEMENT AND PLANNING

MP 8–"Should You Lease or Buy Equipment?" ($.50)

CHAPTER 15

MANAGING THE COMPANY'S FINANCES—II

In the prior chapter, you were introduced to such significant aspects of the financial end of business management as ratio analysis, recordkeeping, cash flow management, and the control of expenses through budgeting. You were then informed about the customary approaches to capital budgeting. A discussion of the credit management area, from the types of credit that firms extend to their customers to a recommended procedure for handling delinquent accounts, brought the chapter to an end.

We begin this second chapter on administering a firm's finances by exploring ways to protect its assets. You will come to appreciate the value of introducing a risk-reduction program and of insuring your company against certain perils. You will also discover some measures to institute that will help you control both internal and external theft. A brief overview of business law is then presented. This is followed by a rather extensive treatment of business taxation. Among other details, it offers specific federal income-tax information for sole proprietorships, partnerships, and corporations.

HOW TO SAFEGUARD YOUR FIRM'S ASSETS

Hopefully, many of the decisions you will make in your new service operation will result in gain. You can, though, expect to suffer an occasional loss. The type of risk involved in your decision making is called *speculative risk.* Speculative risk exists when an action can lead to either a gain or a loss. It is characteristic of all forms of gambling activity.

There is another kind of risk, known as *pure risk,* that you as a business owner should be wary of. Situations involving pure risk offer only the possibility of loss, not gain. A fire at your place of business that causes property damage is an example of just such a situation. So is a lawsuit initiated by someone who suffered an injury on your premises and accuses you of negligence.

How can you protect your company assets against such threats? Two approaches are common:

1. Introduce a risk-reduction program that will lower the likelihood of property damage as well as the occurrence of accidental injuries.
2. Buy protection in the form of insurance policies against the more serious kinds of threats your company may face.

An effective risk-reduction program will consist of a well planned and well-coordinated series of steps. Suggestions for such a program are offered later in this chapter, in the section on "Low-Cost Safety Measures." At this point, though, we begin our discussion of business insurance.

What Kinds of Insurance Policies Should You Buy?

If you are like most new entrepreneurs, you are starting off with limited capital and a tight budget. Because of this, you should seek at first only those insurance coverages that are absolutely essential to the health of your business. Once you have gotten off to a successful start and are clearly on a growth track, you might consider looking into additional types of protection. (Figure 15–1 offers an overview of other kinds of policies you may want to consider at a later date.)

For most companies, three types of insurance coverage are imperatives: fire, liability, and workers compensation.

Fire Insurance—Be sure to purchase fire insurance even though you may be convinced that the odds against the occurrence of a serious conflagration on your premises may far exceed 1,000 to 1. A fire can force you entirely out of business within a matter of minutes. Buy a *comprehensive fire policy.* Although you will pay a somewhat higher premium, this type will also safeguard your assets against such perils as smoke, windstorm, explosion, and vandalism. You may also want to consider one or more "floater" policies to insure cash, bonds, property deeds, or other assets that are not usually protected under your basic fire policy.

Your fire policy premium will be affected by the location and condition of your premises. Be sure to insure your property for its *replacement value,* not for what it cost you initially.

Coinsurance—Generally, a specific "coinsurance clause" appears in the fire policy. Its aim is to induce you to purchase and maintain—as minimum coverage—a specified percentage of your property's current value. Most often, the

FIGURE 15–1
Other types of insurance to consider later on

Name of Insurance	Nature of Coverage
Boiler and Machinery	Covers losses due to the explosion of boilers, engines, and other machinery.
Burglary	Compensates the firm for property stolen after forced entry of the premises.
Business interruption	Offers compensation for fixed expenses that usually need to be paid while business activities are shut down (as in the case of a fire or some other catastrophe).
Comprehensive crime	Reimburses the firm for losses due to robbery, burglary, and other types of property disappearance.
Glass	Provides for the replacement of broken windows, showcases, glass doors, mirrors, and the like.
Group Health	Provides basic medical benefits and hospitalization for both management and employees. Also usually provides disability income.
Key Person	Compensates the firm for any loss in profits due to the demise of a key employee. Will also cover the expense of finding, hiring, and training that person's replacement.
Life	Several different kinds of life insurance policies are available for providing financial protection to the families of employees as well as to those of the business owners. With some types, cash accumulations can be tapped for unexpected contingencies. Coverage is also of value to partners who have signed "buy/sell" agreements. Payment upon the death of one partner enables the remaining partners to carry on the business without interruption.
Robbery	Reimburses firm for property taken by force or under the threat of violence.
Water Damage	Covers accidental water damage to property from leaks through roofs or basements, escaping steam, overflows from refrigeration equipment, and so on.

figure is set at 80 percent of the value. If a firm buys less insurance than is required by the coinsurance clause and then suffers a loss because of fire, the insurance carrier will penalize the firm in proportion to the deficiency.

By way of illustration, let us assume that the replacement value of your place of business, along with its contents (equipment, furnishings, machinery, supplies, and inventory), amounts to $350,000. To protect your assets fully, then, you should purchase a comprehensive fire policy in the face amount of $350,000. However, you discover that you can shave your annual fire premium by nearly $1,000 by requesting no more than $200,000 worth of insurance. After all, you may then reason, only the slimmest of chances exists that a fire at your place will destroy as much as $200,000 worth of assets.

Be forewarned! Should a fire subsequently cause damage to the tune of, say, $60,000, the insurance company will not reimburse you for that amount. Why? The reason is clear: you were *underinsured.* The value of your assets totaled $350,000; 80 percent of that figure would come to $280,000. If your policy had been written for $280,000, there would have been no problem. But, with coverage of only $200,000, you failed to meet the required minimum of 80 percent of the property valuation. If we divide $200,000 by $350,000, the result reads 57.14 percent.

You did suffer a loss of $60,000, but since you were underinsured–you will be reimbursed for exactly 57.14 percent of your loss, or $34,284.

Liability Insurance–Lawsuits may be brought against you and your business by persons who claim to have suffered injuries because of your negligence. The outcome of these lawsuits may or may not be in your favor. Liability insurance will protect your assets by paying for the plaintiffs' medical and surgical expenses, reimbursing them for court costs, and compensating them for the loss of future earnings.

Workers Compensation Insurance–As an employer, you are required by law to maintain safe working conditions at your place of business for your personnel. If an employee is injured on the job, whether or not you have been negligent in any way, that individual may apply for compensation benefits. Workers' compensation insurance not only reimburses the injured person for medical expenses but also seeks to replace some of the lost wages. Premiums for this kind of insurance are based on such factors as the types of jobs in the organization, the kinds of hazards that may be present on the premises, and the size of the firm's payroll.

SENSIBLE, LOW-COST SAFETY MEASURES YOU SHOULD TAKE

In addition to buying insurance to safeguard your company against fire and casualty losses, you can take many other steps to minimize risk. You can, for example:

- Arrange for the regular disposal of waste
- Check for frayed or exposed wires that carry electricity
- Clean up spills immediately
- Clearly mark all exits and fire doors
- Consider installing a sprinkler system

- Do not allow smoking on your premises. Post "No Smoking" signs conspicuously.
- From time to time, hold a fire drill for your employees
- Guard against leaving cabinet doors open
- In rainy weather, lay down nonskid mats and keep entrances dry
- Install smoke alarms wherever necessary
- Institute a procedure for handling accidental injuries
- Keep aisles open and free from encumbrances
- Keep storerooms well illuminated
- Maintain all machines and equipment in good working condition
- Open doors slowly
- Place fire extinguishers in appropriate locations throughout your premises
- Train all employees thoroughly
- Use the right implements when opening cases or cartons

HOW TO INSTITUTE EFFECTIVE THEFT CONTROL

You can expect that your new service enterprise, like every other business, may suffer occasional losses due to external or internal theft. Among the thieves who perpetrate external crimes are burglars, robbers, shoplifters, passers of counterfeit money or bad checks, and short-change artists. Employee pilferage (of cash, supplies, or merchandise), check-kiting, and embezzlement are instances of internal theft.

Regardless of its source, theft will adversely affect your operation. As an example, the nation's retailers lose many billions of dollars each year to shoplifters. To cover these losses, the retailers are forced to raise their prices to the consumer.

Reducing the Threat–The business owner can institute many measures to hold down losses due to criminal activity. If, for example, you operate a store, you can reduce shoplifting activity by putting up anti-shoplifting signs ("Shoplifters Will Be Prosecuted!"), installing convex mirrors so that all areas of the store can be watched, keeping expensive goods under lock and key, and training your personnel to be alert at all times.

Here are just a few of the steps that can help you to reduce the threat of theft:

- Teach your employees how to identify counterfeit bills and how to avoid being duped by short-change thieves.
- Institute a foolproof check-acceptance procedure.
- Have employees get your approval before giving a discount to anyone.
- Have all outer doors inspected and their door frames reinforced.

FIGURE 15–2
Sixteen ways to cut down on losses from theft

1. When hiring, make certain your selection and screening procedures are good. Make it known from the start that you expect honesty in all your employees. Set a personal example with your own behavior at all times.
2. Train your employees to be calm and cooperative in the event of a holdup. A life is a precious thing that no amount of money can replace.
3. Schedule at least two individuals to open up in the morning and close at night, and to make bank deposits.
4. Train your employees to be alert: to watch people who enter your premises with coats over their arms or carrying shopping bags or bulky packages; to keep an eye on those who look or act suspicious; to wait promptly on customers.
5. Keep good records in accordance with good accounting procedures.
6. If possible, sign all checks yourself. Never sign blank checks to leave behind when traveling or on vacation.
7. Make certain all cash disbursements have your personal approval.
8. Try to reconcile all bank statements throughout the year. Review all canceled checks and their endorsements.
9. Keep close watch over the shipping and receiving functions. This includes setting up tight recordkeeping systems within both departments, supervising the loading and unloading of trucks, and even fencing off the two areas from other departments.
10. Always remove excess cash from the cash register and place it in the safe. Bank regularly, and at different times from day to day. Leave the cash drawer empty and open at night to avoid possible forced entry that might damage the equipment.
11. Keep all keys locked up when not in use. Issue as few as you have to, in order to avoid unnecessary duplication.
12. Prosecute any shoplifter who is apprehended and any employee caught stealing. If there's any doubt whatsoever in a particular incident, it might be wiser to avoid prosecution because of the possibility of a lawsuit for false arrest.
13. To prevent employees from pocketing change or bills from the register, insist on issuing register receipts to all customers. An even better arrangement is making out sales slips for each and every sale.
14. Install a good alarm system, preferably a central system, on the premises. In high-risk areas, consider additional safeguards, such as a private patrol service, gratings, and so on.
15. Protect all doors and entrances with properly installed, pin-tumbler type cylinder locks and deadbolts.
16. Safes should be of high quality, fire resistant, and fastened to the building itself.

Source: Adapted from THE SMALL BUSINESS HANDBOOK, Revised, by Irving Burstiner. © 1989. Reprinted by permission of the publisher: Prentice Hall Press/A division of Simon & Schuster, Englewood Cliffs, N.J.

- If your business is in a high-risk area, have gratings or screens installed over windows and outer doors.
- At your premises, keep one or more lights on throughout the night.
- Issue keys only to those employees who must use them and who you believe are completely trustworthy.
- Do not identify your firm on keys or key chains.
- Should you or an employee lose a key, change the lock it fits at once.

Fig. 15–2 offers additional suggestions for reducing theft.

SOME BASICS OF BUSINESS LAW

The roots of modern American law extend way back in time to the rules, regulations, and prevailing customs of the Roman Empire. Over the centuries, this body of "customary" or "common" Roman law found its way to England. Subsequently, it was refined and greatly expanded by the English. Brought over to the American colonies, this broadened base served as the foundation of our own legal system. Much more has since been added as governments at all levels enacted countless numbers of statutes, or written laws.

Business Law

In Chapter 5, we reviewed the procedure for registering the several legal forms of business operation and then enumerated the major federal laws that were designed to protect the consumer. A summary of legislation pertaining to business employees appeared in Chapter 9. Now, in this next section, we discuss several additional legal aspects of interest to the new business owner. The treatment is necessarily brief; any more detailed coverage of business law lies well beyond the scope of this book.

Contract Law

The law of contracts is one of the more significant aspects of business law. A contract is "a mutual agreement between two or more people to perform or not perform certain acts."*

Here are a few of the kinds of situations that call for a signed contract:

- Parents enroll their eight-year-old child in a ballet school
- A homeowner arranges to have the living-room furniture reupholstered
- A large publishing house hires a business machines repair company to service its equipment for the next three years

*John A. Reinecke and William F. Schoell, *Introduction to Business: A Contemporary View,* 4th ed. (Boston: Allyn and Bacon, 1984), 594.

- A young adult applies to a health club for a one-year membership
- A franchisor of beauty salons requests a booth at a "business opportunities" convention
- A national transportation company asks an advertising agency to handle its account
- At a travel agency, newlyweds schedule a six-day Caribbean cruise
- A construction firm agrees to build a warehouse for a large wholesaler
- At an airport, a business executive rents a Lincoln Town Car from a car-rental agency

To be enforceable in court, a contract must satisfy all of the following conditions:

1. It contains a proposal or an offer by one party to another.
2. The purpose of the offer or proposal is a legal one.
3. Both parties accept the offer or proposal.
4. Acceptance is completely voluntary; no intimidation, coercion, or threat has been involved.
5. Each party offers the other one something of value. (Note: This aspect is known as "extending consideration.")
6. Both parties are of legal age and sound of mind.

Agency Law

Agency is "a contractual relationship involving an agent and a principal, in which the agent is given the authority to represent the principal in dealings with third parties."* This authorization may be granted orally or put into written form.

Property Law

The law of property applies to all kinds of real and personal property including land, homes, and other buildings; mortgages; wills and estates; patents, trademarks, and copyrights; and situations involving bankruptcy.

Patents and Trademarks—If you should invent a new product and would like to have exclusive rights to its manufacture and sale, you will need to secure a patent on your invention. Your first step should be to have a patent attorney conduct a search to ascertain whether or not a similar item has already been registered. If nothing is found, you should then submit an application to the Commissioner of Patents and Trademarks, Washington, DC 20231.

Companies register and use trademarks to differentiate their products and/or services, as well as their organizations, from those of competitors. Any of the

*John Jude Moran, *Practical Business Law* (Englewood Cliffs, N.J.: Prentice-Hall, 1985), 332.

following can serve alone as a trademark, or in combination with any of the others: a letter of the alphabet, a word, a symbol, a device, a sound, or a mark.

Copyrights–According to the Copyright Act of 1976, original works or compositions (writings, paintings, music, photographs, and the like) belong to their creators for the rest of their lives and for 50 years thereafter. Yet, even though you are the legal owner of any innovative work you produce, you should register your creation. This step can give you additional protection against the unauthorized use of your work. You may secure an application from The Register of Copyrights, Library of Congress, Washington, DC 20559. Fill it out and then mail it, along with two copies of your work and the required fee to the Register of Copyrights.

Bankruptcy–Bankruptcy is a legal procedure by which business organizations (or people)–can gain relief from accumulated debt that they cannot possibly pay back. Most often, application for this relief is made voluntarily–under Chapter 7 of the Federal Bankruptcy Code. The court subsequently appoints a trustee to liquidate the firm's (or person's) assets and distribute monies collected therefrom among the creditors. A company can also file under Chapter 11 of the Code, and submit a plan to the court for reorganization.

KNOW YOUR TAX RESPONSIBILITIES

Taxes are an indispensable feature of modern civilization. As a new-business owner, you will quickly discover that you need to learn much more about taxes than you knew while you were still an employee. For the majority of businesspeople, the federal tax burden stems largely from the income, FICA, and FUTA taxes. Many owners are also responsible for paying self-employment tax; some are liable for excise tax. State and local governments as well impose a variety of taxes on individuals and organizations. Real estate, sales, and income taxes are examples.

The complexities of tax law are, of course, far beyond the scope of this book. We can offer only a skeletal treatment of a few of the more significant details in the remaining pages of this chapter. For additional information, be sure to contact the Internal Revenue Service. Request a copy of their "Publication 334–Tax Guide for Small Business." Updated each year, this 8-½″ by 11″ book serves as an excellent resource for your use in preparing your annual tax returns.*

Consulting a good tax advisor would be an even wiser move.

Federal Income Tax

Whether you derive your earnings from a job you hold or from a business that you own, those earnings are subject to federal income tax rules and regulations. Where businesses, rather than individuals, are concerned, different regulations

*For a listing of useful IRS publications, see Figure 15–3.

FIGURE 15–3
Tax publications available free from the IRS

Publication Number	Title
334	Tax Guide for Small Business
463	Travel, Entertainment, and Gift Expenses
505	Tax Withholding and Estimated Tax
525	Taxable and Nontaxable Income
526	Charitable Contributions
533	Self-Employment Tax
534	Depreciation
535	Business Expenses
536	Net Operating Losses
537	Installment Sales
538	Accounting Periods and Methods
541	Tax Information on Partnerships
542	Tax Information on Corporations
544	Sales and Other Dispositions of Assets
551	Basis of Assets
560	Retirement Plans for the Self-Employed
575	Pension and Annuity Income
583	Taxpayers Starting a Business
586A	The Collection Process (Income Tax Accounts)
587	Business Use of Your Home
589	Tax Information on S Corporations
590	Individual Retirement Arrangements (IRAs)
594	The Collection Process (Employment Tax Accounts)
910	Guide to Free Tax Services
911	Tax Information for Direct Sellers
917	Business Use of a Car
924	Reporting of Real Estate Transactions to IRS
937	Business Reporting (Employment Taxes and Information Returns)

apply to each of the three legal forms of operation. Only corporations are required to pay taxes on their earnings. Neither the sole proprietorship nor the partnership directly incurs any tax liability.

Federal tax forms for sole proprietorships, partnerships, and corporations are shown in the Appendix. As you read through the next few pages, it would be helpful for you to refer to each form as it is mentioned.

Income Tax Information for Sole Proprietorships

Internal Revenue Service regulations do not differentiate between the sole proprietorship and its owner. If you have selected this legal form, you are not required to file a separate income tax return for your business. However, you must submit your personal income tax information on Form 1040 ("Individual Income Tax Return"). This is the same form you used as an employee.

Form 1040 must be filed each year before April 15th. The IRS will assess penalties for failure to file your return on time or if you neglect to show all the necessary information on your return.

Should you need more time for completing your return, you can apply for a four-month extension by filing Form 4868 ("Application for Automatic Extension of Time to File U.S. Individual Income Tax Return") by April 15th. Timely submission of Form 4868 does not, however, extend the time for paying any tax due.

Schedule C–You are required to submit an additional schedule with your Form 1040. This is Schedule C–"Profit or Loss from Business (Sole Proprietorship)." This calls for details about your firm's performance for the year just ended including gross revenue, your cost of goods sold (if any), a summary of all business expenses incurred, and the net profit (or loss).

To calculate your income tax liability, you must add the income produced because of your business activity to any other earnings you may have received during the same year.

If you operate two or more sole proprietorships, you will need to furnish separate Schedule C's for each business.

Estimated Tax–To guard against possible delinquency, you are required to estimate the amount of tax you will most likely incur during the current year. Payment of estimated tax in advance is the norm. To help you in determining and submitting estimated tax payments each year, the IRS will provide instructions for the procedure, along with a worksheet and four declaration vouchers (Form 1040ES–"Declaration of Estimated Tax for Individuals"). You will need to file the vouchers, each in turn, before the 15th of April, June, September, and January. A partial tax payment must accompany each voucher.

When you calculate your estimated tax liability, you must also take into account the amount of *self-employment tax* you expect to have to pay for the year. (See the section on "Self-Employment Tax" later in this chapter.) If you underpay your tax liability or fail to file your estimated tax vouchers before their due dates, you will incur a penalty.

Income Tax Information for Partnerships*

Our government does not directly tax either the sole proprietorship or the partnership. Instead, those who operate under either legal form incur personal income tax liability. As we have already seen, sole proprietors declare their income on Form 1040. Partners, too, report their personal income–along with their distributive share of business' profits–on the selfsame Form 1040.

Form 1065–Every partnership is also required to submit an annual *information* return: Form 1065–"U.S. Partnership Return of Income." Only a general partner may sign the form. (Note: Form 1065 is due each year by April 15th. If, however, you operate your firm on a fiscal year basis, the due date becomes the 15th of the fourth month following the close of your fiscal year.)

The company must also issue to each partner a copy of Schedule K-1, Form 1065 ("Partner's Share of Income, Credits, Deductions, Etc.").

An automatic extension of time (three months) may be granted upon filing Form 8736 ("Application for Automatic Extension of Time to File Return for a U.S. Partnership, REMIC, or for Certain Trusts").

Estimated Tax–Like the sole proprietor, partners must also comply with the regulations covering estimated tax. They need to submit the earlier-mentioned Form 1040ES each quarter, along with part payment of their tax.

Income Tax Information for Corporations**

Corporations are taxable entities. They have an existence of their own, apart from the people who own or manage them. Whether or not it has earned taxable income, every corporation must file annual tax returns.

Several different income tax report forms are available for corporate use:

Form 1120 – "U. S. Corporation Income Tax Return"
Form 1120A – "U.S. Corporation Short-Form Income Tax Return"
Form 1120S – "U.S. Income Tax Return for an S Corporation"

Form 1120 is the income tax reporting form commonly filed by corporations. Form 1120A may be used by a corporation with less than $500,000 in all three of these categories: gross receipts, total income, and total assets. (Certain other requirements also apply.) S corporations (discussed later in this chapter) submit Form 1120S.

Ordinarily, your corporate tax return should be filed on or before March 15th of each year. If you are set up on a fiscal-year basis, your return is due by the 15th of the third month following the close of your fiscal year. You will need to file your corporate tax return with the IRS center that serves the area where your principal office, books, and records are located.

---

*For more details, send for IRS Publication 541–"Tax Information on Partnerships."

**For more information, order IRS Publication 542–"Tax Information on Corporations."

If you need more time, you can apply for an automatic six-month extension by submitting Form 7004 ("Application for Automatic Extension of Time to File Corporation Income Tax Return") by the due date of your return.

Corporate Tax Rates–These are based on the level of taxable income and graduated, as indicated below:

On taxable income of:	The tax rate is:
$50,000 or less	15%
$50,001–$75,000	25%
Over $75,000	34%

Note, however, these additional points:

1. On taxable income that exceeds $100,000, the corporation must pay an additional 5 percent tax. This additional tax is capped at $11,750.
2. The rate for a corporation with taxable income of $335,000 or more is a flat 34 percent.
3. If your firm is a "qualified personal service corporation," the above rates do not apply.* Your tax rate is 34 percent.

Estimated Tax Payments–A corporation that incurs a tax liability of $500 or more must deposit its payments of estimated tax with an authorized financial institution or a federal reserve bank. A federal tax deposit coupon is to accompany each payment. The deposits are to be made on or before the 15th of the following months of the firm's tax year: the fourth, sixth, ninth, and twelfth months.

*The S Corporation***–A singular disadvantage of the typical corporate form is the "double taxation" problem. First, the company itself must pay tax on any earned income. If the corporation then distributes dividends to its shareholders, these people will have to declare those dividends on their Form 1040 returns and pay income tax accordingly.

Eligible firms can avoid this problem by electing to be treated as S corporations. To gain this status, an organization must meet specific criteria, among them:

- It must be a domestic corporation.
- It must have only one class of stock.
- It can have no more than 35 shareholders.

*It is a qualified personal service corporation if: (a) employees–or their estates and beneficiaries–hold at least 95 percent of the value of the corporation's stock and (b) the employees perform services at least 95 percent of the time in any of the following fields: health, law, engineering, architecture, accounting, actuarial science, performing arts, or consulting.

**For more details, see IRS Publication 589–"Tax Information on S Corporations."

- Shareholders must be citizens or residents of the United States.
- All shareholders must give their consent to S corporation status.

To be treated as an S corporation, the firm must file Form 2553 ("Election by a Small Business Corporation") with the IRS.

Information on Other Federal Taxes

Regardless of your legal form, income tax is not the only federal tax liability you face. You will also need to comply with the provisions of two other major laws: (1) the Federal Insurance Contributions Act (FICA) and (2) the Federal Unemployment Tax Act (FUTA). Moreover, if you are the sole proprietor of your business, you are also liable for self-employment tax. In addition, some types of operations may be responsible for collecting and paying excise tax.

The Federal Insurance Contributions Act (FICA)—This law provides for a federal system of old age, survivors, disability, and hospital insurance. The first three are financed by the social security tax; the hospital insurance is financed by the Medicare tax. The social security and Medicare taxes are levied on both employee and employer (who must match the amount).

Two significant aspects of FICA regulations control the amount of tax to be paid: (1) the specified percentage of earnings to be taxed, and (2) the "wage base," or top limit on earnings, to which the rate is to be applied. Both of these may change from one year to the next. In 1991, the tax rate for social security was 6.2 percent each for employers and employees (12.4 percent total). The 1991 wage base of $53,400 was scheduled to rise to $55,500 for 1992. The 1991 Medicare tax rate was 1.45 percent each for employers and employees (2.9 percent total). In 1991, the wage base for this tax was $125,000; for 1992, this was due to be increased to $130,200.*

You must withhold the required FICA amount from every employee's paycheck. Useful tables for determining the amount of each deduction are available in IRS *Publication 15* ("Circular E—Employer's Tax Guide").

File your FICA tax reports four times each year, within a month after the end of each quarter. For this purpose, use Form 941 ("Employer's Quarterly Federal Tax Return").** FICA monies collected and matching amounts contributed by your firm must be deposited periodically throughout the year. Each deposit, accompanied by a federal tax deposit coupon, is to be made to a federal reserve bank or other authorized financial institution.

The Federal Unemployment Tax Act (FUTA)—This law offers unemployment insurance to workers who lose their jobs. Only the employer, not the employee, pays this tax. The FUTA tax rate, 6.2 percent for 1992, applies to the first $7,000

*Meals, lodging, services, and other payments in kind are subject to the same FICA tax as are wages paid in cash.

***Note:* Withholding income tax monies are also to be included in this report.

in wages paid to each employee in the organization. In 1991, employers were credited with up to 5.4 percent of the 6.2 percent rate for the state unemployment tax they paid.

You incur FUTA tax liability if: (a) you pay employees $1,500 or more in any calendar quarter or (b) you have had an employee for at least part of a day in each of 20 different weeks.

Within a month following your year's end, be sure to file Form 940 ("Employer's Annual Federal Unemployment (FUTA) Tax Return"). Smaller companies may use Form 940-EZ.

Self-Employment Tax–This is a social security tax that is imposed on the sole proprietor. If you are self-employed and expect to net $400 or more for the year, you are responsible for paying this tax.

In 1991, the self-employment tax rate was 15.3 percent of net earnings, up to a maximum of $53,400. Included in this rate was 12.4 percent for "Social Security" (old-age, survivors', and disability insurance) and 2.9 percent for "Medicare" tax. The maximum net earnings subject to the Medicare portion for 1991 was $125,000.

If you own more than one sole proprietorship, you need to combine your net earnings from each to determine your total self-employment income.

In figuring your adjusted gross income for the year, you can deduct one-half of your self-employment tax (7.65 percent of your net earnings) as a business expense. You may use this deduction only to determine your self-employment tax liability; it is *not* an income tax deduction.

Excise Tax–Federal excise tax is placed on the sale of some products, certain types of transactions, and certain occupations.* Some examples are:

- Environmental taxes on certain chemicals
- Air transportation taxes
- Communications taxes (Example: on local telephone service)
- Manufacturers' taxes (Examples: on sport fishing equipment, on firearms)
- Fuel (Examples: gas, diesel fuel)

Manufacturers and retailers who are responsible for collecting excise taxes must quote the tax amount separately from the selling price. If your company is required to collect excise taxes, you will need to file four times each year on Form 720 ("Quarterly Federal Excise Tax Return").

State and Local Tax Liabilities

As a business owner, your tax liabilities are much broader than those imposed by the federal government. Most states and a few cities levy taxes on business income. Many states require the payment of an unincorporated business tax or

*For more details, see IRS Publication 510–"Excise Taxes for 1992."

a corporation tax even when the firm has no income whatsoever. Sales taxes must be collected when goods are sold and, in a few cases, in connection with the purchase of services. Local governments tax real estate to help pay toward the many services they provide.

Sole proprietors and partners are not permitted to deduct as a business expense any state income tax they may have paid. They can, however, deduct the amount on their individual 1040s when computing their tax liability if they itemize all deductions. Property taxes are also deductible. Corporations can deduct any state income tax they pay.

Retailers and service firms required to collect sales taxes from their customers must maintain records of their collections and forward the amounts collected to their local taxing authorities.

Withholding Taxes

Every business is required to withhold a designated percentage of each employee's pay for both income tax and FICA tax purposes. The firm must turn over the amounts it withholds on a regular basis throughout each year. (See previous section on FICA tax.) Tables that indicate the correct percentages for the company to withhold (based on weekly, biweekly, or monthly pay periods) are available in *IRS Publication 15*–"Circular E–Employer's Tax Guide."

Note that records of taxes withheld must be retained for at least four years after the due date of the return or after the date the tax is paid, whichever is later. Among other details, these records should show: the employee's name, address, and social security number; the total amount of each wage payment and the date paid; the amount subject to withholding; a copy of the W-4 form ("Employee's Withholding Allowance Certificate"; and information on FICA and FUTA taxes.

FOR FURTHER INFORMATION

Books

Anderson, Ronald et al., *Business Law and the Legal Environment,* 14th ed. Cincinnati: South-Western, 1989.

Crane, Frederick G., *Insurance Principles and Practice,* 2d ed. New York: Wiley, 1984.

Foster, Frank H. and Robert L. Shook, *Everything You Need to Know about Patents, Copyrights, and Trademarks.* New York: Wiley, 1989.

Greene, Mark R. and James S. Trieschmann, *Risk and Insurance,* 7th ed. Cincinnati: South-Western, 1988.

Lane, Marc J., *Legal Handbook for Small Business,* rev. ed. New York: AMACOM, 1989.

Lieberman, Jethro K., *The Legal Environment of Business.* San Diego: Harcourt Brace Jovanovich, 1989.

Mehr, Robert I., *Fundamentals of Insurance,* 2d ed. Homewood, Ill.: Irwin, 1986.

Moran, John Jude, *Practical Business Law,* 2d ed. Englewood Cliffs, N. J.: Prentice-Hall, 1989.

Prentice-Hall Editorial Staff, *Federal Tax Handbook, 1989 Edition.* Englewood Cliffs, N. J.: Prentice-Hall, 1989.

Raby, William L. et al., *Introduction to Federal Taxation, 1990 Edition.* Englewood Cliffs, N. J.: Prentice-Hall, 1990.

Research Institute of America, *Master Federal Tax Manual.* New York: Prentice Hall Press, 1991.

Spiro, G., *The Legal Environment of Business.* Englewood Cliffs, N. J.: Prentice-Hall, 1989.

Williams, C. Arthur, Jr. and Richard M. Heins, *Risk Management and Insurance,* 6th ed. New York: McGraw-Hill, 1988.

Wood, Robert W., *The Ultimate Tax Planning Guide for Growing Companies.* Homewood, Ill.: Business One Irwin, 1990.

Business Development Publications Available from the U.S. Small Business Administration

FINANCIAL MANAGEMENT

FM 7–"Analyze Your Records to Reduce Costs" ($.50)

FM 10–"Record Keeping in a Small Business" ($1.00)

MANAGEMENT AND PLANNING

MU 28–"Small Business Risk Management Guide" ($1.00)

CRIME PREVENTION

CP 2–"Curtailing Crime–Inside and Out" ($1.00)

CP 3–"A Small Business Guide to Computer Security" ($1.00)

PRODUCTS/IDEAS/INVENTIONS

PI 1–"Ideals into Dollars" ($2.00)

PI 2–"Avoiding Patent, Trademark, and Copyright Problems" ($1.00)

PI 3–"Trademarks and Business Goodwill" ($1.00)

Part Six

PLANNING THE FUTURE OF YOUR BUSINESS

CHAPTER 16

PLANNING AHEAD: WHAT DOES THE FUTURE HOLD?

This final chapter is devoted to the future of your service enterprise. We begin by introducing the concept of the business life cycle. You will come to understand how each stage of the cycle tends to shape the marketing behavior of the successful organization. You will then learn about the importance of consolidating your position and reviewing your firm's strengths and weaknesses before embarking on an expansion route. You will be made aware of the available options to choose among in your quest for company growth. Finally, we address the problems associated with management succession and bringing family members into the operation.

REVIEWING THE BUSINESS LIFE CYCLE CONCEPT

Much like people, and like all the products and services that ever have been or will be placed on the market, every business organization has a life cycle of its own. Over its limited, circumscribed lifetime, the successful enterprise can be expected to pass through four stages: (1) introduction, (2) growth, (3) maturity, and (4) decline. These phases of the business life cycle are depicted by the graph displayed in Figure 16–1. Note that the passage of time is marked off along the graph's horizontal axis and that company revenues are plotted along its vertical axis.

FIGURE 16–1
The business life cycle

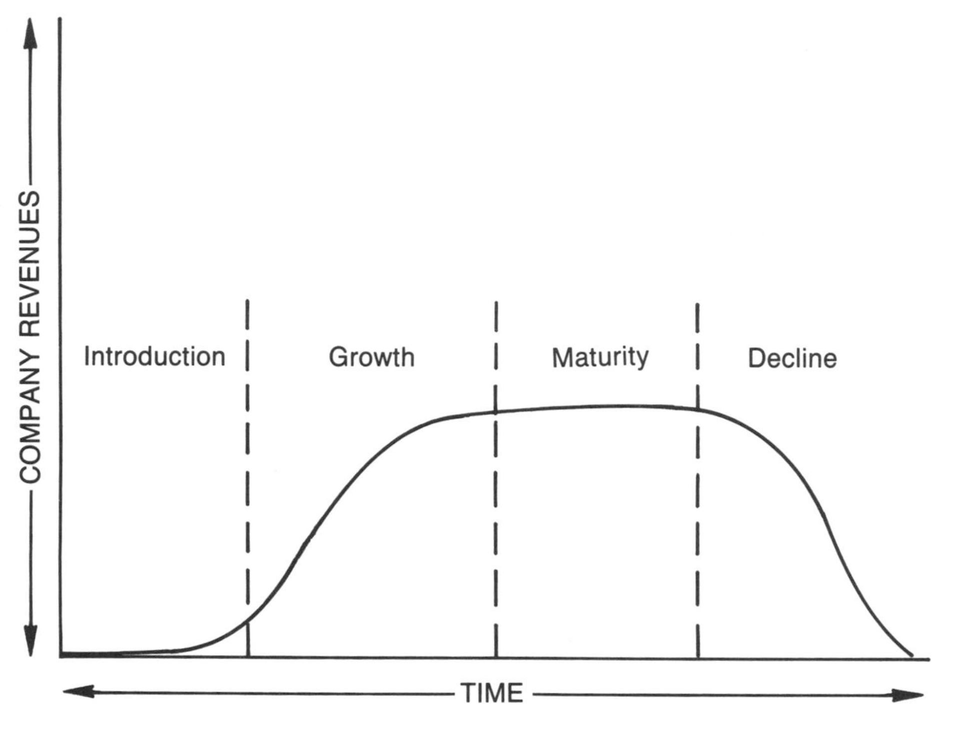

As your business enters each new stage, you will most likely need to reconsider your strategies and devise new tactics to cope with the ever-changing marketing environment. No one can, of course, know in advance how long a company will remain in existence or the length of each stage in its life cycle. Far too many variables, internal as well as external, are bound to influence the organization's progress all along the way.

Introductory Stage–Giving birth to your business and securing your foothold in the economy are the major challenges you face at this stage of the business life cycle. Heavy promotion is the critical element in meeting these challenges; you need to tell your targeted prospects about your company and your service(s).

Every year, as many as half a million people start new ventures. Unfortunately, many are unable to survive; these firms never reach the second, or growth, stage.

Growth Stage–During this phase, look to solidify your initial success and the subsequent gains you made. Continue modifying and improving upon your marketing approaches to the pricing, promotion, and distribution of your service(s). Resist the temptation to seek rapid expansion externally; go after internal growth first. Explore ways to increase revenues without straying from your present premises. Develop strategies for attracting more clients. If you have not as yet tried direct mail approaches to find additional customers, do so. If you already have, and they have been productive, increase the size and frequency of your mailings. Step up your publicity efforts; work on improving your public relations programs. If you operate out of a retail location, display posters or banners in or on your windows.

Maturity Stage—At some indeterminate date, your firm will attain its maturity. By that time, your organization may have grown considerably; business is brisk; and watching your competition will occupy much of your time. Competitive actions may compel you to devise effective counter moves. You may find that you need to increase your promotion budget to maintain a good level of sales and to keep your company's name before the public.

This stage of the business life cycle may, or may not, last for many years.

Decline Stage—Regardless of how large your company may grow, the time must come when your business will begin an irreversible slide into the decline stage of its life cycle. Sales volume falls off; profits drop sharply. You will, of course, go through all the right cost-cutting motions. You will even try to effect drastic reductions in your overhead by shutting down entire sections and departments that no longer contribute their proportionate share of company profits (or, perhaps, are being supported by other sections and departments).

Some of the marketing tactics you resort to may help to stave off your firm's demise for a year of two, or perhaps even longer. Sooner or later, though, you can expect that the company life cycle will run out.

TIPS ON PLANNING FOR COMPANY GROWTH

As soon as your new enterprise moves into the growth stage of its life cycle, you would do well to restrain your eagerness to run off in pursuit of fast company growth. This is the moment when you must begin to examine carefully the state of your affairs.

Take Stock Before Planning for Growth

Like many entrepreneurs, you may begin to think about expansion soon after having successfully launched your new business. Caution is indicated. Bear in mind that, before you attempt to gamble on your future, you need to take time out for some intensive long-range planning.

As you will recall, planning entails visualizing some future state of affairs; selecting attainable objectives; developing a timetable for reaching those goals; working out sales projections; preparing budgets for all facets of the business; making proforma balance sheets, income statements, and cash flow analyses; and much, much more.

Take complete stock of your business before you begin. You will need to review your financial situation to determine whether or not—and when—you will be able to take your first tentative step toward expansion. Will you be able to cover your initial financial requirements by reinvesting the profits you expect your firm to generate? Will you need to seek additional loan or equity capital to get you started?

Check your organization, too. Do you have enough employees at this time to launch an expansion plan? Or, as is more likely, will you need to hire and train additional personnel? If this is the case, you should start preparing a comprehensive human resources program for your company. Among other things, you will need to:

- Anticipate all new positions that will have to be filled between now and your target date(s)
- Develop job descriptions and prepare job specifications for those anticipated openings
- Schedule the retraining of some of your current employees to handle new responsibilities
- Project the number of additional employees you will need to hire
- Locate and recruit a sufficient number of candidates for the openings you expect to have
- Institute a pay plan (or plans) that will help you to attain your objectives
- Devise curricula, methods, and procedures for the different training programs you will need

What Paths Are Open to You?

You may choose to follow any one (or more) of these popular avenues to company growth:

Branch out—Open a branch of your service enterprise at a different location. If the new unit proves successful, you can continue adding other branches to your budding chain.

Make an acquisition—Purchase someone else's established and profitable business, one that offers the same service(s) as you do.

Seek a merger—Look to combine your company with another organization that is in the same business as you.

Diversify—Launch a second, different type of business.

Integrate backwards—Control your distribution by establishing your own wholesaling operation and/or manufacturing plant.

Franchise your operation—Many entrepreneurs who were fortunate enough to have started successful businesses soon begin dreaming about the opportunities that franchising offers. The temptation to move in this direction stems from the realization that they can use other people's money, rather than their own capital, to expand rapidly into a multi-unit chain.

Franchising, however, is never an easy avenue to company growth. The planning alone for such an undertaking is a formidable task. By way of illustrating this point, consider just these preliminary challenges that management will face:

- work out the details of the franchise offer
- decide on how much the franchise fee is to be
- establish the percentage of gross sales that franchisees will be required to pay—plus a smaller percentage for advertising and promotion
- prepare a prospectus for distribution
- hire a capable franchise sales manager
- hunt for suitable locations
- locate and contact prospective franchisees

MANAGEMENT SUCCESSION

Some day, hopefully in the not-too-distant future, you will become convinced that you have finally secured your proper niche in the service sector. Your sales curve has been ascending steadily, your profits continue to mount, and you are beginning to chafe at the bit toward implementing your plans for expansion. Along about the same time, though, you may discover that a growing backlog of work is plaguing you. It seems to be taking its toll on you; you feel that you can never catch up. Happily, before you reach the point of utter exhaustion, you come to realize that you need a capable assistant.

Well, it's about time! Think about what might have happened to your new business if, Heaven forbid, you had fallen ill two or three months ago? Would it not have been more prudent of you to have taken an assistant on board six months (or a year) earlier?

This is something for you to think about right now. Who can you count on to take over your operation, should a calamity befall you? Give this problem a great deal of thought. Compose a list of the qualities, background, and experience this individual should possess.

Review your present employees. Is there anyone now working for you whom you can train to take over the reins in an emergency? Or, is there a family member who not only meets most of your requirements but is also willing to work with you? If neither alternative is available, you will be compelled to search for the right person outside your organization.

At any event, you may need to put your new assistant through several years of training, under your close supervision. It will, of course, be up to you to improve on that individual's weak points and enhance his or her strengths.

KEEPING THE FAMILY BUSINESS RUNNING

Most owners are anxious to keep their successful business operations in the family. They look forward to transferring their enterprises some day, along with its assets and its cash flow, to their spouses, children, and/or other relatives. One of the more common problems they run across is a lack of interest in the operation on the part of some family members. In many cases where an entrepreneur unfortunately passes away, the spouse and/or the children prefer to sell off the business rather than stepping in and continuing to run it. It is also unfortunate that those relatives who eagerly join the business while you are still at its helm may not prove to be competent enough to take over, should the need ever arise.

If you would like to keep it all in the family, be sure to begin planning for this many years before the time to turn over the reins draws near. If you want your children to succeed you, start your preparations while they are young. Work at instilling in them a set of useful values that will help them throughout their adult years. Foster enthusiasm for the work ethic. Teach them to be responsible citizens–and hold them accountable for their actions both at home and at school. Provide them with a fine education. Get them involved in your business at as early an age as you can, preferably before your firm enters the growth stage of its life cycle. Assist them in acquiring those interpersonal and leadership skills they will need to handle increasing responsibilities. Then, take this major forward step: delegate a substantial share of the managerial workload to these new executives!

FOR FURTHER INFORMATION

Books

Benson, Benjamin, et al., *Your Family Business: A Success Guide for Growth and Survival.* Homewood, Ill.: Dow Jones-Irwin, 1990.

Hagendorf, S., *Tax Guide for Buying and Selling a Business,* 6th ed. Englewood Cliffs, N. J.: Prentice-Hall, 1986.

Reed, Stanley Foster and Lane & Edson, P.C., *The Art of M&A: A Merger/Acquisition/ Buyout Guide.* Homewood, Ill.: Business One Irwin, 1989.

Rock, Milton L., ed., *The Mergers and Acquisitions Handbook.* New York: McGraw-Hill, 1987.

Scharf, Charles A. et al., *Acquisitions, Mergers, Sales, Buyouts, Takeovers: A Handbook with Forms,* 3d ed. Englewood Cliffs, N. J.: Prentice-Hall, 1985.

Business Development Publications Available from the U.S. Small Business Administration

MANAGEMENT AND PLANNING

MP 3–"Problems in Managing a Family-Owned Business: ($.50)

MP 20–"Business Continuation Planning" ($1.00)

APPENDIX

FIGURE A–1
Schedule C (Form 1040)

SCHEDULE C (Form 1040)
Department of the Treasury Internal Revenue Service (T)

Profit or Loss From Business

(Sole Proprietorship)
▶ Partnerships, joint ventures, etc., must file Form 1065.
▶ Attach to Form 1040 or Form 1041. ▶ See Instructions for Schedule C (Form 1040).

OMB No. 1545-0074
1991
Attachment Sequence No. 09

Name of proprietor: Susan J. Brown — Social security number (SSN): 111 : 00 : 1111

A Principal business or profession, including product or service (see instructions): Retail Ladies Apparel — B Enter principal business code (from page 2) ▶ 3 9 1 3

C Business name: Milady Fashions — D Employer ID number (Not SSN): 10 : 1234567

E Business address (including suite or room no.) ▶ 725 Big Sur Drive
City, town or post office, state, and ZIP code: Franklin, NY 18725

F Accounting method: (1) ☐ Cash (2) ☐ Accrual (3) ☑ Other (specify) ▶ Hybrid

G Method(s) used to value closing inventory: (1) ☑ Cost (2) ☐ Lower of cost or market (3) ☐ Other (attach explanation) (4) ☐ Does not apply (if checked, skip line H)

	Yes	No
H Was there any change in determining quantities, costs, or valuations between opening and closing inventory? (If "Yes," attach explanation.)		✓
I Did you "materially participate" in the operation of this business during 1991? (If "No," see instructions for limitations on losses.)	✓	

J If this is the first Schedule C filed for this business, check here ▶ ☐

Part I Income

		Line	Amount
1	Gross receipts or sales. **Caution:** *If this income was reported to you on Form W-2 and the "Statutory employee" box on that form was checked, see the instructions and check here* ▶ ☐	1	397,742
2	Returns and allowances	2	1,442
3	Subtract line 2 from line 1	3	396,300
4	Cost of goods sold (from line 40 on page 2)	4	239,349
5	Subtract line 4 from line 3 and enter the **gross profit** here	5	156,951
6	Other income, including Federal and state gasoline or fuel tax credit or refund (see instructions)	6	
7	**Add lines 5 and 6. This is your gross income** ▶	7	156,951

Part II Expenses *(Caution: Enter expenses for business use of your home on line 30.)*

		Line	Amount			Line	Amount
8	Advertising	8	3,500	21	Repairs and maintenance	21	964
9	Bad debts from sales or services (see instructions)	9	479	22	Supplies (not included in Part III)	22	1,203
10	Car and truck expenses (see instructions—also attach Form 4562)	10	3,849	23	Taxes and licenses	23	5,727
11	Commissions and fees	11		24	Travel, meals, and entertainment: a Travel	24a	
12	Depletion	12			b Meals and entertainment		
13	Depreciation and section 179 expense deduction (not included in Part III) (see instructions)	13	2,731		c Enter 20% of line 24b subject to limitations (see instructions)		
14	Employee benefit programs (other than on line 19)	14			d Subtract line 24c from line 24b	24d	
15	Insurance (other than health)	15	238	25	Utilities	25	3,570
16	Interest:			26	Wages (less jobs credit)	26	59,050
a	Mortgage (paid to banks, etc.)	16a		27a	Other expenses (list type and amount):		
b	Other	16b	2,633		Bank service charges 180		
17	Legal and professional services	17			Chamber of commerce 60		
18	Office expense	18	216		Free Credit Card Co. 6,000		
19	Pension and profit-sharing plans	19			Trash removal 1,600		
20	Rent or lease (see instructions):				Window washing 238		
a	Vehicles, machinery, and equipment	20a					
b	Other business property	20b	12,000	27b	Total other expenses	27b	8,078

		Line	Amount
28	Add amounts in columns for lines 8 through 27b. These are your **total expenses** before expenses for business use of your home ▶	28	104,238
29	Tentative profit (loss). Subtract line 28 from line 7	29	52,713
30	Expenses for business use of your home (attach **Form 8829**)	30	
31	**Net profit or (loss).** Subtract line 30 from line 29. If a profit, enter here and on Form 1040, line 12. Also enter the net profit on Schedule SE, line 2 (statutory employees, see instructions). If a loss, you MUST go on to line 32 (fiduciaries, see instructions)	31	52,713

32 If you have a loss, you MUST check the box that describes your investment in this activity (see instructions)
If you checked 32a, enter the loss on Form 1040, line 12, and Schedule SE, line 2 (statutory employees, see instructions). If you checked 32b, you MUST attach Form 6198.
32a ☐ All investment is at risk.
32b ☐ Some investment is not at risk.

Source: "Tax Guide for Small Business—1991 Edition," *Publication 334* (Washington, D.C.: Internal Revenue Service, rev. November 1991), 138–39.

FIGURE A–1
(Continued)

Schedule C (Form 1040) 1991 — Page 2

Part III — Cost of Goods Sold *(See instructions.)*

33	Inventory at beginning of year. (If different from last year's closing inventory, attach explanation.)	33	42,843
34	Purchases less cost of items withdrawn for personal use	34	240,252
35	Cost of labor. (Do not include salary paid to yourself.)	35	
36	Materials and supplies	36	
37	Other costs	37	
38	Add lines 33 through 37	38	283,095
39	Inventory at end of year	39	43,746
40	**Cost of goods sold.** Subtract line 39 from line 38. Enter the result here and on page 1, line 4	40	239,349

Part IV — Principal Business or Professional Activity Codes

Locate the major category that best describes your activity. Within the major category, select the activity code that most closely identifies the business or profession that is the principal source of your sales or receipts. Enter this 4-digit code on page 1, line B. *For example, real estate agent is under the major category of* ***"Real Estate,"*** *and the code is "5520."* **(Note:** *If your principal source of income is from farming activities, you should file* ***Schedule F*** *(Form 1040), Profit or Loss From Farming.)*

Agricultural Services, Forestry, Fishing

Code

1990 Animal services, other than breeding
1933 Crop services
2113 Farm labor & management services
2246 Fishing, commercial
2238 Forestry, except logging
2212 Horticulture & landscaping
2469 Hunting & trapping
1974 Livestock breeding
0836 Logging
1958 Veterinary services, including pets

Construction

0018 Operative builders (for own account)

Building Trade Contractors, Including Repairs

0414 Carpentering & flooring
0455 Concrete work
0273 Electrical work
0299 Masonry, dry wall, stone, & tile
0257 Painting & paper hanging
0232 Plumbing, heating, & air conditioning
0430 Roofing, siding & sheet metal
0885 Other building trade contractors (excavation, glazing, etc.)

General Contractors

0075 Highway & street construction
0059 Nonresidential building
0034 Residential building
3889 Other heavy construction (pipe laying, bridge construction, etc.)

Finance, Insurance, & Related Services

6064 Brokers & dealers of securities
6080 Commodity contracts brokers & dealers; security & commodity exchanges
6148 Credit institutions & mortgage bankers
5702 Insurance agents or brokers
5744 Insurance services (appraisal, consulting, inspection, etc.)
6130 Investment advisors & services
5777 Other financial services

Manufacturing, Including Printing & Publishing

0679 Apparel & other textile products
1115 Electric & electronic equipment
1073 Fabricated metal products
0638 Food products & beverages
0810 Furniture & fixtures
0695 Leather footwear, handbags, etc.
0836 Lumber & other wood products
1099 Machinery & machine shops
0877 Paper & allied products
1057 Primary metal industries
0851 Printing & publishing
1032 Stone, clay, & glass products
0653 Textile mill products
1883 Other manufacturing industries

Mining & Mineral Extraction

1537 Coal mining
1511 Metal mining
1552 Oil & gas
1719 Quarrying & nonmetallic mining

Real Estate

5538 Operators & lessors of buildings, including residential
5553 Operators & lessors of other real property
5520 Real estate agents & brokers
5579 Real estate property managers
5710 Subdividers & developers, except cemeteries
6155 Title abstract offices

Services: Personal, Professional, & Business Services

Amusement & Recreational Services

9670 Bowling centers
9688 Motion picture & tape distribution & allied services
9597 Motion picture & video production
9639 Motion picture theaters
8557 Physical fitness facilities
9696 Professional sports & racing, including promoters & managers
9811 Theatrical performers, musicians, agents, producers & related services
9613 Video tape rental
9837 Other amusement & recreational services

Automotive Services

8813 Automotive rental or leasing, without driver
8953 Automotive repairs, general & specialized
8839 Parking, except valet
8896 Other automotive services (wash, towing, etc.)

Business & Personal Services

7658 Accounting & bookkeeping
7716 Advertising, except direct mail
7682 Architectural services
8318 Barber shop (or barber)
8110 Beauty shop (or beautician)
8714 Child day care
6676 Communication services
7872 Computer programming, processing, data preparation & related services
7922 Computer repair, maintenance, & leasing
7286 Consulting services
7799 Consumer credit reporting & collection services
8755 Counseling (except health practitioners)
6395 Courier or package delivery
7732 Employment agencies & personnel supply
7518 Engineering services
7773 Equipment rental & leasing (except computer or automotive)
8532 Funeral services & crematories
7633 Income tax preparation
7914 Investigative & protective services
7617 Legal services (or lawyer)
7856 Mailing, reproduction, commercial art, photography, & stenographic services
7245 Management services
8771 Ministers & chaplains
8334 Photographic studios
7260 Public relations
6536 Public warehousing
7708 Surveying services
8730 Teaching or tutoring
6510 Trash collection without own dump
6692 Utilities (dumps, snowplowing, road cleaning, etc.)
7880 Other business services
6882 Other personal services

Hotels & Other Lodging Places

7237 Camps & camping parks
7096 Hotels, motels, & tourist homes
7211 Rooming & boarding houses

Laundry & Cleaning Services

7450 Carpet & upholstery cleaning
7419 Coin-operated laundries & dry cleaning
7435 Full-service laundry, dry cleaning, & garment service
7476 Janitorial & related services (building, house, & window cleaning)

Medical & Health Services

9274 Chiropractors
9233 Dentist's office or clinic
9217 Doctor's (M.D.) office or clinic
9456 Medical & dental laboratories
9472 Nursing & personal care facilities
9290 Optometrists
9258 Osteopathic physicians & surgeons
9241 Podiatrists
9415 Registered & practical nurses
9431 Offices & clinics of other health practitioners (dieticians, midwives, speech pathologists, etc.)
9886 Other health services

Miscellaneous Repair, Except Computers

9019 Audio equipment & TV repair
9035 Electrical & electronic equipment repair, except audio & TV
9050 Furniture repair & reupholstery
2881 Other equipment repair

Trade, Retail—Selling Goods to Individuals & Households

3038 Catalog or mail order
3012 Selling door to door, by telephone or party plan, or from mobile unit
3053 Vending machine selling

Selling From Showroom, Store, or Other Fixed Location

Apparel & Accessories

3921 Accessory & specialty stores & furriers for women
3939 Clothing, family
3772 Clothing, men's & boys'
3913 Clothing, women's
3756 Shoe stores
3954 Other apparel & accessory stores

Automotive & Service Stations

3558 Gasoline service stations
3319 New car dealers (franchised)
3533 Tires, accessories, & parts
3335 Used car dealers
3517 Other automotive dealers (motorcycles, recreational vehicles, etc.)

Building, Hardware, & Garden Supply

4416 Building materials dealers
4457 Hardware stores
4473 Nurseries & garden supply stores
4432 Paint, glass, & wallpaper stores

Food & Beverages

0612 Bakeries selling at retail
3086 Catering services
3095 Drinking places (bars, taverns, pubs, saloons, etc.)
3079 Eating places, meals & snacks
3210 Grocery stores (general line)
3251 Liquor stores
3236 Specialized food stores (meat, produce, candy, health food, etc.)

Furniture & General Merchandise

3988 Computer & software stores
3970 Furniture stores
4317 Home furnishings stores (china, floor coverings, drapes)
4119 Household appliance stores
4333 Music & record stores
3996 TV, audio & electronic stores
3715 Variety stores
3731 Other general merchandise stores

Miscellaneous Retail Stores

4812 Boat dealers
5017 Book stores, excluding newsstands
4853 Camera & photo supply stores
3277 Drug stores
5058 Fabric & needlework stores
4655 Florists
5090 Fuel dealers (except gasoline)
4630 Gift, novelty & souvenir shops
4838 Hobby, toy, & game shops
4671 Jewelry stores
4895 Luggage & leather goods stores
5074 Mobile home dealers
4879 Optical goods stores
4697 Sporting goods & bicycle shops
5033 Stationery stores
4614 Used merchandise & antique stores (except motor vehicle parts)
5884 Other retail stores

Trade, Wholesale—Selling Goods to Other Businesses, etc.

Durable Goods, Including Machinery Equipment, Wood, Metals, etc.

2634 Agent or broker for other firms—more than 50% of gross sales on commission
2618 Selling for your own account

Nondurable Goods, Including Food, Fiber, Chemicals, etc.

2675 Agent or broker for other firms—more than 50% of gross sales on commission
2659 Selling for your own account

Transportation Services

6619 Air transportation
6312 Bus & limousine transportation
6361 Highway passenger transportation (except chartered service)
6114 Taxicabs
6635 Travel agents & tour operators
6338 Trucking (except trash collection)
6551 Water transportation
6650 Other transportation services

8888 **Unable to classify**

FIGURE A–1
(Continued)

SCHEDULE SE (Form 1040) Department of the Treasury Internal Revenue Service (T)	**Self-Employment Tax** ▶ See Instructions for Schedule SE (Form 1040). ▶ Attach to Form 1040.	OMB No. 1545-0074 **1991** Attachment Sequence No. 17
Name of person with self-employment income (as shown on Form 1040) Susan J. Brown	Social security number of person with self-employment income ▶	111 : 00 : 1111

Who Must File Schedule SE

You must file Schedule SE if:

- Your *net earnings from self-employment from other than church employee income* (line 4 of Short Schedule SE or line 4c of Long Schedule SE) were $400 or more; **OR**
- You had church employee income (as defined in the instructions) of $108.28 or more;

AND

- Your wages (and tips) subject to social security AND Medicare tax (or railroad retirement tax) were less than $125,000.

Exception: If your only self-employment income was from earnings as a minister, member of a religious order, or Christian Science practitioner, AND you filed **Form 4361** and received IRS approval not to be taxed on those earnings, DO NOT file Schedule SE. Instead, write "Exempt–Form 4361" on Form 1040, line 47.

Note: *Most people can use Short Schedule SE on this page. But you may have to use Long Schedule SE on the back.*

Who MUST Use Long Schedule SE (Section B)

You must use Long Schedule SE if ANY of the following apply:

- You received wages or tips **and** the total of all of your wages (and tips) subject to social security, Medicare, or railroad retirement tax plus your net earnings from self-employment is more than $53,400;
- You use either "optional method" to figure your net earnings from self-employment (see Section B, Part II, and the instructions);
- You are a minister, member of a religious order, or Christian Science practitioner and you received IRS approval (by filing Form 4361) not to be taxed on your earnings from these sources, but you owe self-employment tax on other earnings;
- You had church employee income of $108.28 or more that was reported to you on Form W-2; **OR**
- You received tips subject to social security, Medicare, or railroad retirement tax, but you did not report those tips to your employer.

Section A—Short Schedule SE (Read above to see if you must use Long Schedule SE on the back (Section B).)

1	Net farm profit or (loss) from Schedule F (Form 1040), line 37, and farm partnerships, Schedule K-1 (Form 1065), line 15a	1	
2	Net profit or (loss) from Schedule C (Form 1040), line 31, and Schedule K-1 (Form 1065), line 15a (other than farming). See instructions for other income to report	2	52,713
3	Combine lines 1 and 2	3	52,713
4	**Net earnings from self-employment.** Multiply line 3 by .9235. If less than $400, **do not** file this schedule; you **do not** owe self-employment tax. **Caution:** *If you received wages or tips, and the total of your wages (and tips) subject to social security, Medicare, or railroad retirement tax plus the amount on line 4 is more than $53,400, you cannot use Short Schedule SE. Instead, use Long Schedule SE on the back* ▶	4	48,680
5	**Self-employment tax.** If the amount on line 4 is: • $53,400 or less, multiply line 4 by 15.3% (.153) and enter the result. • More than $53,400, but less than $125,000, multiply the amount in excess of $53,400 by 2.9% (.029). Add $8,170.20 to the result and enter the total. • $125,000 or more, enter $10,246.60. Also enter this amount on Form 1040, line 47	5	7,448

Note: *Also enter one-half of the amount from line 5 on* ***Form 1040, line 25.***

For Paperwork Reduction Act Notice, see Form 1040 instructions. Cat. No. 11358Z **Schedule SE (Form 1040) 1991**

FIGURE A-2
Form 4562 (to be submitted along with schedule C)

Form **4562** | **Depreciation and Amortization** (Including Information on Listed Property) | OMB No. 1545-0172 | **1991**

Department of the Treasury Internal Revenue Service (T) | ▶ See separate instructions. ▶ Attach this form to your return. | Attachment Sequence No. 67

Name(s) shown on return: Susan J. Brown — Identifying number: 111-00-1111

Business or activity to which this form relates: Milady Fashions / Retail Ladies' Apparel

Part I — **Election To Expense Certain Tangible Property (Section 179)** (**Note:** *If you have any "Listed Property," complete Part V.*)

		Line	Amount
1	Maximum dollar limitation (see instructions)	1	$10,000
2	Total cost of section 179 property placed in service during the tax year (see instructions)	2	7,500
3	Threshold cost of section 179 property before reduction in limitation	3	$200,000
4	Reduction in limitation—Subtract line 3 from line 2, but do not enter less than -0-	4	
5	Dollar limitation for tax year—Subtract line 4 from line 1, but do not enter less than -0-	5	10,000

	(a) Description of property	(b) Cost	(c) Elected cost
6	Adding machine	200	200

		Line	Amount
7	Listed property—Enter amount from line 26	7	
8	Total elected cost of section 179 property—Add amounts in column (c), lines 6 and 7	8	200
9	Tentative deduction—Enter the lesser of line 5 or line 8	9	200
10	Carryover of disallowed deduction from 1990 (see instructions)	10	
11	Taxable income limitation—Enter the lesser of taxable income or line 5 (see instructions)	11	10,000
12	Section 179 expense deduction—Add lines 9 and 10, but do not enter more than line 11	12	200
13	Carryover of disallowed deduction to 1992—Add lines 9 and 10, less line 12 ▶	13	

Note: *Do not use Part II or Part III below for automobiles, certain other vehicles, cellular telephones, computers, or property used for entertainment, recreation, or amusement (listed property). Instead, use Part V for listed property.*

Part II — **MACRS Depreciation For Assets Placed in Service ONLY During Your 1991 Tax Year (Do Not Include Listed Property)**

(a) Classification of property	(b) Mo. and yr. placed in service	(c) Basis for depreciation (Business/investment use only—see instructions)	(d) Recovery period	(e) Convention	(f) Method	(g) Depreciation deduction
14 General Depreciation System (GDS) (see instructions):						
a 3-year property						
b 5-year property						
c 7-year property		800	7	HY	200 DB	114
d 10-year property						
e 15-year property						
f 20-year property						
g Residential rental property			27.5 yrs.	MM	S/L	
			27.5 yrs.	MM	S/L	
h Nonresidential real property			31.5 yrs.	MM	S/L	
			31.5 yrs.	MM	S/L	
15 Alternative Depreciation System (ADS) (see instructions):						
a Class life					S/L	
b 12-year			12 yrs.		S/L	
c 40-year			40 yrs.	MM	S/L	

Part III — **Other Depreciation (Do Not Include Listed Property)**

		Line	Amount
16	GDS and ADS deductions for assets placed in service in tax years beginning before 1991 (see instructions)	16	
17	Property subject to section 168(f)(1) election (see instructions)	17	
18	ACRS and other depreciation (see instructions)	18	1,117

Part IV — **Summary**

		Line	Amount
19	Listed property—Enter amount from line 25	19	1,300
20	Total—Add deductions on line 12, lines 14 and 15 in column (g), and lines 16 through 19. Enter here and on the appropriate lines of your return. (Partnerships and S corporations—see instructions)	20	2,731
21	For assets shown above and placed in service during the current year, enter the portion of the basis attributable to section 263A costs (see instructions)	21	

For Paperwork Reduction Act Notice, see page 1 of the separate instructions. Cat. No. 12906N Form 4562 (1991)

Source: "Tax Guide for Small Business—1991 Edition," *Publication 334* (Washington, D.C.: Internal Revenue Service, rev. November 1991), 140–42.

FIGURE A–2 (Continued)

Form 4562 (1991) Page 2

Part V Listed Property.—Automobiles, Certain Other Vehicles, Cellular Telephones, Computers, and Property Used for Entertainment, Recreation, or Amusement

If you are using the standard mileage rate or deducting vehicle lease expense, complete columns (a) through (c) of Section A, all of Section B, and Section C if applicable.

Section A.—Depreciation (Caution: *See instructions for limitations for automobiles.)*

22a Do you have evidence to support the business/investment use claimed? ☐ Yes ☐ No 22b If "Yes," is the evidence written? ☐ Yes ☐ No

(a) Type of property (list vehicles first)	(b) Date placed in service	(c) Business/investment use percentage	(d) Cost or other basis	(e) Basis for depreciation (business/investment use only)	(f) Recovery period	(g) Method/Convention	(h) Depreciation deduction	(i) Elected section 179 cost
23 *Property used more than 50% in a qualified business use (see instructions):*								
USA 280 S Van	3/20/91	75%	8,667	6,500	5 YRS	200 DB/HY	1,300	0
		%						
		%						
24 *Property used 50% or less in a qualified business use (see instructions):*								
		%				S/L –		
		%				S/L –		
		%				S/L –		

25 Add amounts in column (h). Enter the total here and on line 19, page 1 . . . . . . 25 1,300

26 Add amounts in column (i). Enter the total here and on line 7, page 1 26

Section B.—Information Regarding Use of Vehicles—*If you deduct expenses for vehicles:*

- *Always complete this section for vehicles used by a sole proprietor, partner, or other "more than 5% owner," or related person.*
- *If you provided vehicles to your employees, first answer the questions in Section C to see if you meet an exception to completing this section for those vehicles.*

	(a) Vehicle 1		(b) Vehicle 2		(c) Vehicle 3		(d) Vehicle 4		(e) Vehicle 5		(f) Vehicle 6	
27 Total business/investment miles driven during the year (DO NOT include commuting miles).	7,500											
28 Total commuting miles driven during the year	2,025											
29 Total other personal (noncommuting) miles driven	475											
30 Total miles driven during the year—Add lines 27 through 29	10,000											
	Yes	No	Yes	No	Yes	No	Yes	No	Yes	No	Yes	No
31 Was the vehicle available for personal use during off-duty hours?	✓											
32 Was the vehicle used primarily by a more than 5% owner or related person? . .	✓											
33 Is another vehicle available for personal use?	✓											

Section C.—Questions for Employers Who Provide Vehicles for Use by Their Employees
(Answer these questions to determine if you meet an exception to completing Section B. **Note:** *Section B must always be completed for vehicles used by sole proprietors, partners, or other more than 5% owners or related persons.)*

	Yes	No
34 Do you maintain a written policy statement that prohibits all personal use of vehicles, including commuting, by your employees?		
35 Do you maintain a written policy statement that prohibits personal use of vehicles, except commuting, by your employees? (See instructions for vehicles used by corporate officers, directors, or 1% or more owners.) .		
36 Do you treat all use of vehicles by employees as personal use?		
37 Do you provide more than five vehicles to your employees and retain the information received from your employees concerning the use of the vehicles?		
38 Do you meet the requirements concerning qualified automobile demonstration use (see instructions)? . .		

Note: *If your answer to 34, 35, 36, 37, or 38 is "Yes," you need not complete Section B for the covered vehicles.*

Part VI Amortization

(a) Description of costs	(b) Date amortization begins	(c) Amortizable amount	(d) Code section	(e) Amortization period or percentage	(f) Amortization for this year
39 Amortization of costs that begins during your 1991 tax year:					

40 Amortization of costs that began before 1991 40

41 Total. Enter here and on "Other Deductions" or "Other Expenses" line of your return 41

FIGURE A-3
Form 1065

Form **1065** Department of the Treasury Internal Revenue Service

U.S. Partnership Return of Income

For calendar year 1991, or tax year beginning ...., 1991, and ending ...., 19....

▶ See separate instructions.

OMB No. 1545-0099

1991

A Principal business activity: Retail	Use the IRS label. Otherwise, please print or type.	10-9876543 DEC91 D71	D Employer identification number: 10-9876543
B Principal product or service: Books		AbleBee Book Store	E Date business started: 10/1/78
		334 WEST MAIN STREET	
C Business code number: 5942		ANYTOWN MD 20904	F Total assets (see Specific Instructions): $ 45,391

G Check applicable boxes: (1) ☐ Initial return (2) ☐ Final return (3) ☐ Change in address (4) ☐ Amended return

H Check accounting method: (1) ☐ Cash (2) ☑ Accrual (3) ☐ Other (specify) ▶ ....

I Number of partners in this partnership ▶ 2

Caution: *Include **only** trade or business income and expenses on lines 1a through 22 below. See the instructions for more information.*

Section	Line	Description	Sub-line	Sub-amount	Line	Amount
Income	1a	Gross receipts or sales	1a	409,465		
	b	Less returns and allowances	1b	3,365	1c	406,100
	2	Cost of goods sold (Schedule A, line 8)			2	267,641
	3	Gross profit. Subtract line 2 from line 1c			3	138,459
	4	Ordinary income (loss) from other partnerships and fiduciaries *(attach schedule)*			4	
	5	Net farm profit (loss) *(attach Schedule F (Form 1040))*			5	
	6	Net gain (loss) from Form 4797, Part II, line 18			6	
	7	Other income (loss) (see instructions) *(attach schedule)*			7	559
	8	**Total income (loss).** Combine lines 3 through 7			8	139,018
Deductions (see instructions for limitations)	9a	Salaries and wages (other than to partners)	9a	29,350		
	b	Less jobs credit	9b		9c	29,350
	10	Guaranteed payments to partners			10	25,000
	11	Rent			11	20,000
	12	Interest			12	1,451
	13	Taxes			13	3,295
	14	Bad debts			14	250
	15	Repairs			15	1,125
	16a	Depreciation (see instructions)	16a	1,174		
	b	Less depreciation reported on Schedule A and elsewhere on return	16b		16c	1,174
	17	Depletion **(Do not deduct oil and gas depletion.)**			17	
	18	Retirement plans, etc.			18	
	19	Employee benefit programs			19	
	20	Other deductions *(attach schedule)*			20	8,003
	21	**Total deductions.** Add the amounts shown in the far right column for lines 9c through 20			21	89,648
	22	**Ordinary income (loss)** from trade or business activities. Subtract line 21 from line 8			22	49,370

Please Sign Here

Under penalties of perjury, I declare that I have examined this return, including accompanying schedules and statements, and to the best of my knowledge and belief, it is true, correct, and complete. Declaration of preparer (other than general partner) is based on all information of which preparer has any knowledge.

▶ Frank W. Able — Signature of general partner ▶ 3/27/92 — Date

Paid Preparer's Use Only

Preparer's signature ▶ | Date | Check if self-employed ▶ ☐ | Preparer's social security no.

Firm's name (or yours if self-employed) and address ▶ | E.I. No. ▶ | ZIP code ▶

For Paperwork Reduction Act Notice, see page 1 of separate instructions. Cat. No. 11390Z Form **1065** (1991)

Source: "Tax Guide for Small Business—1991 Edition," *Publication 334* (Washington, D.C.: Internal Revenue Service, rev. November 1991), 145–47.

FIGURE A-3
(Continued)

Form 1065 (1991) Page 2

Schedule A Cost of Goods Sold

1	Inventory at beginning of year	1	18,125
2	Purchases less cost of items withdrawn for personal use	2	268,741
3	Cost of labor	3	
4	Additional section 263A costs (see instructions) *(attach schedule)*	4	
5	Other costs *(attach schedule)*	5	
6	**Total.** Add lines 1 through 5	6	286,866
7	Inventory at end of year	7	19,225
8	**Cost of goods sold.** Subtract line 7 from line 6. Enter here and on page 1, line 2	8	267,641

9a Check all methods used for valuing closing inventory:
(i) ☐ Cost
(ii) ☑ Lower of cost or market as described in Regulations section 1.471-4
(iii) ☐ Writedown of "subnormal" goods as described in Regulations section 1.471-2(c)
(iv) ☐ Other (specify method used and attach explanation) ▶
b Check this box if the LIFO inventory method was adopted this tax year for any goods *(if checked, attach Form 970)* ▶ ☐
c Do the rules of section 263A (for property produced or acquired for resale) apply to the partnership? ☐ **Yes** ☑ **No**
d Was there any change in determining quantities, cost, or valuations between opening and closing inventory? ☐ **Yes** ☑ **No**
If "Yes," attach explanation.

Schedule B Other Information

		Yes	No
1	Is this partnership a limited partnership?		✓
2	Are any partners in this partnership also partnerships?		✓
3	Is this partnership a partner in another partnership?		✓
4	Is this partnership subject to the consolidated audit procedures of sections 6221 through 6233? If "Yes," see **Designation of Tax Matters Partner** below		✓
5	Does this partnership meet **all** the requirements shown in the instructions for **Question 5?**		✓
6	Does this partnership have any foreign partners?		✓
7	Is this partnership a publicly traded partnership as defined in section 469(k)(2)?		✓
8	Has this partnership filed, or is it required to file, **Form 8264,** Application for Registration of a Tax Shelter?		✓
9	At any time during the tax year, did the partnership have an interest in or a signature or other authority over a financial account in a foreign country (such as a bank account, securities account, or other financial account)? (See the instructions for exceptions and filing requirements for form TD F 90-22.1.) If "Yes," enter the name of the foreign country. ▶		✓
10	Was the partnership the grantor of, or transferor to, a foreign trust which existed during the current tax year, whether or not the partnership or any partner has any beneficial interest in it? If "Yes," you may have to file Forms 3520, 3520-A, or 926		✓
11	Was there a distribution of property or a transfer (for example, by sale or death) of a partnership interest during the tax year? If "Yes," you may elect to adjust the basis of the partnership's assets under section 754 by attaching the statement described under **Elections** on page 5 of the instructions		✓

Designation of Tax Matters Partner (See instructions.)

Enter below the general partner designated as the tax matters partner (TMP) for the tax year of this return.

Name of designated TMP ▶ Identifying number of TMP ▶

Address of designated TMP ▶

FIGURE A–3 (Continued)

Form 1065 (1991) Page 3

Schedule K Partners' Shares of Income, Credits, Deductions, Etc.

	(a) Distributive share items		(b) Total amount
Income (Loss)	1 Ordinary income (loss) from trade or business activities (page 1, line 22)	1	49,370
	2 Net income (loss) from rental real estate activities *(attach Form 8825)*	2	
	3a Gross income from other rental activities — 3a		
	b Less expenses *(attach schedule)* — 3b		
	c Net income (loss) from other rental activities	3c	
	4 Portfolio income (loss) (see instructions):		
	a Interest income	4a	
	b Dividend income	4b	150
	c Royalty income	4c	
	d Net short-term capital gain (loss) *(attach Schedule D (Form 1065))*	4d	
	e Net long-term capital gain (loss) *(attach Schedule D (Form 1065))*	4e	
	f Other portfolio income (loss) *(attach schedule)*	4f	
	5 Guaranteed payments to partners	5	25,000
	6 Net gain (loss) under section 1231 (other than due to casualty or theft) *(attach Form 4797)*	6	
	7 Other income (loss) *(attach schedule)*	7	
Deductions	8 Charitable contributions (see instructions) *(attach list)*	8	650
	9 Section 179 expense deduction *(attach Form 4562)*	9	
	10 Deductions related to portfolio income (see instructions) (itemize)	10	
	11 Other deductions *(attach schedule)*	11	
Investment Interest	12a Interest expense on investment debts	12a	
	b (1) Investment income included on lines 4a through 4f above	12b(1)	150
	(2) Investment expenses included on line 10 above	12b(2)	
Credits	13a Credit for income tax withheld	13a	
	b Low-income housing credit (see instructions):		
	(1) From partnerships to which section 42(j)(5) applies for property placed in service before 1990	13b(1)	
	(2) Other than on line 13b(1) for property placed in service before 1990	13b(2)	
	(3) From partnerships to which section 42(j)(5) applies for property placed in service after 1989	13b(3)	
	(4) Other than on line 13b(3) for property placed in service after 1989	13b(4)	
	c Qualified rehabilitation expenditures related to rental real estate activities *(attach Form 3468)*	13c	
	d Credits (other than credits shown on lines 13b and 13c) related to rental real estate activities (see instructions)	13d	
	e Credits related to other rental activities (see instructions)	13e	
	14 Other credits (see instructions)	14	
Self-Employment	15a Net earnings (loss) from self-employment	15a	74,370
	b Gross farming or fishing income	15b	
	c Gross nonfarm income	15c	
Adjustments and Tax Preference Items	16a Accelerated depreciation of real property placed in service before 1987	16a	
	b Accelerated depreciation of leased personal property placed in service before 1987	16b	
	c Depreciation adjustment on property placed in service after 1986	16c	
	d Depletion (other than oil and gas)	16d	
	e (1) Gross income from oil, gas, and geothermal properties	16e(1)	
	(2) Deductions allocable to oil, gas, and geothermal properties	16e(2)	
	f Other adjustments and tax preference items *(attach schedule)*	16f	
Foreign Taxes	17a Type of income ▶ .... b Foreign country or U.S. possession ▶		
	c Total gross income from sources outside the U.S. *(attach schedule)*	17c	
	d Total applicable deductions and losses *(attach schedule)*	17d	
	e Total foreign taxes (check one): ▶ ☐ Paid ☐ Accrued	17e	
	f Reduction in taxes available for credit *(attach schedule)*	17f	
	g Other foreign tax information *(attach schedule)*	17g	
Other	18a Total expenditures to which a section 59(e) election may apply	18a	
	b Type of expenditures ▶		
	19 Other items and amounts required to be reported separately to partners (see instructions) *(attach schedule)*		
Analysis	20a Income (loss). Combine lines 1 through 7 in column (b). From the result, subtract the sum of lines 8 through 12a, 17e, and 18a	20a	73,870

b Analysis by type of partner:	(a) Corporate	(b) Individual i. Active	(b) Individual ii. Passive	(c) Partnership	(d) Exempt organization	(e) Nominee/Other
(1) General partners		73,870				
(2) Limited partners						

FIGURE A–4
Schedule K-1 (Form 1065)

SCHEDULE K-1 (Form 1065) Department of the Treasury Internal Revenue Service

Partner's Share of Income, Credits, Deductions, Etc.

▶ See separate instructions.

For calendar year 1991 or tax year beginning , 1991, and ending , 19

OMB No. 1545-0099 — **1991**

Partner's identifying number ▶ 123 - 00 - 6789 | **Partnership's identifying number ▶** 10 - 9876543

Partner's name, address, and ZIP code: Frank W. Able, 10 Green Street, Anytown, MD 20904

Partnership's name, address, and ZIP code: AbleBee Book Store, 334 West Main Street, Anytown, MD 20904

A Is this partner a general partner? ☑ Yes ☐ No

B Partner's share of liabilities (see instructions):
Nonrecourse . . . $
Qualified nonrecourse financing . . $
Other . . . $ 10,900

C What type of entity is this partner? ▶ Individual

D Is this partner a ☑ domestic or a ☐ foreign partner?

E IRS Center where partnership filed return: Philadelphia

F Enter partner's percentage of: (i) Before change or termination / (ii) End of year
Profit sharing . . . % 50 %
Loss sharing . . . % 50 %
Ownership of capital . . . % 50 %

G(1) Tax shelter registration number ▶ N/A

(2) Type of tax shelter ▶

H Check here if this partnership is a publicly traded partnership as defined in section 469(k)(2) . . . . ☐

I Check applicable boxes: (1) ☐ Final K-1 (2) ☐ Amended K-1

J **Analysis of partner's capital account:**

(a) Capital account at beginning of year	(b) Capital contributed during year	(c) Partner's share of lines 3, 4, and 7, Form 1065, Schedule M-2	(d) Withdrawals and distributions	(e) Capital account at end of year (combine columns (a) through (d))
14,050		24,460	(26,440)	12,070

	(a) Distributive share item		(b) Amount	(c) 1040 filers enter the amount in column (b) on:
Income (Loss)	1 Ordinary income (loss) from trade or business activities	1	24,685	(See Partner's Instructions for Schedule K-1 (Form 1065).)
	2 Net income (loss) from rental real estate activities	2		
	3 Net income (loss) from other rental activities	3		
	4 Portfolio income (loss):			
	a Interest	4a		Sch. B, Part I, line 1
	b Dividends	4b	75	Sch. B, Part II, line 5
	c Royalties	4c		Sch. E, Part I, line 4
	d Net short-term capital gain (loss)	4d		Sch. D, line 4, col. (f) or (g)
	e Net long-term capital gain (loss)	4e		Sch. D, line 11, col. (f) or (g)
	f Other portfolio income (loss) *(attach schedule)*	4f		(Enter on applicable line of your return.)
	5 Guaranteed payments to partner	5	20,000	(See Partner's Instructions for Schedule K-1 (Form 1065).)
	6 Net gain (loss) under section 1231 (other than due to casualty or theft)	6		
	7 Other income (loss) *(attach schedule)*	7		(Enter on applicable line of your return.)
Deductions	8 Charitable contributions (see instructions) *(attach schedule)*	8	325	Sch. A, line 13 or 14
	9 Section 179 expense deduction	9		(See Partner's Instructions for Schedule K-1 (Form 1065).)
	10 Deductions related to portfolio income *(attach schedule)*	10		
	11 Other deductions *(attach schedule)*	11		
Investment Interest	12a Interest expense on investment debts	12a		Form 4952, line 1
	b (1) Investment income included on lines 4a through 4f above	b(1)	75	(See Partner's Instructions for Schedule K-1 (Form 1065).)
	(2) Investment expenses included on line 10 above	b(2)		
Credits	13a Credit for income tax withheld	13a		(See Partner's Instructions for Schedule K-1 (Form 1065).)
	b Low-income housing credit:			
	(1) From section 42(j)(5) partnerships for property placed in service before 1990	b(1)		Form 8586, line 5
	(2) Other than on line 13b(1) for property placed in service before 1990	b(2)		
	(3) From section 42(j)(5) partnerships for property placed in service after 1989	b(3)		
	(4) Other than on line 13b(3) for property placed in service after 1989	b(4)		
	c Qualified rehabilitation expenditures related to rental real estate activities (see instructions)	13c		(See Partner's Instructions for Schedule K-1 (Form 1065).)
	d Credits (other than credits shown on lines 13b and 13c) related to rental real estate activities (see instructions)	13d		
	e Credits related to other rental activities (see instructions)	13e		
	14 Other credits (see instructions)	14		

For Paperwork Reduction Act Notice, see Instructions for Form 1065. Cat. No. 11394R **Schedule K-1 (Form 1065) 1991**

Source: "Tax Guide for Small Business—1991 Edition," *Publication 334* (Washington, D.C.: Internal Revenue Service, rev. November 1991), 148–50.

FIGURE A-4
(Continued)

Schedule K-1 (Form 1065) 1991 Page 2

		(a) Distributive share item		(b) Amount	(c) 1040 filers enter the amount in column (b) on:
Self-employment	15a	Net earnings (loss) from self-employment	15a	44,685	Sch. SE, Section A or B
	b	Gross farming or fishing income	15b		(See Partner's Instructions for Schedule K-1 (Form 1065).)
	c	Gross nonfarm income	15c		
Adjustments and Tax Preference Items	16a	Accelerated depreciation of real property placed in service before 1987	16a		(See Partner's Instructions for Schedule K-1 (Form 1065) and Instructions for Form 6251.)
	b	Accelerated depreciation of leased personal property placed in service before 1987	16b		
	c	Depreciation adjustment on property placed in service after 1986	16c		
	d	Depletion (other than oil and gas)	16d		
	e	(1) Gross income from oil, gas, and geothermal properties	e(1)		
		(2) Deductions allocable to oil, gas, and geothermal properties	e(2)		
	f	Other adjustments and tax preference items *(attach schedule)*	16f		
Foreign Taxes	17a	Type of income ▶			Form 1116, Check boxes
	b	Name of foreign country or U.S. possession ▶			Form 1116, Part I
	c	Total gross income from sources outside the U.S. *(attach schedule)*	17c		
	d	Total applicable deductions and losses *(attach schedule)*	17d		
	e	Total foreign taxes (check one): ▶ ☐ Paid ☐ Accrued	17e		Form 1116, Part II
	f	Reduction in taxes available for credit *(attach schedule)*	17f		Form 1116, Part III
	g	Other foreign tax information *(attach schedule)*	17g		See Instructions for Form 1116.
Other	18a	Total expenditures to which a section 59(e) election may apply	18a		See Partner's Instructions for Schedule K-1 (Form 1065).
	b	Type of expenditures ▶			
	19	Recapture of low-income housing credit:			
	a	From section 42(j)(5) partnerships	19a		Form 8611, line 8
	b	Other than on line 19a	19b		

Supplemental Information

20 Supplemental information required to be reported separately to each partner *(attach additional schedules if more space is needed)*:

$25 Tax-exempt Interest – Municipal Bonds

FIGURE A–4
(Continued)

Form 1065 (1991) Page **4**

Caution: *Read the instructions for* ***Question 5*** *of Schedule B on page 14 of the instructions before completing Schedules L, M-1, and M-2.*

Schedule L **Balance Sheets**

Assets	Beginning of tax year (a)	(b)	End of tax year (c)	(d)
1 Cash		3,455		3,350
2a Trade notes and accounts receivable	7,150		10,990	
b Less allowance for bad debts		7,150		10,990
3 Inventories		18,125		19,225
4 U.S. government obligations				
5 Tax-exempt securities		1,000		1,000
6 Other current assets *(attach schedule)*				
7 Mortgage and real estate loans				
8 Other investments *(attach schedule)*		1,000		1,000
9a Buildings and other depreciable assets	15,000		15,000	
b Less accumulated depreciation	4,000	11,000	5,174	9,826
10a Depletable assets				
b Less accumulated depletion				
11 Land (net of any amortization)				
12a Intangible assets (amortizable only)				
b Less accumulated amortization				
13 Other assets *(attach schedule)*				
14 **Total** assets		41,730		45,391
Liabilities and Capital				
15 Accounts payable		10,180		10,462
16 Mortgages, notes, bonds payable in less than 1 year		4,000		3,600
17 Other current liabilities *(attach schedule)*				
18 All nonrecourse loans				
19 Mortgages, notes, bonds payable in 1 year or more				7,739
20 Other liabilities *(attach schedule)*				
21 Partners' capital accounts		27,550		23,590
22 **Total** liabilities and capital		41,730		45,391

Schedule M-1 **Reconciliation of Income per Books With Income per Return**

1 Net income per books	48,920	5 Income recorded on books this year not included on Schedule K, lines 1 through 7 (itemize): a Tax-exempt interest $ 50	50
2 Income included on Schedule K, lines 1 through 7, not recorded on books this year (itemize): Guaranteed Payments	25,000	6 Deductions included on Schedule K, lines 1 through 12a, 17e, and 18a, not charged against book income this year (itemize): a Depreciation $	
3 Expenses recorded on books this year not included on Schedule K, lines 1 through 12a, 17e, and 18a (itemize): a Depreciation $ b Travel and entertainment $		7 Total of lines 5 and 6	50
4 Total of lines 1 through 3	73,920	8 Income (loss) (Schedule K, line 20a). Line 4 less line 7	73,870

Schedule M-2 **Analysis of Partners' Capital Accounts**

1 Balance at beginning of year	27,550	6 Distributions: a Cash	52,880
2 Capital contributed during year		b Property	
3 Net income per books	48,920	7 Other decreases (itemize):	
4 Other increases (itemize):			
		8 Total of lines 6 and 7	52,880
5 Total of lines 1 through 4	76,470	9 Balance at end of year. Line 5 less line 8	23,590

FIGURE A–5
Form 1120

Form **1120** — Department of the Treasury, Internal Revenue Service

U.S. Corporation Income Tax Return

For calendar year 1991 or tax year beginning ...., 1991, ending ...., 19 ...
► **Instructions are separate. See page 1 for Paperwork Reduction Act Notice.**

OMB No. 1545-0123 — **1991**

A Check if a—
(1) Consolidated return (attach Form 851) ☐
(2) Personal holding co. (attach Sch. PH) ☐
(3) Personal service corp. (as defined in Temp. Regs. sec. 1.441-4T—see instructions) ☐

Use IRS label. Otherwise, please print or type.

10-0395674 DEC91 071 3998
TENTEX TOYS, INC.
36 DIVISION STREET
ANYTOWN, IL 60930

B Employer identification number
C Date incorporated: 3-1-72
D Total assets (see Specific Instructions): $ 879,417

E Check applicable boxes: (1) ☐ Initial return (2) ☐ Final return (3) ☐ Change in address

Income

Line	Description		Amount
1a	Gross receipts or sales 2,010,000 b Less returns and allowances 20,000 c Bal ►	1c	1,990,000
2	Cost of goods sold (Schedule A, line 7)	2	1,520,000
3	Gross profit. Subtract line 2 from line 1c	3	470,000
4	Dividends (Schedule C, line 19)	4	10,000
5	Interest	5	5,500
6	Gross rents	6	
7	Gross royalties	7	
8	Capital gain net income (attach Schedule D (Form 1120))	8	
9	Net gain or (loss) from Form 4797, Part II, line 18 (attach Form 4797)	9	
10	Other income (see instructions—attach schedule)	10	
11	**Total income.** Add lines 3 through 10 ►	11	485,500

Deductions (See instructions for limitations on deductions.)

Line	Description		Amount
12	Compensation of officers (Schedule E, line 4)	12	70,000
13a	Salaries and wages 44,000 b Less jobs credit 6,000 c Balance ►	13c	38,000
14	Repairs	14	800
15	Bad debts	15	1,600
16	Rents	16	9,200
17	Taxes	17	15,000
18	Interest	18	27,200
19	Contributions (**see instructions for 10% limitation**)	19	23,150
20	Depreciation (attach Form 4562) — 20: 17,600		
21	Less depreciation claimed on Schedule A and elsewhere on return — 21a: 12,400	21b	5,200
22	Depletion	22	
23	Advertising	23	8,700
24	Pension, profit-sharing, etc., plans	24	
25	Employee benefit programs	25	
26	Other deductions (attach schedule)	26	78,300
27	**Total deductions.** Add lines 12 through 26 ►	27	277,150
28	Taxable income before net operating loss deduction and special deductions. Subtract line 27 from line 11	28	208,350
29	**Less:** a Net operating loss deduction (see instructions) — 29a		
	b Special deductions (Schedule C, line 20) — 29b: 8,000	29c	8,000

Tax and Payments

Line	Description		Amount
30	**Taxable income.** Subtract line 29c from line 28	30	200,350
31	**Total tax** (Schedule J, line 10)	31	55,387
32	**Payments:** a 1990 overpayment credited to 1991 — 32a		
b	1991 estimated tax payments — 32b: 69,117		
c	Less 1991 refund applied for on Form 4466 — 32c ( ) d Bal ► 32d: 69,117		
e	Tax deposited with Form 7004 — 32e		
f	Credit from regulated investment companies (attach Form 2439) — 32f		
g	Credit for Federal tax on fuels (attach Form 4136). See instructions — 32g	32h	69,117
33	Estimated tax penalty (see page 4 of instructions). Check if Form 2220 is attached ► ☐	33	
34	**Tax due.** If the total of lines 31 and 33 is larger than line 32h, enter amount owed	34	
35	**Overpayment.** If line 32h is larger than the total of lines 31 and 33, enter amount overpaid	35	13,730
36	Enter amount of line 35 you want: **Credited to 1992 estimated tax** ► 13,730 **Refunded** ►	36	

Please Sign Here

Under penalties of perjury, I declare that I have examined this return, including accompanying schedules and statements, and to the best of my knowledge and belief, it is true, correct, and complete. Declaration of preparer (other than taxpayer) is based on all information of which preparer has any knowledge.

James Q. Barclay — Signature of officer | 3-7-92 — Date | President — Title

Paid Preparer's Use Only

Preparer's signature | Date | Check if self-employed ☐ | Preparer's social security number
Firm's name (or yours if self-employed) and address | E.I. No. ► | ZIP code ►

Cat. No. 11450Q

Source: "Tax Guide for Small Business—1991 Edition," *Publication 334* (Washington, D.C.: Internal Revenue Service, rev. November 1991), 156–59.

FIGURE A-5
(Continued)

Form 1120 (1991) Page 2

Schedule A **Cost of Goods Sold** (See instructions.)

1	Inventory at beginning of year	1	126,000
2	Purchases	2	1,127,100
3	Cost of labor	3	402,000
4a	Additional section 263A costs (see instructions—attach schedule)	4a	40,000
b	Other costs (attach schedule)	4b	123,300
5	**Total.** Add lines 1 through 4b	5	1,818,400
6	Inventory at end of year	6	298,400
7	**Cost of goods sold.** Subtract line 6 from line 5. Enter here and on line 2, page 1	7	1,520,000

8a Check all methods used for valuing closing inventory:
(i) ☐ Cost (ii) ☑ Lower of cost or market as described in Regulations section 1.471-4 (see instructions)
(iii) ☐ Writedown of "subnormal" goods as described in Regulations section 1.471-2(c) (see instructions)
(iv) ☐ Other (Specify method used and attach explanation.) ▶

b Check if the LIFO inventory method was adopted this tax year for any goods (If checked, attach Form 970) ▶ ☐

c If the LIFO inventory method was used for this tax year, enter percentage (or amounts) of closing inventory computed under LIFO | 8c |

d Do the rules of section 263A (for property produced or acquired for resale) apply to the corporation? ☑ Yes ☐ No

e Was there any change in determining quantities, cost, or valuations between opening and closing inventory? If "Yes," attach explanation ☐ Yes ☑ No

Schedule C **Dividends and Special Deductions** (See instructions.)

		(a) Dividends received	(b) %	(c) Special deductions: (a) × (b)
1	Dividends from less-than-20%-owned domestic corporations that are subject to the 70% deduction (other than debt-financed stock)		70	
2	Dividends from 20%-or-more-owned domestic corporations that are subject to the 80% deduction (other than debt-financed stock)	10,000	80	8,000
3	Dividends on debt-financed stock of domestic and foreign corporations (section 246A)		see instructions	
4	Dividends on certain preferred stock of less-than-20%-owned public utilities		41.176	
5	Dividends on certain preferred stock of 20%-or-more-owned public utilities		47.059	
6	Dividends from less-than-20%-owned foreign corporations and certain FSCs that are subject to the 70% deduction		70	
7	Dividends from 20%-or-more-owned foreign corporations and certain FSCs that are subject to the 80% deduction		80	
8	Dividends from wholly owned foreign subsidiaries subject to the 100% deduction (section 245(b))		100	
9	**Total.** Add lines 1 through 8. See instructions for limitation			8,000
10	Dividends from domestic corporations received by a small business investment company operating under the Small Business Investment Act of 1958		100	
11	Dividends from certain FSCs that are subject to the 100% deduction (section 245(c)(1))		100	
12	Dividends from affiliated group members subject to the 100% deduction (section 243(a)(3))		100	
13	Other dividends from foreign corporations not included on lines 3, 6, 7, 8, or 11			
14	Income from controlled foreign corporations under subpart F (attach Forms 5471)			
15	Foreign dividend gross-up (section 78)			
16	IC-DISC and former DISC dividends not included on lines 1, 2, or 3 (section 246(d))			
17	Other dividends			
18	Deduction for dividends paid on certain preferred stock of public utilities (see instructions)			
19	**Total dividends.** Add lines 1 through 17. Enter here and on line 4, page 1 ▶	10,000		
20	**Total deductions.** Add lines 9, 10, 11, 12, and 18. Enter here and on line 29b, page 1 ▶			8,000

Schedule E **Compensation of Officers** (See instructions for line 12, page 1.)

Complete Schedule E only if total receipts (line 1a plus lines 4 through 10 of page 1, Form 1120) are $500,000 or more.

	(a) Name of officer	(b) Social security number	(c) Percent of time devoted to business	Percent of corporation stock owned (d) Common	(e) Preferred	(f) Amount of compensation
1	James Q. Barclay	581-00-0936	100 %	45 %	%	55,000
			%	%	%	
	George M. Collins	447-00-2604	100 %	15 %	%	31,000
			%	%	%	
	Samuel Adams	401-00-2611	50 %	2 %	%	14,000
2	Total compensation of officers					100,000
3	**Less:** Compensation of officers claimed on Schedule A and elsewhere on return					(30,000)
4	Compensation of officers deducted on line 12, page 1					70,000

FIGURE A–5
(Continued)

Form 1120 (1991) Page 3

Schedule J — Tax Computation

1	Check if you are a member of a controlled group (see sections 1561 and 1563) . . . . ▶ ☐		
2	If the box on line 1 is checked:		
a	Enter your share of the $50,000 and $25,000 taxable income bracket amounts (in that order): (i) $ (ii) $		
b	Enter your share of the additional 5% tax (not to exceed $11,750) . . . . ▶ $		
3	Income tax (see instructions to figure the tax). Check this box if the corporation is a qualified personal service corporation (see instructions on page 13) . . . ▶ ☐	3	61,387
4a	Foreign tax credit (attach Form 1118) . . . 4a		
b	Possessions tax credit (attach Form 5735) . . . 4b		
c	Orphan drug credit (attach Form 6765) . . . 4c		
d	Credit for fuel produced from a nonconventional source (see instructions) . . . 4d		
e	General business credit. Enter here and check which forms are attached: ☐ Form 3800 ☐ Form 3468 ☑ Form 5884 ☐ Form 6478 ☐ Form 6765 ☐ Form 8586 ☐ Form 8830 ☐ Form 8826 . . . 4e 6,000		
f	Credit for prior year minimum tax (attach Form 8827) . . . 4f		
5	**Total.** Add lines 4a through 4f . . .	5	6,000
6	Subtract line 5 from line 3 . . .	6	55,387
7	Personal holding company tax (attach Schedule PH (Form 1120)) . . .	7	
8	Recapture taxes. Check if from: ☐ Form 4255 ☐ Form 8611 . . .	8	
9a	Alternative minimum tax (attach Form 4626). See instructions . . .	9a	
b	Environmental tax (attach Form 4626) . . .	9b	
10	**Total tax.** Add lines 6 through 9b. Enter here and on line 31, page 1 . . .	10	55,387

Schedule K — Other Information (See page 15 of the instructions.)

		Yes	No
1	Check method of accounting: a ☐ Cash b ☑ Accrual c ☐ Other (specify) ▶		
2	Refer to the list in the instructions and state the principal: a Business activity code no. ▶ 3998 b Business activity ▶ Manufacturing c Product or service ▶ Toys		
3	Did the corporation at the end of the tax year own, directly or indirectly, 50% or more of the voting stock of a domestic corporation? (For rules of attribution, see section 267(c).) . . . If "Yes," attach a schedule showing: (a) name, address, and identifying number; (b) percentage owned; and (c) taxable income or (loss) before NOL and special deductions of such corporation for the tax year ending with or within your tax year.		✓
4	Did any individual, partnership, corporation, estate, or trust at the end of the tax year own, directly or indirectly, 50% or more of the corporation's voting stock? (For rules of attribution, see section 267(c).) If "Yes," complete a and b . . . a Attach a schedule showing name, address, and identifying number. b Enter percentage owned ▶		✓
5	Did one foreign person (see instructions for definition) at any time during the tax year own at least 25% of: a The total voting power of all classes of stock of the corporation entitled to vote, or b The total value of all classes of stock of the corporation? If "Yes," the corporation may have to file Form 5472. If "Yes," enter owner's country(ies) ▶ .... Enter number of Forms 5472 attached ▶		✓
6	Was the corporation a U.S. shareholder of any controlled foreign corporation? (See sections 951 and 957.) . . If "Yes," attach Form 5471 for each such corporation. Enter number of Forms 5471 attached ▶		✓
7	At any time during the tax year, did the corporation have an interest in or a signature or other authority over a financial account in a foreign country (such as a bank account, securities account, or other financial account)? (See page 15 of the instructions for more information, including filing requirements for Form TD F 90-22.1.) If "Yes," enter name of foreign country ▶		✓
8	Was the corporation the grantor of, or transferor to, a foreign trust that existed during the current tax year, whether or not the corporation has any beneficial interest in it? . . . If "Yes," the corporation may have to file Forms 3520, 3520-A, or 926.		✓
9	During this tax year, did the corporation pay dividends (other than stock dividends and distributions in exchange for stock) in excess of the corporation's current and accumulated earnings and profits? (See sections 301 and 316.) . . . If "Yes," file Form 5452. If this is a consolidated return, answer here for parent corporation and on **Form 851,** Affiliations Schedule, for each subsidiary.		✓
10	Check this box if the corporation issued publicly offered debt instruments with original issue discount . . ▶ ☐ If so, the corporation may have to file Form 8281.		
11	Enter the amount of tax-exempt interest received or accrued during the tax year ▶ $ 5,000		
12	**If there were 35 or fewer shareholders at the end of the tax year, enter the number ▶**		

FIGURE A–5
(Continued)

Form 1120 (1991) Page 4

Schedule L — Balance Sheets

Assets		Beginning of tax year (a)	(b)	End of tax year (c)	(d)
1	Cash		14,700		28,331
2a	Trade notes and accounts receivable	98,400		103,700	
b	Less allowance for bad debts	( )	98,400	( )	103,700
3	Inventories		126,000		298,400
4	U.S. government obligations				
5	Tax-exempt securities (see instructions)		100,000		120,000
6	Other current assets (attach schedule)		26,300		17,266
7	Loans to stockholders				
8	Mortgage and real estate loans				
9	Other investments (attach schedule)		100,000		80,000
10a	Buildings and other depreciable assets	272,400		296,700	
b	Less accumulated depreciation	(88,300)	184,100	(104,280)	192,420
11a	Depletable assets				
b	Less accumulated depletion	( )		( )	
12	Land (net of any amortization)		20,000		20,000
13a	Intangible assets (amortizable only)				
b	Less accumulated amortization	( )		( )	
14	Other assets (attach schedule)		14,800		19,300
15	Total assets		684,300		879,417
	Liabilities and Stockholders' Equity				
16	Accounts payable		28,500		34,834
17	Mortgages, notes, bonds payable in less than 1 year		4,300		4,300
18	Other current liabilities (attach schedule)		6,800		7,400
19	Loans from stockholders				
20	Mortgages, notes, bonds payable in 1 year or more		176,700		264,100
21	Other liabilities (attach schedule)				
22	Capital stock: a Preferred stock				
	b Common stock	200,000	200,000	200,000	200,000
23	Paid-in or capital surplus				
24	Retained earnings—Appropriated (attach schedule)		30,000		40,000
25	Retained earnings—Unappropriated		238,000		328,783
26	Less cost of treasury stock		( )		( )
27	Total liabilities and stockholders' equity		684,300		879,417

Schedule M-1 — Reconciliation of Income per Books With Income per Return *(This schedule does not have to be completed if the total assets on line 15, column (d), of Schedule L are less than $25,000.)*

1	Net income per books	147,783	7	Income recorded on books this year not included on this return (itemize): a Tax-exempt interest $ 5,000 b Insurance Proceeds 9,500	14,500
2	Federal income tax	55,387			
3	Excess of capital losses over capital gains	3,600			
4	Income subject to tax not recorded on books this year (itemize):		8	Deductions on this return not charged against book income this year (itemize): a Depreciation $ 1,620 b Contributions carryover $	1,620
5	Expenses recorded on books this year not deducted on this return (itemize): a Depreciation $ b Contributions carryover $ 850 c Travel and entertainment $ See Itemized statement attached 16,850	17,700	9	Add lines 7 and 8	16,120
6	Add lines 1 through 5	224,470	10	Income (line 28, page 1)—line 6 less line 9	208,350

Schedule M-2 — Analysis of Unappropriated Retained Earnings per Books (Line 25, Schedule L) *(This schedule does not have to be completed if the total assets on line 15, column (d), of Schedule L are less than $25,000.)*

1	Balance at beginning of year	238,000	5	Distributions: a Cash	65,000
2	Net income per books	147,783		b Stock	
3	Other increases (itemize): Refund of 1989 Income Tax Due to I.R.S. Examination	18,000		c Property	
			6	Other decreases (itemize): Reserve for Contingencies	10,000
			7	Add lines 5 and 6	75,000
4	Add lines 1, 2, and 3	403,783	8	Balance at end of year (line 4 less line 7)	328,783

FIGURE A–6
Form 1120A

Form **1120-A** — Department of the Treasury, Internal Revenue Service

U.S. Corporation Short-Form Income Tax Return

Instructions are separate. See them to make sure you qualify to file Form 1120-A.

For calendar year 1991 or tax year beginning ...., 1991, ending ...., 19 .....

OMB No. 1545-0890 — **1991**

A Check this box if corp. is a personal service corp. (as defined in Temp. Regs. sec. 1.441-4T—see instructions) ▶ ☐

10-2134567 DEC91 D91 5995
ROSE FLOWER SHOP, INC.
38 SUPERIOR LANE
FAIR CITY, MD 20715

B Employer identification number

C Date incorporated: 7-1-82

D Total assets (see Specific Instructions): $ 65,987

E Check applicable boxes: (1) ☐ Initial return (2) ☐ Change in address

F Check method of accounting: (1) ☐ Cash (2) ☑ Accrual (3) ☐ Other (specify) . . ▶

Income

Line	Description		Amount
1a	Gross receipts or sales 248,000 b Less returns and allowances 7,500 c Balance ▶	1c	240,500
2	Cost of goods sold (see instructions)	2	144,000
3	Gross profit. Subtract line 2 from line 1c	3	96,500
4	Domestic corporation dividends subject to the 70% deduction	4	
5	Interest	5	942
6	Gross rents	6	
7	Gross royalties	7	
8	Capital gain net income (attach Schedule D (Form 1120))	8	
9	Net gain or (loss) from Form 4797, Part II, line 18 (attach Form 4797)	9	
10	Other income (see instructions)	10	
11	**Total income.** Add lines 3 through 10 ▶	11	97,442

Deductions (See instructions for limitations on deductions.)

Line	Description		Amount
12	Compensation of officers (see instructions)	12	23,000
13a	Salaries and wages 24,320 b Less jobs credit c Balance ▶	13c	24,320
14	Repairs	14	
15	Bad debts	15	
16	Rents	16	6,000
17	Taxes	17	3,320
18	Interest	18	1,340
19	Contributions (see instructions for 10% limitation)	19	1,820
20	Depreciation (attach Form 4562) — 20		
21	Less depreciation claimed elsewhere on return — 21a	21b	
22	Other deductions (attach schedule) (Advertising)	22	3,000
23	**Total deductions.** Add lines 12 through 22 ▶	23	62,800
24	Taxable income before net operating loss deduction and special deductions. Subtract line 23 from line 11	24	34,642
25	Less: a Net operating loss deduction (see instructions) — 25a; b Special deductions (see instructions) — 25b	25c	

Tax and Payments

Line	Description		Amount
26	**Taxable income.** Subtract line 25c from line 24	26	34,642
27	**Total tax** (from page 2, Part I, line 7)	27	5,196
28	**Payments:**		
a	1990 overpayment credited to 1991 — 28a		
b	1991 estimated tax payments — 28b 6,000		
c	Less 1991 refund applied for on Form 4466 — 28c ( ) Bal ▶ 28d 6,000		
e	Tax deposited with Form 7004 — 28e		
f	Credit from regulated investment companies (attach Form 2439) — 28f		
g	Credit for Federal tax on fuels (attach Form 4136). See instructions — 28g		
h	**Total payments.** Add lines 28d through 28g	28h	6,000
29	Estimated tax penalty (see page 4 of instructions). Check if Form 2220 is attached ▶ ☐	29	
30	**Tax due.** If the total of lines 27 and 29 is larger than line 28h, enter amount owed	30	
31	**Overpayment.** If line 28h is larger than the total of lines 27 and 29, enter amount overpaid	31	804
32	Enter amount of line 31 you want: **Credited to 1992 estimated tax** ▶ 804 **Refunded** ▶	32	

Please Sign Here

Under penalties of perjury, I declare that I have examined this return, including accompanying schedules and statements, and to the best of my knowledge and belief, it is true, correct, and complete. Declaration of preparer (other than taxpayer) is based on all information of which preparer has any knowledge.

▶ George Rose | 2-15-92 | ▶ President
Signature of officer | Date | Title

Paid Preparer's Use Only

Preparer's signature ▶ | Date | Check if self-employed ▶ ☐ | Preparer's social security number

Firm's name (or yours if self-employed) and address ▶ | E.I. No. ▶ | ZIP code ▶

For Paperwork Reduction Act Notice, see page 1 of the instructions. Cat. No. 11456E Form **1120-A** (1991)

Source: "Tax Guide for Small Business—1991 Edition," *Publication 334* (Washington, D.C.: Internal Revenue Service, rev. November 1991), 152–53.

FIGURE A-6
(Continued)

Form 1120-A (1991) Page 2

Part I Tax Computation

1 Income tax (see instructions to figure the tax). Check this box if the corp. is a qualified personal service corp. (see instructions) . . . ▶ ☐		1	5,196
2a General business credit. Check if from: ☐ Form 3800 ☐ Form 3468 ☐ Form 5884 ☐ Form 6478 ☐ Form 6765 ☐ Form 8586 ☐ Form 8830 ☐ Form 8826	2a		
b Credit for prior year minimum tax (attach Form 8827) . . .	2b		
3 Total credits. Add lines 2a and 2b . . .		3	
4 Subtract line 3 from line 1 . . .		4	5,196
5 Recapture taxes. Check if from: ☐ Form 4255 ☐ Form 8611 . . .		5	
6 Alternative minimum tax (attach Form 4626). See instructions . . .		6	
7 Total tax. Add lines 4 through 6. Enter here and on line 27, page 1 . . .		7	5,196

Part II Other Information (See page 15 of the instructions.)

1 Refer to the list in the instructions and state the principal:
  a Business activity code no. ▶ 5995
  b Business activity ▶ Flower Shop
  c Product or service ▶ Flowers

2 Did any individual, partnership, estate, or trust at the end of the tax year own, directly or indirectly, 50% or more of the corporation's voting stock? (For rules of attribution, see section 267(c).) . . . ☑ Yes ☐ No

If "Yes," attach schedule showing name, address, and identifying number. (Schedule not illustrated)

3 Enter the amount of tax-exempt interest received or accrued during the tax year . . . ▶ $ -0-

4 Enter amount of cash distributions and the book value of property (other than cash) distributions made in this tax year . . . ▶ $ -0-

5a If an amount is entered on line 2, page 1, see the worksheet on page 11 for amounts to enter below:
  (1) Purchases (see instructions) . . . 134,034
  (2) Additional sec. 263A costs (see instructions—attach schedule) . . .
  (3) Other costs (attach schedule) . . . 9,466

b Do the rules of section 263A (for property produced or acquired for resale) apply to the corporation? . . . ☐ Yes ☑ No

6 At any time during the tax year, did the corporation have an interest in or a signature or other authority over a financial account in a foreign country (such as a bank account, securities account, or other financial account)? (See page 15 of the instructions for filing requirements for Form TD F 90-22.1.). . . . ☐ Yes ☑ No

If "Yes," enter the name of the foreign country ▶

Part III Balance Sheets

		(a) Beginning of tax year		(b) End of tax year	
Assets	1 Cash . . .	20,540		18,498	
	2a Trade notes and accounts receivable . . .				
	b Less allowance for bad debts . . .	(	)	(	)
	3 Inventories . . .	2,530		2,010	
	4 U.S. government obligations . . .	13,807		45,479	
	5 Tax-exempt securities (see instructions) . . .				
	6 Other current assets (attach schedule) . . .				
	7 Loans to stockholders . . .				
	8 Mortgage and real estate loans . . .				
	9a Depreciable, depletable, and intangible assets . . .				
	b Less accumulated depreciation, depletion, and amortization	(	)	(	)
	10 Land (net of any amortization) . . .				
	11 Other assets (attach schedule) . . .				
	12 Total assets . . .	36,877		65,987	
Liabilities and Stockholders' Equity	13 Accounts payable . . .	6,415		6,079	
	14 Other current liabilities (attach schedule) . . .				
	15 Loans from stockholders . . .				
	16 Mortgages, notes, bonds payable . . .				
	17 Other liabilities (attach schedule) . . .				
	18 Capital stock (preferred and common stock) . . .	20,000		20,000	
	19 Paid-in or capital surplus . . .				
	20 Retained earnings . . .	10,462		39,908	
	21 Less cost of treasury stock . . .	(	)	(	)
	22 Total liabilities and stockholders' equity . . .	36,877		65,987	

Part IV Reconciliation of Income per Books With Income per Return (Must be completed by all filers.)

1 Net income per books . . .	29,446	6 Income recorded on books this year not included on this return (itemize)	
2 Federal income tax . . .	5,196		
3 Excess of capital losses over capital gains . . .		7 Deductions on this return not charged against book income this year (itemize)	
4 Income subject to tax not recorded on books this year (itemize)			
5 Expenses recorded on books this year not deducted on this return (itemize)		8 Income (line 24, page 1). Enter the sum of lines 1 through 5 less the sum of lines 6 and 7 . . .	34,642

FIGURE A–7
Form 1120S

Form **1120S** — Department of the Treasury, Internal Revenue Service

U.S. Income Tax Return for an S Corporation

For calendar year 1991, or tax year beginning .... , 1991, and ending .... , 19 .....

▶ See separate instructions.

OMB No. 1545-0130 — **1991**

A Date of election as an S corporation: 12-1-90

B Business code no. (see Specific Instructions): 5008

Use IRS label. Otherwise, please print or type.

10-4487965 DEC91 D74 3070
STRATOTECH, INC.
482 WINSTON STREET
METRO CITY OH 43705

C Employer identification number: 10-4487965

D Date incorporated: 3-1-73

E Total assets (see Specific Instructions): $ 825,714

F Check applicable boxes: (1) ☑ Initial return (2) ☐ Final return (3) ☐ Change in address (4) ☐ Amended return

G Check this box if this S corporation is subject to the consolidated audit procedures of sections 6241 through 6245 (see instructions before checking this box) . ▶ ☐

H Enter number of shareholders in the corporation at end of the tax year . . . ▶ 6

Caution: *Include only trade or business income and expenses on lines 1a through 21. See the instructions for more information.*

Income	1a	Gross receipts or sales 1,545,700 b Less returns and allowances 21,000 c Bal ▶	1c	1,524,700
	2	Cost of goods sold (Schedule A, line 8)	2	954,700
	3	Gross profit. Subtract line 2 from line 1c	3	570,000
	4	Net gain (loss) from Form 4797, Part II, line 18 *(attach Form 4797)*	4	-0-
	5	Other income (see instructions) *(attach schedule)*	5	-0-
	6	Total income (loss). Combine lines 3 through 5 ▶	6	570,000
Deductions (See instructions for limitations.)	7	Compensation of officers	7	170,000
	8a	Salaries and wages 144,000 b Less jobs credit 6,000 c Bal ▶	8c	138,000
	9	Repairs	9	800
	10	Bad debts	10	1,600
	11	Rents	11	9,200
	12	Taxes	12	15,000
	13	Interest	13	24,200
	14a	Depreciation (see instructions) 14a 5,200		
	b	Depreciation claimed on Schedule A and elsewhere on return 14b -0-		
	c	Subtract line 14b from line 14a	14c	5,200
	15	Depletion (Do not deduct oil and gas depletion.)	15	-0-
	16	Advertising	16	8,700
	17	Pension, profit-sharing, etc., plans	17	-0-
	18	Employee benefit programs	18	-0-
	19	Other deductions *(attach schedule)*	19	78,300
	20	Total deductions. Add lines 7 through 19 ▶	20	451,000
	21	Ordinary income (loss) from trade or business activities. Subtract line 20 from line 6	21	119,000
Tax and Payments	22	Tax:		
	a	Excess net passive income tax *(attach schedule)* 22a		
	b	Tax from Schedule D (Form 1120S) 22b		
	c	Add lines 22a and 22b (see instructions for additional taxes)	22c	-0-
	23	Payments:		
	a	1991 estimated tax payments 23a		
	b	Tax deposited with Form 7004 23b		
	c	Credit for Federal tax on fuels *(attach Form 4136)* 23c		
	d	Add lines 23a through 23c	23d	-0-
	24	Estimated tax penalty (see page 3 of instructions). Check if Form 2220 is attached ▶ ☐	24	
	25	Tax due. If the total of lines 22c and 24 is larger than line 23d, enter amount owed. See instructions for depositary method of payment ▶	25	-0-
	26	Overpayment. If line 23d is larger than the total of lines 22c and 24, enter amount overpaid ▶	26	-0-
	27	Enter amount of line 26 you want: Credited to 1992 estimated tax ▶ Refunded ▶	27	-0-

Please Sign Here

Under penalties of perjury, I declare that I have examined this return, including accompanying schedules and statements, and to the best of my knowledge and belief, it is true, correct, and complete. Declaration of preparer (other than taxpayer) is based on all information of which preparer has any knowledge.

▶ *John H. Green* (Signature of officer) | 3-10-92 (Date) | ▶ President (Title)

Paid Preparer's Use Only

Preparer's signature ▶ | Date | Check if self-employed ▶ ☐ | Preparer's social security number

Firm's name (or yours if self-employed) and address ▶ | E.I. No. ▶ | ZIP code ▶

For Paperwork Reduction Act Notice, see page 1 of separate instructions. Cat. No. 11510H Form 1120S (1991)

Source: "Tax Guide for Small Business—1991 Edition," *Publication 334* (Washington, D.C.: Internal Revenue Service, rev. November 1991), 163–65.

FIGURE A–7
(Continued)

Form 1120S (1991) Page 2

Schedule A Cost of Goods Sold (See instructions.)

1	Inventory at beginning of year	1	126,000
2	Purchases	2	1,127,100
3	Cost of labor	3	-0-
4	Additional section 263A costs (see instructions) *(attach schedule)*	4	-0-
5	Other costs *(attach schedule)*	5	-0-
6	**Total.** Add lines 1 through 5	6	1,253,100
7	Inventory at end of year	7	298,400
8	**Cost of goods sold.** Subtract line 7 from line 6. Enter here and on line 2, page 1	8	954,700

9a Check all methods used for valuing closing inventory:

(i) ☐ Cost

(ii) ☑ Lower of cost or market as described in Regulations section 1.471-4

(iii) ☐ Writedown of "subnormal" goods as described in Regulations section 1.471-2(c)

(iv) ☐ Other (specify method used and attach explanation) ▶ ....

b Check if the LIFO inventory method was adopted this tax year for any goods *(if checked, attach Form 970)* ▶ ☐

c If the LIFO inventory method was used for this tax year, enter percentage (or amounts) of closing inventory computed under LIFO . . . 9c

d Do the rules of section 263A (for property produced or acquired for resale) apply to the corporation? ☐ Yes ☑ No

e Was there any change in determining quantities, cost, or valuations between opening and closing inventory? ☐ Yes ☑ No
If "Yes," attach explanation.

Schedule B Other Information

		Yes	No
1	Check method of accounting: (a) ☐ Cash (b) ☑ Accrual (c) ☐ Other (specify) ▶		
2	Refer to the list in the instructions and state your principal: (a) Business activity ▶ 5008 - Distributor (b) Product or service ▶ Heavy Equipment		
3	Did you at the end of the tax year own, directly or indirectly, 50% or more of the voting stock of a domestic corporation? (For rules of attribution, see section 267(c).) If "Yes," attach a schedule showing: (a) name, address, and employer identification number and (b) percentage owned.		✓
4	Were you a member of a controlled group subject to the provisions of section 1561?		✓
5	At any time during the tax year, did you have an interest in or a signature or other authority over a financial account in a foreign country (such as a bank account, securities account, or other financial account)? (See instructions for exceptions and filing requirements for form TD F 90-22.1.) If "Yes," enter the name of the foreign country ▶		✓
6	Were you the grantor of, or transferor to, a foreign trust that existed during the current tax year, whether or not you have any beneficial interest in it? If "Yes," you may have to file Forms 3520, 3520-A, or 926		✓
7	Check this box if the corporation has filed or is required to file **Form 8264,** Application for Registration of a Tax Shelter ▶ ☐		
8	Check this box if the corporation issued publicly offered debt instruments with original issue discount ▶ ☐ If so, the corporation may have to file **Form 8281,** Information Return for Publicly Offered Original Issue Discount Instruments.		
9	If the corporation: (a) filed its election to be an S corporation after 1986, (b) was a C corporation before it elected to be an S corporation **or** the corporation acquired an asset with a basis determined by reference to its basis (or the basis of any other property) in the hands of a C corporation, and (c) has net unrealized built-in gain (defined in section 1374(d)(1)) in excess of the net recognized built-in gain from prior years, enter the net unrealized built-in gain reduced by net recognized built-in gain from prior years (see instructions) ▶ $ 37,200		
10	Check this box if the corporation had subchapter C earnings and profits at the close of the tax year (see instructions) ▶ ☑		

Designation of Tax Matters Person (See instructions.)

Enter below the shareholder designated as the tax matters person (TMP) for the tax year of this return:

Name of designated TMP ▶ John H. Green   Identifying number of TMP ▶ 458-00-0827

Address of designated TMP ▶ 4340 Holmes Parkway, Metro City, OH 43704

FIGURE A–7
(Continued)

Form 1120S (1991) Page 3

Schedule K Shareholders' Shares of Income, Credits, Deductions, etc.

	(a) Pro rata share items		(b) Total amount
Income (Loss)	1 Ordinary income (loss) from trade or business activities (page 1, line 21)	1	119,000
	2 Net income (loss) from rental real estate activities *(attach Form 8825)*	2	
	3a Gross income from other rental activities — 3a		
	b Less expenses *(attach schedule)* — 3b		
	c Net income (loss) from other rental activities	3c	
	4 Portfolio income (loss):		
	a Interest income	4a	4,000
	b Dividend income	4b	16,000
	c Royalty income	4c	
	d Net short-term capital gain (loss) *(attach Schedule D (Form 1120S))*	4d	
	e Net long-term capital gain (loss) *(attach Schedule D (Form 1120S))*	4e	
	f Other portfolio income (loss) *(attach schedule)*	4f	
	5 Net gain (loss) under section 1231 (other than due to casualty or theft) *(attach Form 4797)*	5	
	6 Other income (loss) *(attach schedule)*	6	
Deductions	7 Charitable contributions (see instructions) *(attach list)*	7	24,000
	8 Section 179 expense deduction *(attach Form 4562)*	8	
	9 Deductions related to portfolio income (loss) (see instructions) (itemize)	9	
	10 Other deductions *(attach schedule)*	10	
Investment Interest	11a Interest expense on investment debts	11a	3,000
	b (1) Investment income included on lines 4a through 4f above	11b(1)	20,000
	(2) Investment expenses included on line 9 above	11b(2)	
Credits	12a Credit for alcohol used as a fuel *(attach Form 6478)*	12a	
	b Low-income housing credit (see instructions):		
	(1) From partnerships to which section 42(j)(5) applies for property placed in service before 1990	12b(1)	
	(2) Other than on line 12b(1) for property placed in service before 1990	12b(2)	
	(3) From partnerships to which section 42(j)(5) applies for property placed in service after 1989	12b(3)	
	(4) Other than on line 12b(3) for property placed in service after 1989	12b(4)	
	c Qualified rehabilitation expenditures related to rental real estate activities *(attach Form 3468)*	12c	
	d Credits (other than credits shown on lines 12b and 12c) related to rental real estate activities (see instructions)	12d	
	e Credits related to other rental activities (see instructions)	12e	
	13 Other credits (see instructions) Jobs Credit	13	6,000
Adjustments and Tax Preference Items	14a Accelerated depreciation of real property placed in service before 1987	14a	
	b Accelerated depreciation of leased personal property placed in service before 1987	14b	
	c Depreciation adjustment on property placed in service after 1986	14c	
	d Depletion (other than oil and gas)	14d	
	e (1) Gross income from oil, gas, or geothermal properties	14e(1)	
	(2) Deductions allocable to oil, gas, or geothermal properties	14e(2)	
	f Other adjustments and tax preference items *(attach schedule)*	14f	
Foreign Taxes	15a Type of income ▶		
	b Name of foreign country or U.S. possession ▶		
	c Total gross income from sources outside the United States *(attach schedule)*	15c	
	d Total applicable deductions and losses *(attach schedule)*	15d	
	e Total foreign taxes (check one): ▶ ☐ Paid ☐ Accrued	15e	
	f Reduction in taxes available for credit *(attach schedule)*	15f	
	g Other foreign tax information *(attach schedule)*	15g	
Other	16a Total expenditures to which a section 59(e) election may apply	16a	
	b Type of expenditures ▶		
	17 Total property distributions (including cash) other than dividends reported on line 19 below	17	65,000
	18 Other items and amounts required to be reported separately to shareholders (see instructions) *(attach schedule)*		
	19 Total dividend distributions paid from accumulated earnings and profits	19	
	20 **Income (loss)** (Required only if Schedule M-1 must be completed.). Combine lines 1 through 6 in column (b). From the result, subtract the sum of lines 7 through 11a, 15e, and 16a	20	112,000

FIGURE A–8
Schedule K-1 (Form 1120S)

SCHEDULE K-1 (Form 1120S)
Department of the Treasury Internal Revenue Service

Shareholder's Share of Income, Credits, Deductions, etc.
▶ See separate instructions.
For calendar year 1991 or tax year beginning , 1991, and ending , 19

OMB No. 1545-0130
1991

Shareholder's identifying number ▶ 458-00-0327	Corporation's identifying number ▶ 10-4487965
Shareholder's name, address, and ZIP code John H. Green 4340 Holmes Parkway Metro City, OH 43704	Corporation's name, address, and ZIP code StratoTech, Inc. 482 Winston Street Metro City, OH 43705

A Shareholder's percentage of stock ownership for tax year (see Instructions for Schedule K-1) ▶ 45 %
B Internal Revenue service center where corporation filed its return ▶ Cincinnati, OH
C (1) Tax shelter registration number (see Instructions for Schedule K-1) ▶
(2) Type of tax shelter ▶
D Check applicable boxes: (1) ☐ Final K-1 (2) ☐ Amended K-1

	(a) Pro rata share items		(b) Amount	(c) Form 1040 filers enter the amount in column (b) on:
Income (Loss)	1 Ordinary income (loss) from trade or business activities	1	53,550	See Shareholder's Instructions for Schedule K-1 (Form 1120S).
	2 Net income (loss) from rental real estate activities	2		
	3 Net income (loss) from other rental activities	3		
	4 Portfolio income (loss):			
	a Interest	4a	1,800	Sch. B, Part I, line 1
	b Dividends	4b	7,200	Sch. B, Part II, line 5
	c Royalties	4c		Sch. E, Part I, line 4
	d Net short-term capital gain (loss)	4d		Sch. D, line 4, col. (f) or (g)
	e Net long-term capital gain (loss)	4e		Sch. D, line 11, col. (f) or (g)
	f Other portfolio income (loss) *(attach schedule)*	4f		(Enter on applicable line of your return.)
	5 Net gain (loss) under section 1231 (other than due to casualty or theft)	5		See Shareholder's Instructions for Schedule K-1 (Form 1120S).
	6 Other income (loss) *(attach schedule)*	6		(Enter on applicable line of your return.)
Deductions	7 Charitable contributions (see instructions) *(attach schedule)*	7	10,800	Sch. A, line 13 or 14
	8 Section 179 expense deduction	8		See Shareholder's Instructions for Schedule K-1 (Form 1120S).
	9 Deductions related to portfolio income (loss) *(attach schedule)*	9		
	10 Other deductions *(attach schedule)*	10		
Investment Interest	11a Interest expense on investment debts	11a	1,350	Form 4952, line 1
	b (1) Investment income included on lines 4a through 4f above	b(1)	9,000	See Shareholder's Instructions for Schedule K-1 (Form 1120S).
	(2) Investment expenses included on line 9 above	b(2)		
Credits	12a Credit for alcohol used as fuel	12a		Form 6478, line 10
	b Low-income housing credit:			
	(1) From section 42(j)(5) partnerships for property placed in service before 1990	b(1)		Form 8586, line 5
	(2) Other than on line 12b(1) for property placed in service before 1990	b(2)		
	(3) From section 42(j)(5) partnerships for property placed in service after 1989	b(3)		
	(4) Other than on line 12b(3) for property placed in service after 1989	b(4)		
	c Qualified rehabilitation expenditures related to rental real estate activities (see instructions)	12c		See Shareholder's Instructions for Schedule K-1 (Form 1120S).
	d Credits (other than credits shown on lines 12b and 12c) related to rental real estate activities (see instructions)	12d		
	e Credits related to other rental activities (see instructions)	12e		
	13 Other credits (see instructions) Jobs Credit	13	2,700	
Adjustments and Tax Preference Items	14a Accelerated depreciation of real property placed in service before 1987	14a		See Shareholder's Instructions for Schedule K-1 (Form 1120S) and Instructions for Form 6251
	b Accelerated depreciation of leased personal property placed in service before 1987	14b		
	c Depreciation adjustment on property placed in service after 1986	14c		
	d Depletion (other than oil and gas)	14d		
	e (1) Gross income from oil, gas, or geothermal properties	e(1)		
	(2) Deductions allocable to oil, gas, or geothermal properties	e(2)		
	f Other adjustments and tax preference items *(attach schedule)*	14f		

For Paperwork Reduction Act Notice, see page 1 of Instructions for Form 1120S. Cat. No. 11520D Schedule K-1 (Form 1120S) 1991

Source: "Tax Guide for Small Business—1991 Edition," *Publication 334* (Washington, D.C.: Internal Revenue Service, rev. November 1991), 166–68.

FIGURE A–8
(Continued)

Schedule K-1 (Form 1120S) (1991) Page **2**

		(a) Pro rata share items		(b) Amount	(c) Form 1040 filers enter the amount in column (b) on:
Foreign Taxes	15a	Type of income ▶			Form 1116, Check boxes
	b	Name of foreign country or U.S. possession ▶			Form 1116, Part I
	c	Total gross income from sources outside the U.S. *(attach schedule)*	15c		
	d	Total applicable deductions and losses *(attach schedule)*	15d		
	e	Total foreign taxes (check one): ▶ ☐ Paid ☐ Accrued	15e		Form 1116, Part II
	f	Reduction in taxes available for credit *(attach schedule)*	15f		Form 1116, Part III
	g	Other foreign tax information *(attach schedule)*	15g		See Instructions for Form 1116
Other	16a	Total expenditures to which a section 59(e) election may apply	16a		See Shareholder's Instructions for Schedule K-1 (Form 1120S).
	b	Type of expenditures ▶			
	17	Property distributions (including cash) other than dividend distributions reported to you on Form 1099-DIV	17	29,250	
	18	Amount of loan repayments for "Loans From Shareholders"	18		
	19	Recapture of low-income housing credit:			
	a	From section 42(j)(5) partnerships	19a		Form 8611, line 8
	b	Other than on line 19a	19b		

Supplemental Information

20 Supplemental information required to be reported separately to each shareholder *(attach additional schedules if more space is needed)*:

Tax-exempt interest $ 2,250

Nondeductible salaries and wages due to jobs credit $ 2,700

FIGURE A-8
(Continued)

Schedule L Balance Sheets

Assets	Beginning of tax year (a)	(b)	End of tax year (c)	(d)
1 Cash		14,700		14,514
2a Trade notes and accounts receivable	98,400		33,700	
b Less allowance for bad debts		98,400		33,700
3 Inventories		126,000		298,400
4 U.S. Government obligations				
5 Tax-exempt securities		100,000		120,000
6 Other current assets *(attach schedule)*		26,300		26,300
7 Loans to shareholders				
8 Mortgage and real estate loans				
9 Other investments *(attach schedule)*		100,000		100,000
10a Buildings and other depreciable assets	204,700		198,700	
b Less accumulated depreciation	6,000	198,700	5,200	193,500
11a Depletable assets				
b Less accumulated depletion				
12 Land (net of any amortization)		20,000		20,000
13a Intangible assets (amortizable only)				
b Less accumulated amortization				
14 Other assets *(attach schedule)*		14,800		19,300
15 Total assets		698,900		825,714
Liabilities and Shareholders' Equity				
16 Accounts payable		28,500		34,834
17 Mortgages, notes, bonds payable in less than 1 year		4,300		4,300
18 Other current liabilities *(attach schedule)*		6,800		7,400
19 Loans from shareholders				
20 Mortgages, notes, bonds payable in 1 year or more		191,300		265,180
21 Other liabilities *(attach schedule)*				
22 Capital stock		200,000		200,000
23 Paid-in or capital surplus				
24 Retained earnings		268,000		314,000
25 Less cost of treasury stock		( )		( )
26 Total liabilities and shareholders' equity		698,900		825,714

Schedule M-1 Reconciliation of Income per Books With Income per Return (You are not required to complete this schedule if the total assets on line 15, column (d), of Schedule L are less than $25,000.)

1 Net income per books	102,270	5 Income recorded on books this year not included on Schedule K, lines 1 through 6 (itemize): a Tax-exempt interest $ 5,000	5,000
2 Income included on Schedule K, lines 1 through 6, not recorded on books this year (itemize):	-0-		
3 Expenses recorded on books this year not included on Schedule K, lines 1 through 11a, 15e, and 16a (itemize): a Depreciation $ b Travel and entertainment $ (Itemized statement attached)	16,350	6 Deductions included on Schedule K, lines 1 through 11a, 15e, and 16a, not charged against book income this year (itemize): a Depreciation $ 1,620	1,620
		7 Add lines 5 and 6	6,620
4 Add lines 1 through 3	118,620	8 Income (loss) (Schedule K, line 20). Line 4 less line 7	112,000

Schedule M-2 Analysis of Accumulated Adjustments Account, Other Adjustments Account, and Shareholders' Undistributed Taxable Income Previously Taxed (See instructions.)

	(a) Accumulated adjustments account	(b) Other adjustments account	(c) Shareholders' undistributed taxable income previously taxed
1 Balance at beginning of tax year	-0-	-0-	
2 Ordinary income from page 1, line 21	119,000		
3 Other additions	20,000	5,000	
4 Loss from page 1, line 21	(-0-)		
5 Other reductions	(33,000)	(-0-)	
6 Combine lines 1 through 5	106,000	5,000	
7 Distributions other than dividend distributions	65,000	-0-	
8 Balance at end of tax year. Subtract line 7 from line 6	41,000	5,000	

INDEX

G

H

I

J

K

L

M

Q

T